FOOTBALL CAMP TRAINING PROGRAM

from the Soccer Italian Style Coaches

WRITTEN BY

MIRKO MAZZANTINI   &   SIMONE BOMBARDIERI

PUBLISHED BY

FOOTBALL CAMP TRAINING PROGRAM

from the Soccer Italian Style Coaches

First Published August 2014 by SoccerTutor.com

Info@soccertutor.com | www.SoccerTutor.com

UK: 0208 1234 007 | **US:** (305) 767 4443 | **ROTW:** +44 208 1234 007
ISBN: 978-1-910491-00-3

Copyright: SoccerTutor.com Limited © 2014. All Rights Reserved.

All rights reserved. No part of this publication may be reproduced, stored in a retrieval system, or transmitted in any form or by any means, electronic, mechanical, photocopy, recording or otherwise, without prior written permission of the copyright owner. Nor can it be circulated in any form of binding or cover other than that in which it is published and without similar condition including this condition being imposed on a subsequent purchaser.

Authors
Mirko Mazzantini and Simone Bombardieri. © 2014

Edited by
Alex Fitzgerald - SoccerTutor.com

Cover Design by
Alex Macrides, Think Out Of The Box Ltd.
email: design@thinkootb.com Tel: +44 (0) 208 144 3550

Diagrams
Diagram designs by SoccerTutor.com. All the diagrams in this book have been created using SoccerTutor.com Tactics Manager Software available from www.SoccerTutor.com

Note: While every effort has been made to ensure the technical accuracy of the content of this book, neither the author nor publishers can accept any responsibility for any injury or loss sustained as a result of the use of this material.

Contents

Soccer Italian Style	8
The Soccer Italian Style Story	9
Soccer Italian Style Coaches	10
Charity Partnership: Soccer Italian Style, Onside Soccer & SoccerTutor.com	11
Onside Soccer	12
Onside Soccer Mentorship Program	14
The Future	16
How to Get Involved	17
Recommendations & Quotes	18
Soccer Italian Style Camps: U9-15	20
Italian Style Soccer Camps Philosophy & Work Methodology	21
Outline of Training Week	23
Session Structure	24
Practice Format	25

WEEK 1 26

Day 01: Running with the Ball 27
1. **Warm Up:** Technical Block 1 27
2. **Technical:** Close Control with Shooting Accuracy 28
3. **Coordination:** Coordination Relay 28
4. **Game Situation:** 1v1 v Defender + 1v1 v Goalkeeper 29
5. **Game with a Theme:** '4 Goals' 4v4 Small Sided Game 29
6. 5v5 Small Sided Games 29

Day 02: Feints / Moves to Beat 30
1. **Warm Up:** Technical Block 2 30
2. **Technical:** Ball Control - Moves / Feints 31
3. **Coordination:** 1v1 Duel - Feints and Dribbling 31
4. **Game Situation:** 1v1 Duel - Feints, Dribbling and Change of Direction 32
5. **Game with a Theme:** 5v5 with 6 Dribble Gates in a SSG 32
6. 5v5 Small Sided Games 32

Day 03: Passing and Receiving 33
1. **Warm Up:** Technical Block 3 33
2. **Technical:** Pass, Move & Receive in a Square 34
3. **Coordination:** Skip, Pass, Receive, Dribble & Run 34
4. **Game Situation:** Passing and Receiving in a 2v1 Duel 35
5. **Game with a Theme:** 5v5 End to End Possession Game 35
6. 5v5 Small Sided Games 35

Day 04: Shooting 36
1. **Warm Up:** Technical Block 4 36
2. **Technical:** One-Two Combination and Shot 37
3. **Coordination:** Shooting Game with a Coordination Circuit 37
4. **Game Situation:** Strength, 1v1 Duels and Finishing 38
5. **Game with a Theme:** 1v1 Marking in a 4v4 SSG 38
6. 5v5 Small Sided Games 38

Day 05: Heading 39
1. **Warm Up:** Technical Block 5 39
2. **Technical:** Heading Accuracy 'Aim for a Corner' 40
3. **Coordination:** Jump, Run, Change of Direction and Headed Pass 40

4. Game Situation: Throw-ins, Heading, 1v1s and Finishing 41
5. Game with a Theme: 6v6 Headers Game with 6 Outside Players 41
6. 11v11 Matches on a Full Pitch 41

WEEK 2 42

Day 01: Running with the Ball 43
1. Warm Up: Technical Block 1 43
2. Technical: Ball Control Exercises 44
3. Coordination: Speed & Agility Training with 1v1 Duels 44
4. Game Situation: Frontal and Back Marking 45
5. Game with a Theme: 5v5 'Rugby Rules' SSG 45
6. 5v5 Small Sided Games 45

Day 02: Feints / Moves to Beat 46
1. Warm Up: Technical Block 2 46
2. Technical: Changing Direction Team Shooting Game 47
3. Coordination: Coordination Relay 47
4. Game Situation: Frontal 1v1 Duel with Coloured Goals 48
5. Game with a Theme: Man to Man Marking in a 5v5 SSG 48
6. 5v5 Small Sided Games 48

Day 03: Passing and Receiving 49
1. Warm Up: Technical Block 3 49
2. Technical: Quick Passing and 1-2 Combinations 50
3. Coordination: Coordination and Passing Relay 50
4. Game Situation: Creating a Numerical Advantage (1v1 > 2v1) 51
5. Game with a Theme: Two Small Sided Games -Rugby / 4 Goals Match 51
6. 5v5 Small Sided Games 51

Day 04: Shooting 52
1. Warm Up: Technical Block 4 52
2. Technical: Ball Control & Shooting with 4 Goals 53
3. Coordination: One-Two and Shoot / 20 Yard Sprints 53
4. Game Situation: 3v2 First Time Shooting Practice 54
5. Game with a Theme: 2v2 Zones in a 4v4 SSG 54
6. 5v5 Small Sided Games 54

Day 05: Heading 55
1. Warm Up: Technical Block 5 55
2. Technical: Heading in Pairs 56
3. Coordination: Jump, Criss-Cross and Heading 56
4. Game Situation: 1v1 Heading in the Penalty Area 57
5. Game with a Theme: Heading with Target Players SSG 57
6. 11v11 Matches on a Full Pitch 57

WEEK 3 58

Day 01: Running with the Ball 59
1. Warm Up: Technical Block 1 59
2. Technical: Dribbling with Different Obstacles 60
3. Coordination: Ball Control and Coordination Relay 60
4. Game Situation: Dribble, Turn & Shoot - 'The 1v1 Duel' 61
5. Game with a Theme: 4v4 (+GK) Attacking Combinations
& Incisive Dribbling in and Around the Penalty Area 61
6. 5v5 Small Sided Games 61

Day 02: Feints / Moves to Beat 62
1. **Warm Up:** Technical Block 2 62
2. **Technical:** Running with the Ball, Feints and Shooting 63
3. **Coordination:** 1v1 RWTB Race - 'Quickest Player Shoots' 63
4. **Game Situation:** 1v1 Back to Goal Duel with Goalkeepers 64
5. **Game with a Theme:** Transition Play / Collective Reactions in a SSG 64
6. **5v5 Small Sided Games** 64

Day 03: Passing and Receiving 65
1. **Warm Up:** Technical Block 3 65
2. **Technical:** Passing Practice for the Right Time of Play 66
3. **Coordination:** Ball Control, Agility, Passing and Receiving with Shooting 66
4. **Game Situation:** Back to Goal 2v1 Dynamic Practice 67
5. **Game with a Theme:** 5v5 Passing Gate Game 67
6. **5v5 Small Sided Games** 67

Day 04: Shooting 68
1. **Warm Up:** Technical Block 4 68
2. **Technical:** Volleying Accuracy - 'Aim for a Corner' 69
3. **Coordination:** Dribble, Shoot, Roll and Save 69
4. **Game Situation:** 1v1 Dribbling and Shooting Duel 70
5. **Game with a Theme:** Shooting Accuracy in a 6v6 SSG 70
6. **5v5 Small Sided Games** 70

Day 05: Receiving in the Air & Finishing 71
1. **Warm Up:** Technical Block 5 71
2. **Technical:** Heading Accuracy 'Against the Crossbar' 72
3. **Coordination:** Roll, Run, Volley Pass and Sprint 72
4. **Game Situation:** Receiving a Long pass & Shielding the Ball 73
5. **Game with a Theme:** Quick Possession and Transition Play to the Striker 73
6. **11v11 Matches on a Full Pitch** 73

WEEK 4 74

Day 01: Running with the Ball 75
1. **Warm Up:** Technical Block 1 75
2. **Technical:** Receiving, Turning and Dribbling with the Back to Goal 76
3. **Coordination:** Dribbling Race with Turning and Shooting 76
4. **Game Situation:** Dribbling Team Game with Numbers 77
5. **Game with a Theme:** 4v4 with 'Scoring Zones' in a SSG 77
6. **5v5 Small Sided Games** 77

Day 02: Feints / Moves to Beat 78
1. **Warm Up:** Technical Block 2 78
2. **Technical:** Feints, Changes of Direction & Accurate Shot 79
3. **Coordination:** Dribbling Coordination and 1v2 Duel 79
4. **Game Situation:** 1v1 Play with Feints / Moves to Beat 80
5. **Game with a Theme:** Collective Tactical Movement in a SSG 80
6. **5v5 Small Sided Games** 80

Day 03: Passing and Receiving 81
1. **Warm Up:** Technical Block 3 81
2. **Technical:** Passing, Receiving and 1v1 Play 82
3. **Coordination:** 'Psycho-Kinetics' Passing in Pairs 82
4. **Game Situation:** Passing Combinations with a 3v2 Advantage 83
5. **Game with a Theme:** 4v4v4 Dynamic 3 Zone Possession Game 83
6. **5v5 Small Sided Games** 83

Day 04: Shooting 84
1. **Warm Up:** Technical Block 4 84
2. **Technical:** Ball Control, Dribbling & Shooting Circuits 85
3. **Coordination:** Speed & Agility Shooting Competition 85
4. **Game Situation:** 2v2 with 4 Goals: 10 Ball Competition in a SSG 86
5. **Game with a Theme:** 3v3 Quick Combinations and Finishing in the Box 86
6. 5v5 Small Sided Games 86

Day 05: Receiving in the Air & Finishing 87
1. **Warm Up:** Technical Block 5 87
2. **Technical:** Heading Accuracy - 'Aim for the Ring' 88
3. **Coordination:** Roll, Receive and Shoot 88
4. **Game Situation:** Passing and Receiving with Good Communication 89
5. **Game with a Theme:** Heading with Target Players SSG (2) 89
6. 11v11 Matches on a Full Pitch 89

WEEK 5 90

Day 01: Running with the Ball 91
1. **Warm Up:** Technical Block 1 91
2. **Technical:** Quick Reactions Man Marking Dribbling Game 92
3. **Coordination:** Quick Reactions Colours Game 92
4. **Game Situation:** Dribbling and Turning - '1v1 Pursuit' 93
5. **Game with a Theme:** Dribbling and RWTB in a SSG 93
6. 5v5 Small Sided Games 93

Day 02: Feints / Moves to Beat 94
1. **Warm Up:** Technical Block 2 94
2. **Technical:** Dribbling with Feints / Moves to Beat 95
3. **Coordination:** Motor Aerobic Exercise - 'Fantasy Track' 95
4. **Game Situation:** 1v1 Situations 96
5. **Game with a Theme:** 5v5 'Nutmeg' Possession Game 96
6. 5v5 Small Sided Games 96

Day 03: Passing and Receiving 97
1. **Warm Up:** Technical Block 3 97
2. **Technical:** Diagonal Passing Square 98
3. **Coordination:** Coordination, Agility and Balance Exercise 98
4. **Game Situation:** 2v2 (+2) Game / Double 2v2 Game 99
5. **Game with a Theme:** 6v3 Speed of Play Dynamic Possession Game 99
6. 5v5 Small Sided Games 99

Day 04: Shooting 100
1. **Warm Up:** Technical Block 4 100
2. **Technical:** Feints / Quick Movements and Shot 101
3. **Coordination:** Roll, Dribble and Shoot with a Goalkeeper 101
4. **Game Situation:** Move, Receive and Score in a 1v1 Duel 102
5. **Game with a Theme:** Shooting Practice in a 7v7 Possession Game 102
6. 5v5 Small Sided Games 102

Day 05: Passing & Receiving in the Air 103
1. **Warm Up:** Technical Block 5 103
2. **Technical:** Accurate Aerial Passing in Pairs 104
3. **Coordination:** Quick Reactions & Speed of Play in a 2v1 Duel Game 104
4. **Game Situation:** 2v1 on the Flanks with Accurate Crossing 105
5. **Game with a Theme:** 4v4 with Long Accurate Passing 105
6. 11v11 Matches on a Full Pitch 105

WEEK 6 106

Day 01: Running with the Ball 107
1. **Warm Up:** Technical Block 1 107
2. **Technical:** Close Control and Turning with Shot 108
3. **Coordination:** Jump, Dribble and Shoot - 'Who's the Fastest?' 108
4. **Game Situation:** Quick Reactions Dribbling Game 109
5. **Game with a Theme:** 4v4 Rugby Game 109
6. **5v5 Small Sided Games** 109

Day 02: Feints / Moves to Beat 110
1. **Warm Up:** Technical Block 2 110
2. **Technical:** Ball Control, Feints & Dribbling 'Star' 111
3. **Coordination:** Dribbling at Speed with 'Nutmeg' 111
4. **Game Situation:** Quick Reactions and Finishing in a 1v2 Frontal Marking Duel 112
5. **Game with a Theme:** Man Marking 6 Goal Dribbling Game 112
6. **5v5 Small Sided Games** 112

Day 03: Passing and Receiving 113
1. **Warm Up:** Technical Block 3 113
2. **Technical:** Passing and Receiving Square 114
3. **Coordination:** Hurdle Agility Training & Volley Passes 114
4. **Game Situation:** 4v2 Possession - Passing, Receiving & Speed of Play 115
5. **Game with a Theme:** Long Passing, Crossing & Finishing in a 7 Zone SSG 115
6. **5v5 Small Sided Games** 115

Day 04: Shooting 116
1. **Warm Up:** Technical Block 4 116
2. **Technical:** Accurate Volleys & Quick Reactions Exercise 117
3. **Coordination:** Sprint, Change Direction and Shooting Race 117
4. **Game Situation:** 1v1 Frontal Duel with 3 Goals15 118
5. **Game with a Theme:** Speed of Play and Shooting SSG 118
6. **5v5 Small Sided Games** 118

Day 05: Passing & Receiving in the Air 119
1. **Warm Up:** Technical Block 5 119
2. **Technical:** 2v2 Football Tennis Tournament 120
3. **Coordination:** Sprinting & Agility with Crossing & Heading 120
4. **Game Situation:** Applying Quick Pressure in a 3 Zone Game 121
5. **Game with a Theme:** 3v3 Attacking / Defending Crosses 121
6. **11v11 Matches on a Full Pitch** 121

Soccer Italian Style

SOCCER ITALIAN STYLE IS WORLDWIDE...WORK WITH US!

SOCCER ITALIAN STYLE has organised youth football events in many countries around the world. If you are a Club Executive, a Coach, a Technical Director or just an individual passionate about the sport and you want your players to have a unique experience, please contact us or visit our website: www.SoccerItalianStyle.it

PROFESSIONAL ITALIAN CAMP is a week of football for boys and girls aged 6 to 18 years old. It is where fun meets the training methodologies of the best Italian academies and is taught by experienced staff who have worked with with some of highest level clubs in Italy.

PROFESSIONAL ITALIAN TEAM CAMP is a weekly team training camp with the work planned around a highly professional methodology which is tested continuously, innovated and adapted based on the level and characteristics of the participating team.

SOCCER ITALIAN STYLE COACHING CLINICS are organised for all different levels and are based on a proven model that creates lots of interest and enjoyment for the participants. The time spent in the classroom is filled with numerous videos from professional training sessions in Italy and it is supported by on-field demonstrations of the concepts discussed.

NEW INITIATIVE: SOCCER AND TOURISM IN ITALY: Soccer Italian Style has a partnership with an important travel agency to provide a unique experience: improve as a player and sightsee the best parts of Tuscany. Firenze, Pisa, Lucca, Siena, and 5 Terre are just some of the magnificent places waiting for you.

If you want your team to have a week of highly professional training and at the same time be immersed in the culture of Italy, Soccer Italian Style can plan your trip in detail, adapting the itinerary and lodging based on the wishes and needs of the players and chaperones.

The Soccer Italian Style Story

Soccer Italian Style was founded in 2005 by 2 passionate professional coaches, Mirko Mazzantini and Simone Bombardieri. Since their first trip overseas, the young coaches' goal has been to share their experiences with passion and professionalism.

The Soccer Italian Style network has spread quickly to many continents through various partnerships, working with youth football clubs, youth football associations and businesses that distribute sports books and videos.

In 2011 Mirko Mazzantini and Simone Bombarideri had the honour to present a lesson at the Coverciano Coaches Training Centre organised by the Italian Football Federation.

Mirko and Simone have received recognition from many countries, and this is reflected in themany contacts and collaborations they have established and by the success of the products developed. This has led to Mirko and Simone visiting many countries throughout the world to share their expertise, particularly in the USA, Canada, Norway, Japan, Australia, New Zealand and many Asian countries. The success enjoyed by Soccer Italian Style has encouraged the founders to increase their efforts with new developments to complement the existing products.

All the initiatives focus on the common denominator; the working philosophy of Soccer Italian Style, as well as the result of personal experiences in professional football clubs, trips around the world and personal experiences.

Numerous coaches, club directors and football fans continuously contact the staff through the website: **www.SoccerItalianStyle.it**

As a result of this interest, Mirko and Simone have welcomed other professional coaches and athletic trainers to their football family to help meet the needs of all that are interested.

Soccer Italian Style Coaches

Mirko Mazzantini
ACF Fiorentina
Academy Coach

Mirko Mazzantini coached at **Empoli FC** for 10 years, working with all the main age groups at academy level. In 2010 he was recruited by AFC Fiorentina to work with the U14/U15 Academy teams.

During the 2010/11 season Mirko won the U15 Italian Academy Serie 'A' championship.

In 2011/12 Mirko was the Assistant of the Fiorentina Reserve team during pre-season and he was the coach of the ACF Fiorentina U14 team who won the Academy Serie 'A' championship and some international tournaments.

Mirko is currently the ACF Fiorentina U15 coach for the 2012/13 season.

He is a qualified football coach through the "Young Players Coach" program and a UEFA 'B' Licenced Coach, as well as an author of many coaching publications, articles, books and DVDs.

Simone Bombardieri
Empoli FC
Academy Coach

Simone Bombardieri played for **Empoli FC** for 5 years. He then started his career as a coach for the club 15 years ago at the age of 22, where he has been coaching various academy age groups from U9-U14.

In the 2011/12 season, Simone was the coach of the Empoli FC U14 team who reached the final of the Nick Cup International Tournament, where they lost in extra time against Inter Milan. They also finished eighth in the Academy Serie 'A' championship.

Simone is currently the Empoli FC U15 coach for the 2012/13 season.

He is also a qualified football coach through the "Young Players Coach" program and a UEFA 'B' Licenced Coach, as well as an author of many coaching publications, articles, books and DVDs.

Charity Partnership:
Soccer Italian Style, Onside Soccer & SoccerTutor.com

Soccer Italian Style have set up of an exciting new partnership with a UK based charity called **Onside Soccer**. **Onside Soccer** provide children from impoverished areas the chance to come along to coaching sessions every week free of charge.

Soccer Italian Style will be working with **Onside Soccer** coaches worldwide to help train and develop them, allowing them to deliver a professional system of coaching for the children who come to their programmes.

Onside Soccer founder Paul Harbinson said:

"We are really pleased to put this partnership in place with Soccer Italian Style. Mirko and Simone are highly respected coaches and having them design this training programme for us will really take our coaching to a new level."

Soccer Italian Style in partnership with **SoccerTutor.com:**

"We are delighted that **50% of the profits from the sale of this book** will be donated to Onside Soccer to allow them to develop and expand their charity programmes."

 of the profits from the sale of this book will be donated to:

Onside Soccer

Onside Soccer is a football charity founded on a Christian ethos. Its purpose is to establish football academies in the developing world to allow children from materially poor backgrounds the opportunity to play a sport they love in a safe, high quality and encouraging environment. It aims to use the young peoples' engagement in the sports programme as an opportunity for them to also be mentored, and receive encouragement in developing positive attitudes both on and off the pitch. Although integrally a Christian charity, Onside Soccer promotes inclusiveness in all training sessions, making sure that everyone who comes along feels welcome and is treated equally irrespective of their beliefs or background.

INSPIRATION AND FOUNDATIONS

Onside Soccer was established in 2009 by Paul Harbinson, who, when travelling to Rwanda with child sponsorship charity Compassion UK, came across a group of children from the slums playing football on a patch of waste ground. After watching the game unfold for a few minutes it became obvious that despite the grinding poverty surrounding them, for these young people football was more then just a game; it was an escape. In their minds, they weren't playing on a potholed, dirt pitch in bare feet, kicking a hand-made football; they were playing at the Emirates or the Nou Camp in the Champions League! After returning to the UK, Paul began exploring the idea of working with children from impoverished backgrounds in the developing world. He sought a method that could combine the seemingly universal passion for football with a life skills programme, thereby equipping these young people with essential skills for life despite their lack of material wealth. A few months later Onside Soccer was born....

HOW ONSIDE STARTED

Since it was in the country of Rwanda that the original idea of Onside Soccer was imagined, Paul's initial plan was to establish the inaugural Onside Soccer project there. Practically however, Paul did not have the necessary contacts there and it quickly became obvious that working in Rwanda wasn't a viable option at that time. However, through a chance meeting with an Indian man named Churchill Joseph, an opportunity presented itself to work in South India instead. Churchill wasn't a rich man by any stretch of the imagination, but he was an inspirational one. A few years previously he had set up the Dr. John Joseph Foundation to help underprivileged children in Chennai, and also ran a small orphanage in the city centre. As a child, Churchill and his mother had been left destitute in a Chennai slum when his father walked out on the family, leaving them penniless, homeless and with little hope. A local church leader named Dr. John Joseph heard of their plight and took them into his home, providing employment for Churchill's mother and granting Churchill an all important education by putting him through school. When Dr. Joseph died, Churchill felt that the most fitting tribute he could pay would be to establish a charitable foundation in his name, offering a helping hand to children in the way that Dr Joseph had helped him. When the Onside team heard about the orphanage and their desire to find a sports programme where the children could engage, it was an easy decision to visit India to try to help out.

KICKING OFF!

By May 2011 sufficient ground work had been achieved and Paul was ready to kick off the first Onside tour!

He and a fellow football coach travelled from England to Chennai to meet Churchill, and together they ran a football summer camp for the local children as a trial project. The summer camp was a great success with approximately 100 children attending each day over a seven day period. Whilst in Chennai, Paul also identified two local football coaches to help the project expand and ensure that a football training session could continue to run for the children each week, for the duration of the year. Onside Soccer Football Academy, Chennai, was established!

By the summer of 2012 groundwork had developed far enough to allow expansion, and a second small team of coaches travelled to Uganda to establish a summer camp in the capital city of Kampala. As in India the camp proved to be very popular, attracting many young people who embraced the opportunity to engage in football and life skills training, and have fun.

Football is very popular in Uganda and it was clear that, in a similar fashion to India, setting up a weekly academy for young people would be possible. A local coach was appointed and under his expert guidance the academy in Kampala is growing from strength to strength.

OVERCOMING BARRIERS

During his experience of delivering football camps in the most impoverished parts of Chennai and Kampala, Paul was able to identify two main barriers that were preventing these young footballers reaching their full potential; local coaches' lack of access to up to date or standardised training methods, and a scarcity of equipment for use during training sessions. Many clubs and leagues exist in these geographical areas and are run by dedicated individuals, but it is often left to each coach to compile whatever training method he or she thinks best and to deliver this with very limited equipment resources.

TEACHING COACHES NEW SKILLS

During the first Onside Soccer trip to Uganda the team spoke with one coach who had been working tirelessly in the slums of Kampala for many years but had been training his youth team from a portion of a manual printed in the UK in the 1970's! The 20 or so drills featured in the manual weren't age appropriate or particularly inspiring but had remained the bedrock of his training programme as this was the only resource available to him. He was also considered quite fortunate by other local coaches to even have this resource!

In order to empower local coaches, Onside Soccer wanted to be able to provide them with a high quality standardised coaching programme which would be appropriate for use in a range of locations across the developing world. To this end the Onside team began researching experts in coaching youth football. On making contact with Soccer Italian Style Academy, the Onside team felt that a partnership could be the ideal solution.

SOCCER ITALIAN STYLE PARTNERSHIP

The SIS Academy was started by successful youth coaches Mirko Mazzantini and Simone Bombardieri, who coach at Italian Serie A sides AFC Fiorentina, and Empoli FC respectively. Both coaches have seen huge success with their training methods and have extensive experience of developing young players. After a consultation process SIS produced a 6 week (30 day) training programme to allow players at Onside Academies the chance to receive up to date and high quality training, equivalent to that being delivered in top European clubs.

The programme is well structured, follows a logical path and is progressive. Furthermore, it is flexible enough that coaches in the developing world can adapt it for their own use and the circumstances of their environment. The structured nature of the training programme also helps to hold the young people's interest week by week, working on many different aspects so they are always stimulated and never bored.

EQUIPMENT PROVISION

Scarcity of football training equipment can be a huge barrier in the development of young football players in less materially wealthy countries. Replacing a couple of footballs or buying a set of bibs for example may not be an option as coaches or clubs simply can not afford to. Many junior teams in poorer areas rely on donations of old kit from teams in the western world who have replaced their own with new ones. Thankfully there are some terrific organisations, such as Kits4Causes and KitAid who approach football clubs at the end of each season and request donations of old kits to be distributed to overseas teams. These organisations have been invaluable in helping to provide the children who attend the Onside Academies with kits. The excitement and gratitude from the children on receiving them has been priceless!

Onside Soccer also provides each of it's academies with good quality football training equipment, such as the footballs themselves, bibs, cones and goals, to ensure that players can be developed to reach their full potential.

PAUL HARBINSON (FOUNDER)

Onside Soccer founder Paul Harbinson said "We value each and every child and young person who attends our training sessions. We believe that just because they live in poverty, it does not mean that they should be denied the chance of receiving the best football training and reach their full potential. That is why using this programme has been so important and fundamental for Onside; it allows us to deliver a high quality level of coaching, in many different parts of the world, to those who would normally have no access to this level of training."

Onside Soccer Mentorship Program

A key element of the Onside Soccer philosophy is that young peoples' universal passion for football can be used as a means to develop in them the positive attitudes they require to go on to transform their own lives and communities. To this end, each training session contains a mentorship element, highlighting lessons that can be learned from sport and translated into lessons for use in everyday life.

The mentorship programme, 'Onside Goals', was complied by the Onside team to comprise 15 interactive talks which can be delivered to players during the rest periods of their football training sessions. Two versions of the mentorship programme have been written, allowing coaches the choice between using either Biblical based or secular presentations. Each of the talks lasts approximately 10-15 minutes and focuses on positive qualities found while playing sports, which are then translated into 'everyday life' context. For example, one session examines how working as a 'team player' can enhance individuals and communities, both on and off the pitch. Coaches use an interactive style to discuss with the children how they felt they had been working as a team during the training session. The integral elements of teamwork, such as communication and supporting colleagues, would then be explored, and a practical application is given to assist the young people in translating these positive qualities to their everyday lives.

The response to Onside Goals mentorship programme so far has been very positive, with many children engaging keenly and positive feedback being received from parents and teachers alike.

"Since they started attending the Onside Soccer Academy, the children who I teach have been much better behaved and their attitude is really good. They really respect the coaches and listen to what they have to say and that has translated into school. We are very happy for them to attend football training and it has been a very positive addition into their lives."

Teacher from Christ Church School, Chennai

THE ONSIDE GOALS
Empowerment through sport

1
- RESPECT
- FRIENDSHIP
- ATTITUDE
- ENTHUSIASM
- TEAM SPIRIT

2
- INTEGRITY
- SKILL
- SELF CONTROL
- FIGHT
- CONFIDENCE

3
- HONESTY
- HARD WORKING
- CONSISTENCY
- SELFLESSNESS
- ENDURANCE

© ONSIDE MINISTRIES | REGISTERED CHARITY 1149686

The Future

Moving forward as an organisation, Onside Soccer has two main aims:

1. To improve and expand their current academies in Chennai and Kampala.
2. To open new academies in different locations in order to reach more children.

Paul Harbinson said this about Onside Soccer's future, "As a small organisation with limited funds we have to marshal our resources as sensibly as possible but, having seen how effective our programmes can be we also want to expand to allow other children the opportunity to come along to our academies.

For us Onside Soccer is about providing an opportunity for young people to attend professional training sessions run by enthusiastic individuals, about creating safe mentorship for them, and about giving children who are materially poor the opportunity to reach their full potential on and off the pitch. We want to provide something consistent in their lives where, no matter what else is going on, they can still come along, get a warm welcome and hopefully learn new skills.

In our camps and training sessions everyone gets the same opportunity to play. We have some really good players who come along and we have some players who are only learning the basics of the game. Everyone works together as a team and everyone is treated with dignity and respect. We want that to continue and to grow.

Currently there are Onside Soccer projects in India and Uganda and Onside also supports a coach in northern Nigeria who is using football as a peace and reconciliation tool between young Christian and Muslim people. Onside have been particularly keen to promote inclusiveness in all of their projects and although we are a Christian charity, anyone who wants to attend our academies is very welcome. Onside have also recently had a basketball coach join them and, in a similar way to our football projects, hope to set up a basketball programme for children in Chennai in the near future".

Quote from Tim Anderson, Onside Volunteer

"I went to Chennai as a volunteer with Onside Soccer to work with them on their annual football camp in May 2014. I didn't have a lot of coaching experience prior to going so was a bit nervous about what I would be able to do but I needn't have worried as the coaches in Chennai were superb.

We ran a week long camp and it was clear from the outset that everything was well organised and professional. The Head Coach in Chennai, Sebastian, has been working for Onside for a few years. He has a really good rapport with the young people who came along and it transpired that most of them had been attending Onside training sessions for at least a couple of years. One of the things that impressed me most was the way the young people engaged with the whole programme. They absolutely loved the football, but they also really enjoyed the mentorship element of things which was great to see.

I was also impressed by the way the Onside team used football to engage with disadvantaged groups in different ways. For example, one afternoon, after our normal training session, we visited a home for young people with learning difficulties to run a training session for some of the kids. It was really amazing to see the impact our visit had and the smiling faces of the kids as they joined in the games. It was just a nice thing to do and it really demonstrated to me that football can be used in all sorts of contexts in a very positive way."

How to Get Involved

As a charity we are always happy to see more people catch our vision and get involved with our work. There are a number of ways to do this:

JOIN US ON A COACHING TOUR

Every year we organise a number of coaching tours to our projects, setting up week long camps and working with local children. Coaching tours also allow participants to see other social action projects going on in the cities we visit. Please check out our website **www.onsidesoccer.com** for further details of current coaching tours.

VOLUNTEER

If you have a passion for helping others and are inspired by what you have read, we are always looking out for people to work with us.

DONATE

We can only run our programmes and keep our projects open through the goodwill and generous donations of our supporters. Everything we provide for the children who come to our projects is free but unfortunately running a charity is anything but!

If you want to support us financially, even in a small way, you can do so through our on-line donations facility which is available on our website at **www.onsidesoccer.com**

"**Sport has the power to change the world...it has the power to inspire. It has the power to unite people in a way that little else does. It speaks to youth in a language they understand. Sport can create hope where once there was only despair.**" *Nelson Mandela*

Recommendations & Quotes

Churchill Joseph

C.E.O. of the Dr John Joseph Foundation, India

'I first came into contact with Onside Soccer in 2010 when I was visiting the UK. I run an orphanage in Chennai (India) providing shelter, food and education for abandoned children but we did not have any kind of sports programme for them, which is very important for children's development. I asked Onside Soccer if they would be interested in helping us out and they agreed to come over to Chennai the following year. When they came across they set up a football summer camp for the local kids. They also trained up a local coach to help us start football classes for the kids every Friday and Saturday.

Since then Onside Soccer have been sending coaches across to help us every year and the number of children coming along each week has really grown rapidly. The kids absolutely love it. They get a chance to play football, which is great, but they also take part in the Onside life skills programme which is designed to help them make positive choices in life and build them up as people. This is really important as a lot of these children come from backgrounds where they don't really receive much positive input into their lives and building them up through sport is a really great way of connecting with them.

Football is also a great way of breaking down social barriers. The children who come along to play football come from varied social and religious backgrounds and we have Hindu, Muslim, Buddhist and Christian kids all playing together on the pitch and making lasting friendships.

Overall, football and sports programmes make a really big difference for us and it is now an integral part of what we do. The Onside Soccer partnership, in building the lives of the less fortunate children in our country, means a lot to us.'

Ivan Kakembo

Vice President of the Uganda Youth Football Association

'Football is huge all across Africa and Uganda is no exception. Everyone loves football and people here play and watch it on TV a lot. There is a lot of natural talent here in Uganda and we have had a few players move overseas and represent clubs all over the world. One of the major problems we have faced is that although we have many people playing the game, we have very few resources and particularly for youth football. We also don't really have a standard way of coaching and, as a result, younger players aren't always receiving the best possible training.

It is important for us that resources like those provided by Onside Soccer and Soccer Italian Style are available. The Uganda Youth Soccer Academy has worked in partnership with Onside Soccer for a number of years and in the past they have provided us with football kits, training equipment and footballs and now they are helping us provide a structured training programme that our coaches can follow.

This is really valuable for us as it means we can distribute a programme which is both easy to follow and up to date with modern training methods.'

Henry Kalungi
Richmond Kickers (USA) and Captain of Uganda National Team

'Football is very important in Uganda. We have many social problems, but football provides hope and a way out. It is great that charitable organisations like Onside Soccer and Soccer Italian Style are providing good programmes for young players to follow and to receive good training.

It benefits everyone - the children, the coaches and hopefully we will see some of these young players progress and represent Uganda at international level in the future.'

'The Onside camp paves the way for many underprivileged children to play and learn soccer without any cost. It is a camp filled with joyfulness! God bless Onside!!'

Asaph Cruz David, Participant at Onside Summer Camp, India

Soccer Italian Style Camps: U9-15

INTRODUCTION

We have produced a six week training program for boys and girls aged 8 - 14 using the 'Soccer Italian Style' method of coaching.

Summer football camps are becoming increasingly popular worldwide and this book was born from the desire to apply the working methodology of SOCCER ITALIAN STYLE to these summer camps. This book can also be adapted to produce a full season training program.

SOCCER ITALIAN STYLE has been organising summer camps all over the world for well over a decade for boys and girls, giving us extensive experience of running camps successfully. It is our hope that this book will be helpful to others who run soccer camps and that they can benefit from our experience and tried and tested methods of coaching.

Italian Style Soccer Camps Philosophy & Work Methodology

To help achieve our goals, Onside Soccer has set up a long term partnership with the Soccer Italian Style (SIS) Academy. Based in Florence, the SIS Academy founders Mirko Mazzantini and Simone Bombardieri have produced a 30 session training programme which is designed to support the Onside coaches, giving them a structure and template to work from which meets their specific needs.

Within Onside Soccer, we have two different types of programs. We have coaches who work with children in 1 week camps and we also have coaches who coach full 30-40 week programs. The 30 sessions in this book produce 6 weeks worth of training.

1 WEEK CAMPS

If you are working with children in a 1 week camp, you can use any of these 6 weeks of training as a ready made program.

FULL SEASON PROGRAMS

If you are coaching a full season program (30-40 weeks) then use these 30 sessions as 6 examples of a week's training and adapt/add your own ideas to create a full program, but make sure to keep the fundamental methods displayed.

You can create and adapt your own sessions which continue to work on the same fundamentals such as ball control, passing/receiving, coordination, game situations, shooting, heading etc.

If you would like more information about Onside Soccer or would even like to visit one of their overseas academies please take a look at their website at **www.onsidesoccer.com**

For more information about Soccer Italian Style please visit their website at **www.socceritalianstyle.it**

PRINCIPLES OF TRAINING CAMPS

Before introducing the 6 weeks of work, we want to explain fully the philosophy and methodology behind these camps. The structure of our camps is based on the principle that there will be 40-60 players participating. Having this number is necessary to maintain proper communication between the players and the coaches at each workstation, ensuring that all of the instructions issued can be followed correctly.

To ensure that a camp functions properly we are also basing drills on a minimum number of 4 coaches. Obviously if more coaches are available then the number of players and workstations can be increased. Training sessions are designed to be held every day and last approximately 2 hours.

Soccer Italian Style has Two Primary Objectives:

- To improve the main/fundamental technical of each player
- The engagement and enjoyment of players through the use of different drills/practices, all of which have a strong competitive element

SIS camps follow the principle of specificity of training. In practical terms this means that every day will have a specific technical objective, with all of the drills used that day designed to work towards that objective. The reason for this is by focusing on inter-linked practices aimed at developing a specific skill or technical objective, we believes there is a much higher chance of a technical improvement.

Outline of Training Week

The philosophy of Soccer Italian Style is expected in every training session. The main themes are the development of the skills of ball control, dribbling and feints/moves to beat. Within the sessions in this book we have enclosed most of the exercises that are fundamental for us to improve these skills.

WARM UP

We split the players into 3 groups in 3 different stations to warm up and assign specific technical topics to be developed. The warm up is always the first practice of the session.

TECHNICAL

The Soccer Italian style technical block focuses on ball control (total control of the ball) and dribbling.

The technical phase is unopposed and works on the individual player's technique.

We work on a specific technique (practice 2) and on coordination (or a conditioning exercise) for practice 3.

TACTICAL

The Soccer Italian style tactical block focuses on feints/moves to beat, dribbling and changes of direction. This is usually the fourth practice in the session as we practice a game situation.

The tactical phase allows the players to use the technical concepts they have learnt and to produce them in a tactical context (game situation) e.g. 1v1 duel. We finish the session with a game and a free small sided game.

DAY 1

On day 1 in all the sessions, we work on ball control and running with the ball. This is to develop the ability of the player to control the ball in various different situations. Make sure to allow ample space for the players to perform the specific coordinative gestures which are essential for the players to develop their motor technique.

DAY 2

On day 2 we work on feints/moves to beat in individual and group practices. We switch the theme to a more tactical concept. The warm up will be entirely focused on the concept of tactical feints and dribbling with exercises designed to reproduce typical situations that especially focus on 1v1 duels.

DAY 3

On day 3 we work on the technique of passing and receiving. We progress through the session to work on tactical concepts such as maintaining possession.

DAY 4

On day 4 we keep working on the same elements from the previous days, but change the focus to shooting. With all the necessary techniques having been already covered, the players can develop their tactical attributes in the game situations and small sided games.

DAY 5

On day 5 we work on the same elements from the previous days, but focus on heading or passing and receiving in the air.

Primary Technical Objective for each Day of the Camp

DAY 1	Running with the Ball
DAY 2	Feints / Moves to Beat
DAY 3	Passing and Receving
DAY 4	Shooting
DAY 5	Heading or Passing/Receving in the Air

Session Structure

INITIAL PHASE - TECHNICAL WARM UP

The initial phase of each session (the technical warm up) lasts about 30 minutes and concentrates on the TECHNICAL BLOCK which Soccer Italian Style has designed for these Onside Soccer programs.

This block includes a series of technical exercises aimed at ball control and domination of the ball. There are 5 different technical warm ups provided for each day. These are repeated for all of the 6 weeks provided in this book.

The concept of the TECHNICAL BLOCK is the cornerstone of the philosophy of SOCCER ITALIAN STYLE and is extremely important to the learning and development of the fundamental techniques. While, day after day, the primary technical objective changes, the first 30 minutes will always be dedicated to these principles.

The players are divided into 2 groups each with 2 coaches. If you have less players or coaches, then just work with 1 group.

CENTRAL PHASE - TECHNICAL AND COORDINATION PRACTICES

At this point, after warming up with the TECHNICAL BLOCK, the group is divided into groups of about 10-15 players. Each group will go to one of the four stations. After 15 minutes there will be a change of station until all 4 groups have completed all 4 workstations.

All 4 stations within a session will have the same primary technical objective but each station will be working from a different perspective:

STATION A focuses on technical skills from a biomechanical point of view and are always unopposed. The coaches will analyse and correct the execution of players' technical movements.

STATION B is a coordination station. The Soccer Italian Style philosophy recognises a strong link between coordination skills and technical movement. Coordination skills are the foundation to each technical gesture.

At this station the coordination exercise is often with the ball and strongly linked to the primary technical gesture of the day. In some sessions, the coordination exercise is replaced with a conditioning exercise.

STATION C focuses on game situations, for example 1v1, 2v2, 3v2 etc. In this workstation, the techniques learnt previously are now tested in a fully opposed situation with active defenders/opponents. This provides a situation which is much close to a real game scenario.

STATION D focuses on game situations similar to Station C but with a greater emphasis on replicating a real match situation. This usually takes the form of a small sided game which is characterised by additional rules to stimulate greater use of the technical skill worked on that day.

FINAL PHASE - FREE SMALL SIDED GAMES

Each training session ends with a small sided game of 5v5 or 6v6 depending on the number of players you are working with. On the final day we suggest ending the camp with 11v11 matches. This is to make sure there is an element of fun for the players and they are allowed space and freedom to play and express themselves on.

Primary Technical Objective for each Day of the Camp

	Technical Warm Up	30 mins
A	Technical	15 mins
B	Coordination	15 mins
C	Game Situation	15 mins
D	Game with a Theme	15 mins
	Free Small Sided Games	30 mins

Practice Format

Each practice in the sessions includes clear diagrams with supporting training notes:

- Session Objective
- Name of Practice
- Description
- Variations/Progressions (if applicable)
- Coaching Points

Key

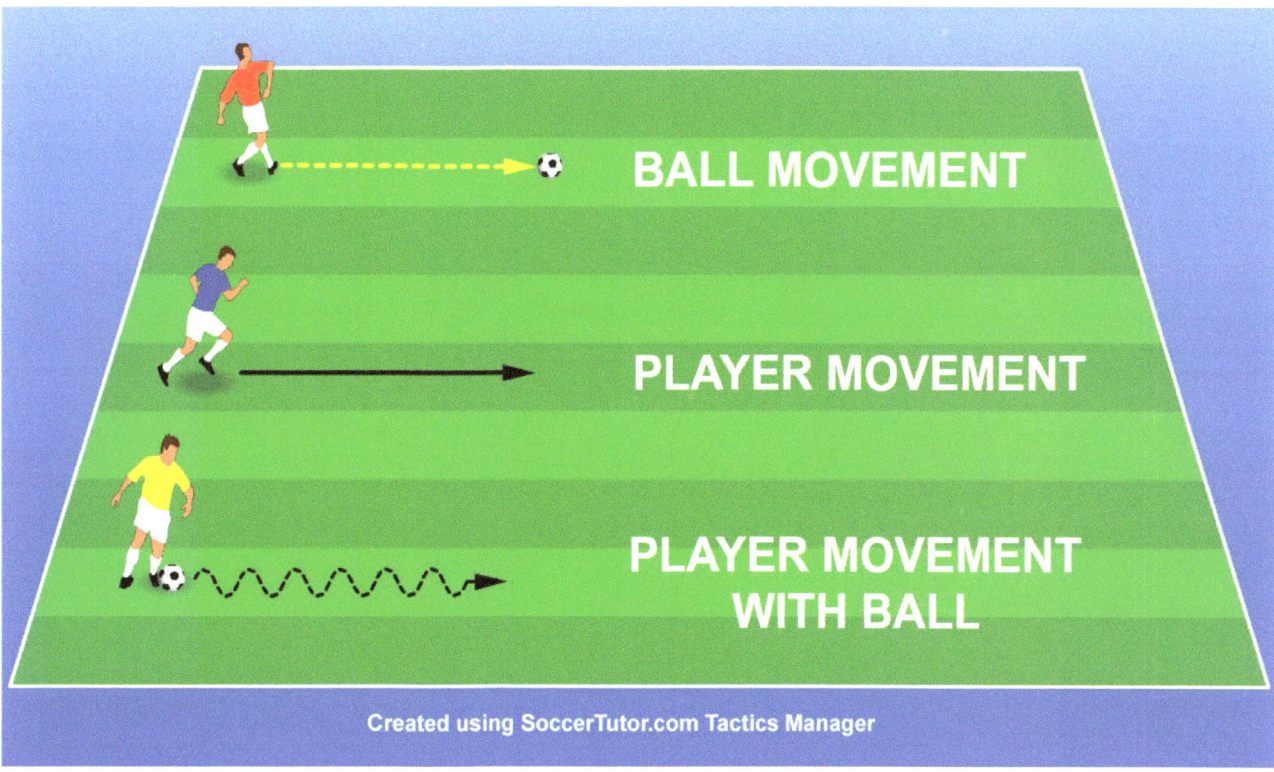

WEEK 1

DAY 01: Running with the Ball

Running with the Ball

Primary Technical Objective: Running with the ball.
Secondary Technical Objective: Coordination, dribbling and shooting.
Tactical Objective: 1v1 Duels.

Duration of Session: 2 hours 15 mins

1. Warm Up: Technical Block 1 — 30 mins

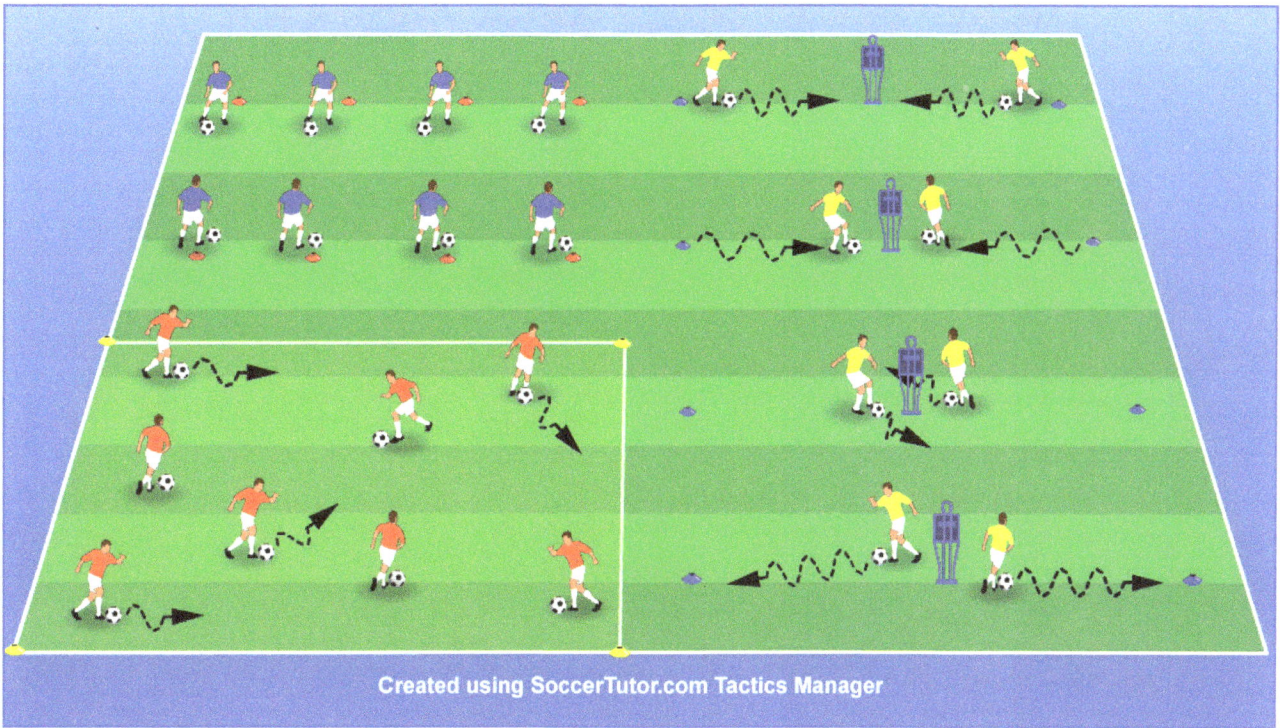

Divide the players into 3 groups with a minimum of 8 players at each station.

Group A

The red players perform different types of dribbling the ball in traffic, making sure to avoid collisions. Keep using variations, making sure that the players use only one foot and then the other when manoeuvring the ball. Vary the part of the foot used - outside, instep, the sole etc. Make sure to also perform different exercises - stretching and joint mobility exercises.

Group B

The blue players are each positioned on a cone. Every player practices different technical ball control exercises on the spot and around the cone. Start slowly and progress to increase the speed of execution. Use exercises such as making an 'L Shape' with the sole, quick outside then inside touches with 1 foot and many more. Each coach can create variants with their own imagination.

Group C

The yellow players line up opposite each other with a mannequin or cone in between them. Each player has a ball and they start simultaneously by dribbling the ball towards the centre and then perform a feint to the right (or left). The coach can determine a specific feint such as a scissor, chop or Maradona move. The players keep the same sequence going and start each time on the coach's whistle.

WEEK 1

2. Technical: Close Control with Shooting Accuracy   15 mins

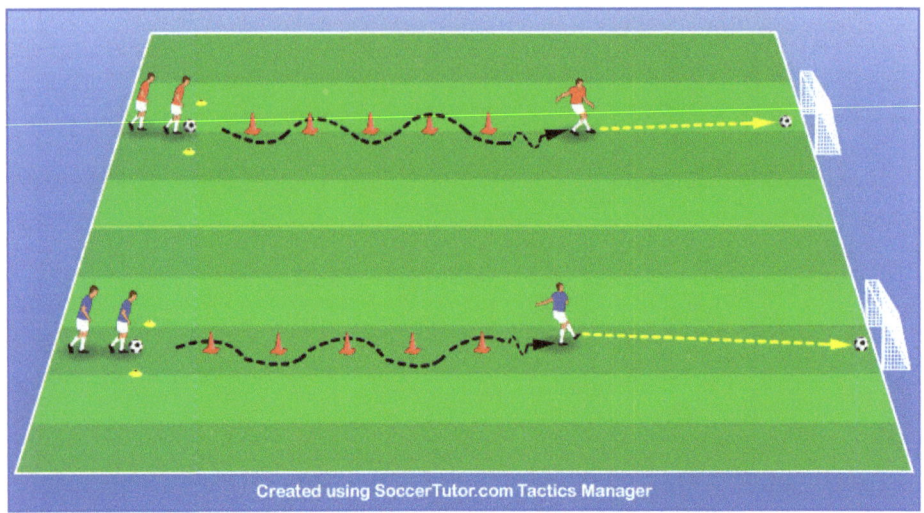

Description
Players dribble through the cones and shoot in the small goals. Vary the sequence of dribbling through the cones and vary the distances between the cones.

Vary the type of ball and use different techniques of running with the ball.

Variations
1. Dribbling only with the right or left foot. 2. Dribbling only with the inside or outside of the feet.

Coaching Points
1. It is necessary to have good control with soft touches at speed to dribble through cones without errors.
2. Players should have slightly bent knees when changing direction, with the ball close to their feet.

---

3. Coordination: Coordination Relay   15 mins

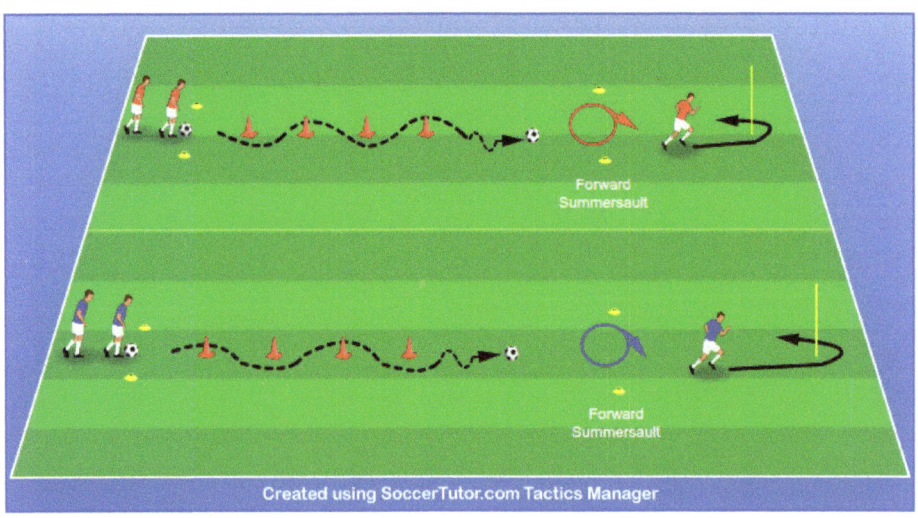

Description
Players must dribble through the cones, stop the ball (leaving it) and do a forward roll.

They then run around the pole and then repeat the exercise back to their teammates (another forward roll and dribble through the cones). The next player then goes.

Variations
1. Play with a goalkeeper. 2. Modify the coordination course. 3. Dribble using different parts of the foot.

Coaching Points
1. Make the exercise a competition to increase the speed of play.
2. Accuracy when dribbling around the cones is key to save time keeping the ball close to their feet.

DAY 01:   Running with the Ball

4. Game Situation: 1v1 v Defender + 1v1 v Goalkeeper   15 mins

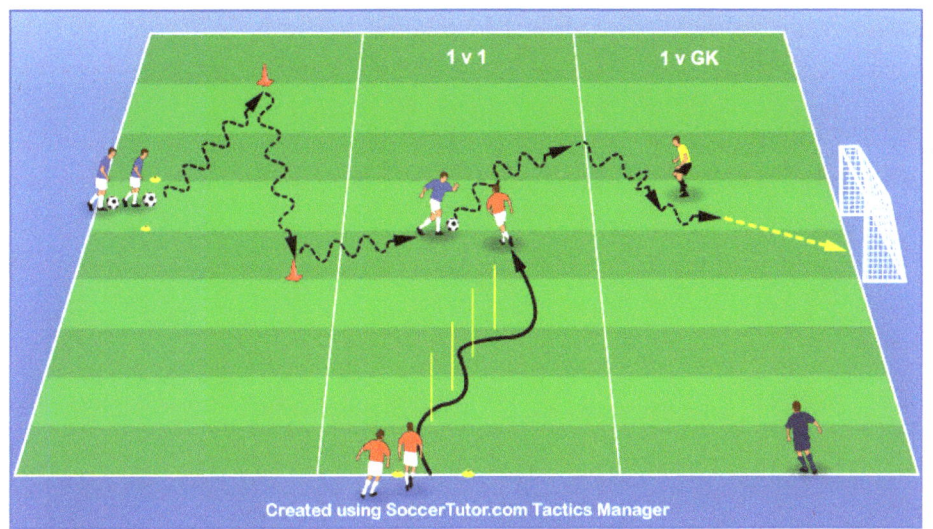

Description

The red player starts by running through the poles. The blue player dribbles and performs some feints and then takes the red player on in a 1v1, before trying to score past the goalkeeper.

If the red player wins the ball from the blue player, he can go into a 1v1 with the goalkeeper.

Variations

1. The goal counts double if a player does a feint specified by the coach.
2. The red players skip through the poles.

Coaching Point

The player with the ball needs to use a change of pace or direction to quickly get into the 1 v GK zone and score.

5. Game with a Theme: '4 Goals 4v4' Small Sided Game   15 mins

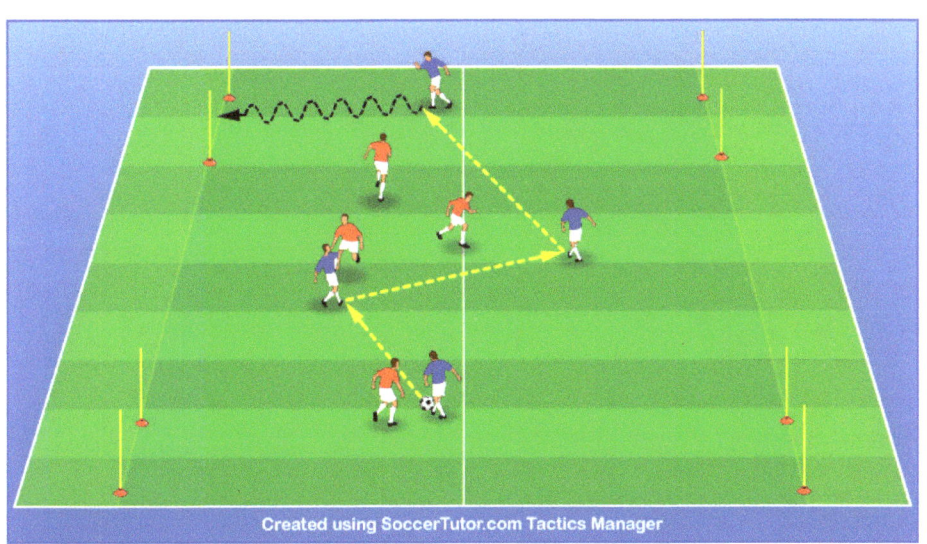

Description

Here we play a free 4v4 small sided game with 4 pole goals in the positions shown.

Each team defends 2 goals.

The players score a goal if they are able to dribble the ball through one of the gates/goals.

Variations

1. Tournament with more teams.
2. Players have to stop the ball on the line to score.
3. Limit the maximum amount of touches.

6. 5v5 Small Sided Games   30 mins

WEEK 1

Feints / Moves to Beat

Primary Technical Objective: Dribbling with the ball and feints/moves to beat.
Secondary Technical Objective: Ball control and shooting.
Coordination Objective: Quickness, adaptation, transformation and reactions.
Tactical Objective: 1v1 Duels and man marking.
Duration of Session: 2 hours 15 mins

1. Warm Up: Technical Block 2 — 30 mins

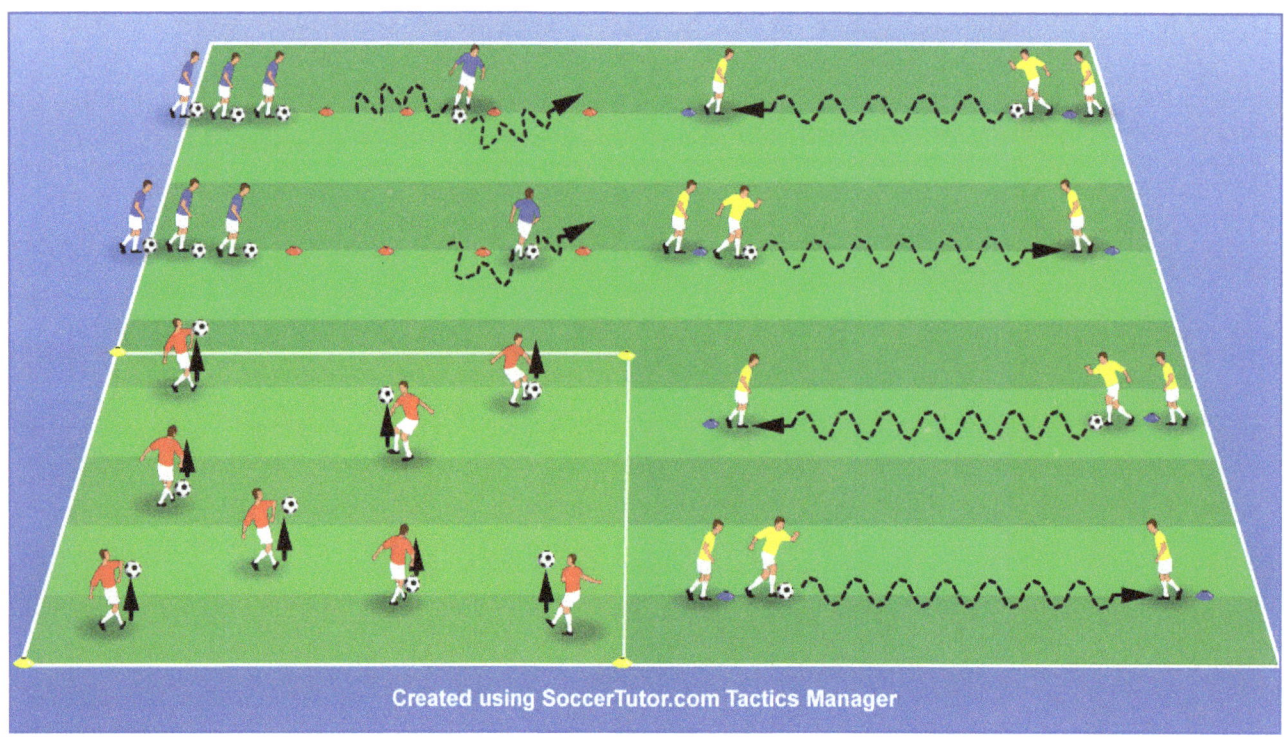

Group A

The red players use a variety of juggling techniques depending on their age/level. If the exercise is too complex for the age/level of their players they can juggle and catch using their hands.

Variations: 1 or 2 touches of the foot and then catch with the hands, juggling with either foot freely, juggle or dribble with alternating rhythm (2 right / 1 left), sequence - foot, thigh, head.

Other Exercises: Juggle at various heights (1 low / 1 high), alternate feet with bounces allowed, juggle followed by acrobatic act e.g. forward roll. You can introduce much more based on ability and propose a points race e.g. first player to complete 20 consecutive alternate touches when juggling.

Group B

The blue players are split into 2 teams and run a relay race dribbling through the cones. When each player arrives at the finish line, they wait there for their teammates to complete. The winning team is the one that finishes quickest. If any player fails to dribble the ball round one of the cones successfully the team receives a time penalty. You can assign rules such as only dribble with left foot, alternate touches etc.

Group C

The yellow players are split into teams of 3 with a ball per team. The first player must dribble the ball to his teammate who is 15 yards away. The player who receives then dribbles the ball to the third player. You can assign points based on whether the players can get the ball to their teammate without losing control of the ball. This exercise can also be done with the players having to juggle the ball.

DAY 02: Feints / Moves to Beat

2. Technical: Ball Control - Moves / Feints

15 mins

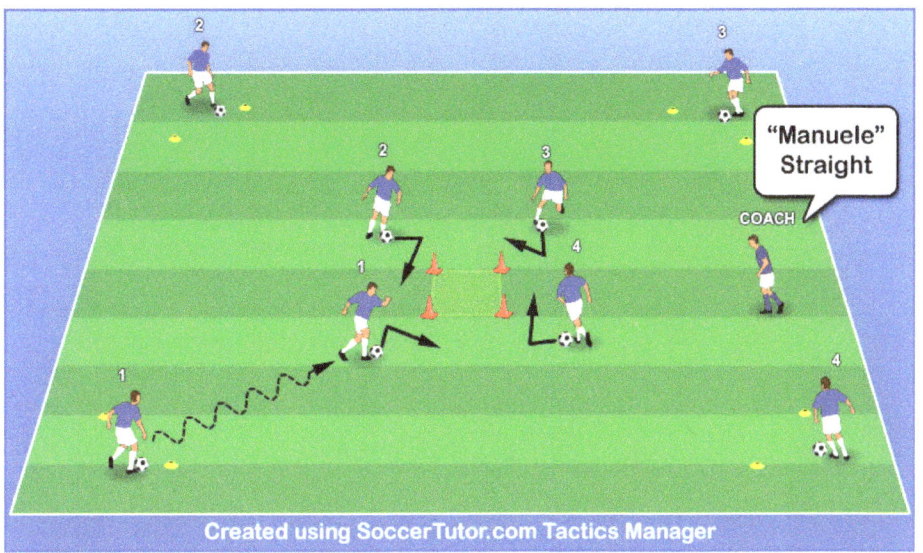

Coaching Points
1. Keep the ball close to the feet.
2. Make many touches with the ball.
3. Dribbling with the ball should be done with soft touches.
4. Move/feint – exaggerate the move making a sharp movement in a different direction.

Description
In a square approximately 10 x 10 yards we have a circle or position cones as shown in the centre. Players are separated into groups in the corners of the square.

On the coaches command, players dribble towards the centre of the square perform a feint before taking the ball away to the LEFT, RIGHT, RETURN or STRAIGHT to the opposite corner.

The different feints and change of position is pre-determined by the coach.

3. Coordination: 1v1 Duel - Feints and Dribbling

15 mins

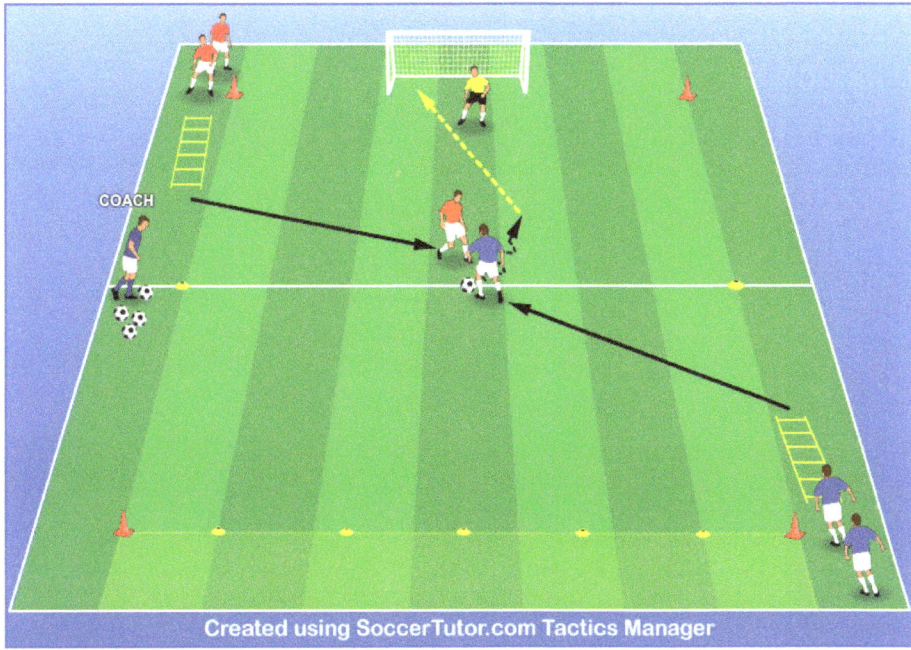

Coaching Points
1. The players need to demonstrate explosive acceleration.
2. Players need to keep the ball close to their feet.
3. The attacker should try to get a shot on goal as quickly as possible.

Description
In an area of 20 x 15 yards two players play against each other in a 1 v 1 practice.

On the coaches signal both players execute fast steps through the speed ladder and then sprint to the centre of the field to gain control of the ball placed there by the coach.

First to the ball becomes the attacker who attempts to beat the defender and shoot at the goal past the goalkeeper. The defender has to attempt to win the ball. If successful, his objective is to score a goal by dribbling into the end zone at the opposite end.

WEEK 1

4. Game Situation: 1v1 Duel - Feints, Dribbling and Change of Direction

15 mins

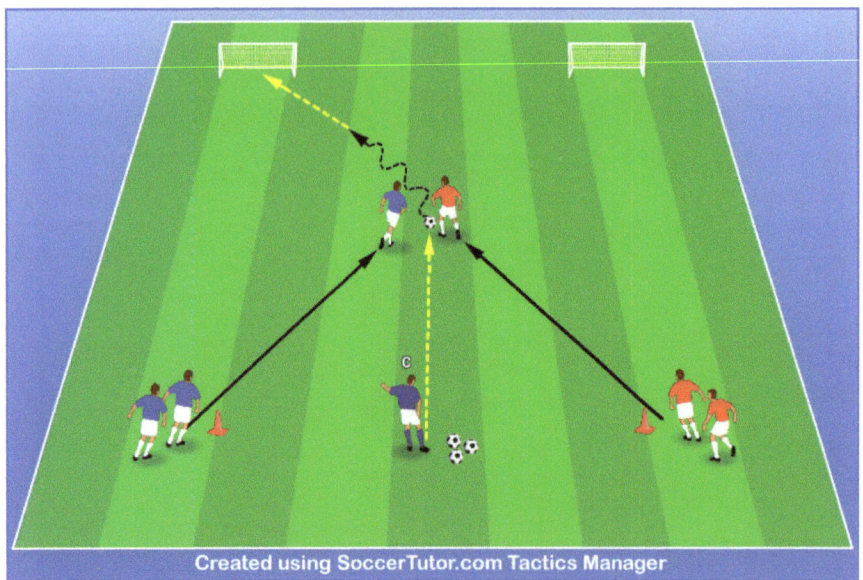

Description

In an area 20 x 15 yards the players compete in 1 v 1 situations. The coach kicks the ball to the centre of the field.

The first player to reach the ball becomes the attacker and aims to score in 1 of the 2 goals. If the defender manages to tackle or intercept the ball he becomes the attacker.

The use of 2 goals in this exercise increases the options for changes in direction and different feints.

Coaching Points

1. The attacker needs to use his body as a barrier between the defender and the ball to protect it.
2. The attacker needs to keep the ball close to their feet using feints and quick changes of direction when needed to get away and score.

5. Game with a Theme: 5v5 with 6 Dribble Gates in a SSG

15 mins

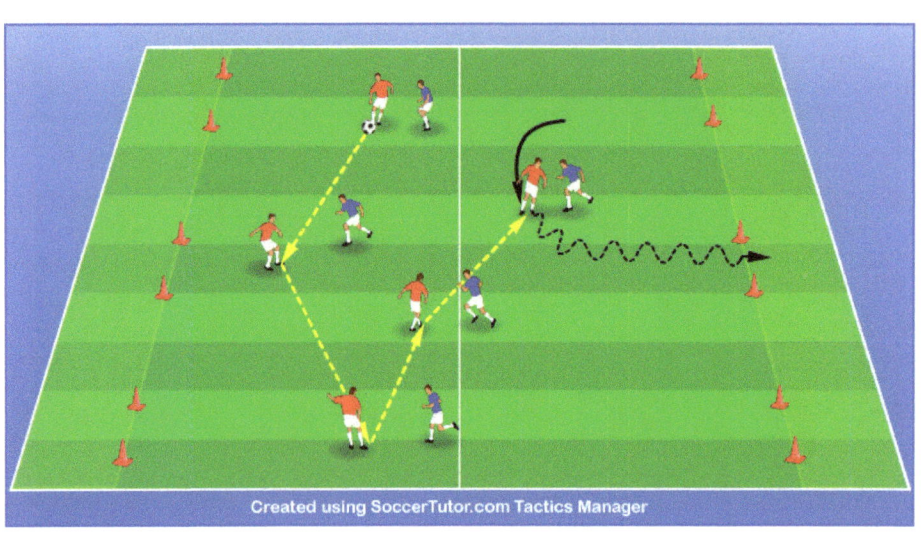

Description

We play a 5v5 free game in an area 30 x 30 yards with 3 goals on each side.

The players must score a goal by dribbling through one of the cone gates.

Variations

1. Tournament with more teams.
2. Stop the ball with the sole on the line to score.
3. Limit the touches.

6. 5v5 Small Sided Games

30 mins

DAY 03: Passing and Receiving

Passing and Receiving

Primary Technical Objective: Passing and receiving on the ground.
Secondary Technical Objective: Dribbling, turning and protecting the ball.
Coordination Objective: Quickness, adaptation, transformation and balance.
Tactical Objective: Creating space, positioning, marking and possession play.

Duration of Session: 2 hours 15 mins

1. Warm Up: Technical Block 3   30 mins

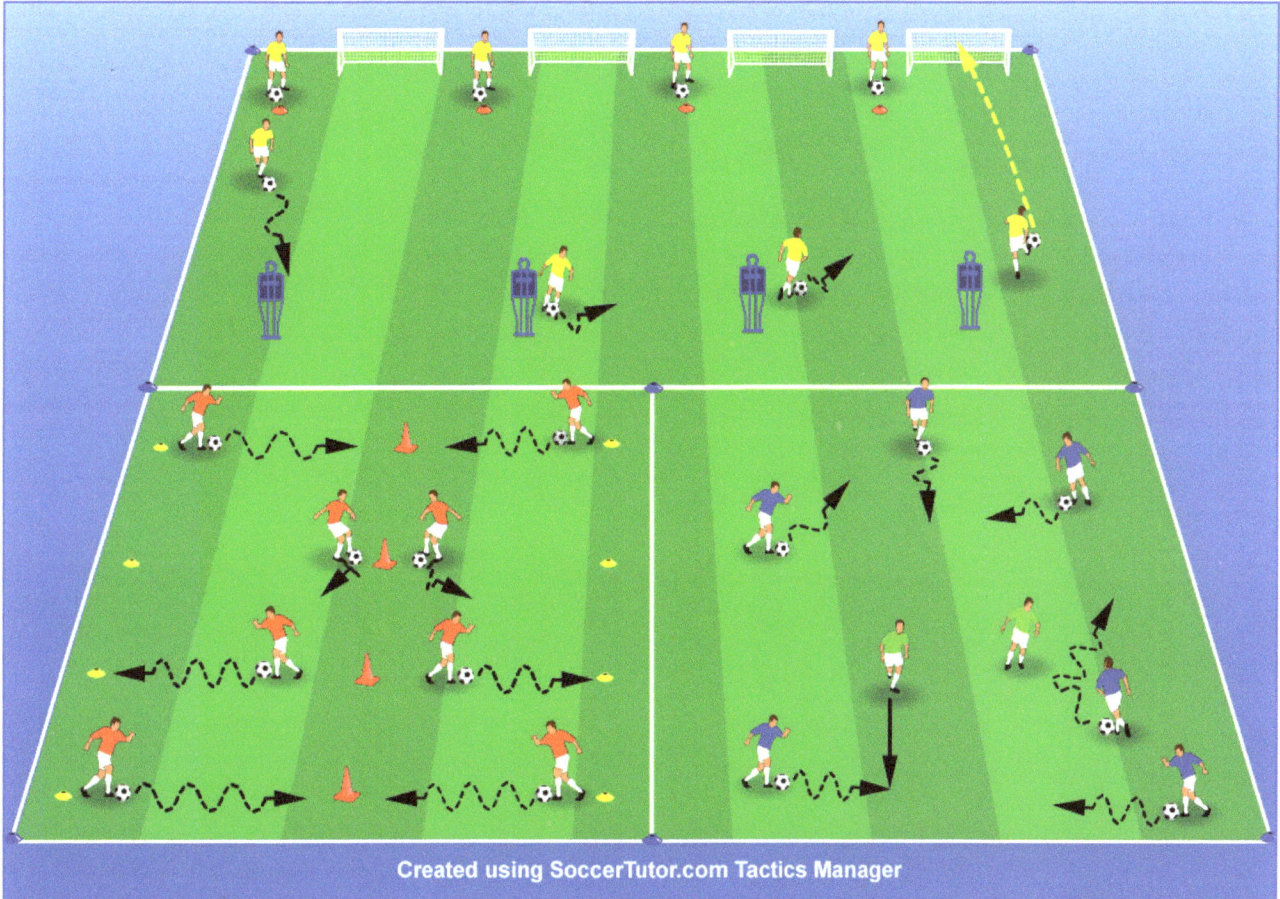

Group A

The red players are in pairs opposite each other 15 yards apart. Both players have a ball and start simultaneously by dribbling the ball towards the centre. At the cone, the players change direction and dribble back to the starting position.

Alternate different types of turns such as turn with the sole, sole 'L' shape, internal cut etc.

Group B

The blue players all have a ball each and move around freely in a 15 x 15 yard area. 2 or more green players are added (depending on the number of players in blue) who try to win the ball from the blue players as quickly as possible. If a blue player loses the ball he is not eliminated, but instead helps the other blue players to maintain possession of the ball. Change the green players every minute.

Group C

The yellow players are divided into 4 groups and compete in a relay competition. Each player dribbles the ball towards the mannequin (or cone) which is 5 yards away, perform a specific turn pre-determined by the coach and then quickly shoot into the goal. The first team to score 10 goals wins the relay.

WEEK 1

2. Technical: Pass, Move & Receive in a Square

15 mins

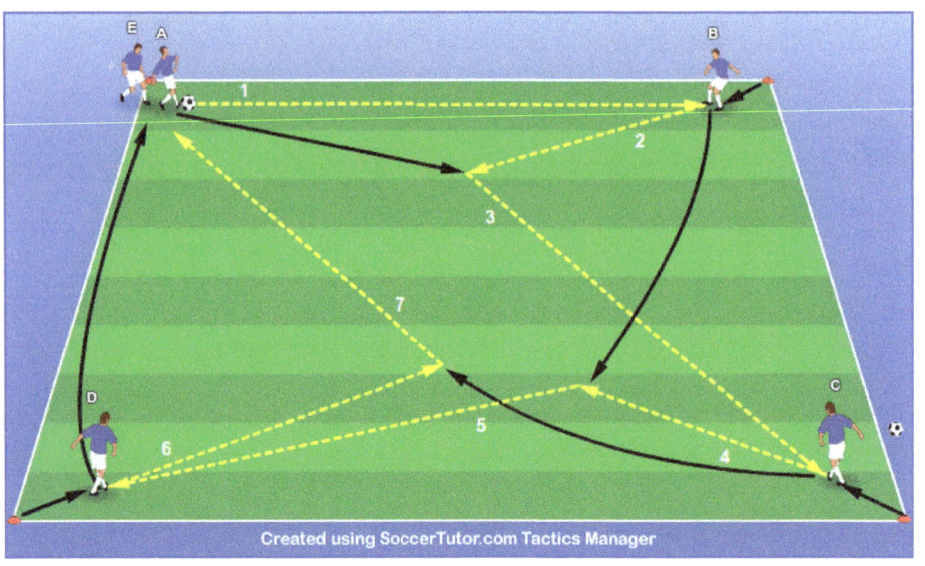

Variations
1. Change the direction.
2. Execute the exercise with volleys starting with the ball in the hands.

Coaching Points
1. The rhythm and timing of the movement together with the pass is key.
2. Players need to make sure their first touch is made on the move to maintain the fluency of the drill.

Description
In a 10 x 10 yard square we have 5 players with 2 players in the starting position.

Player A passes to B who plays the ball back into A's path.

Player A passes to C who lays the ball back for B's run. B then passes to D who plays it into Player C's path to make the final pass back to the starting position.

All players move to the next position after their last pass (A to B, B to C, C to D and D to E).

E starts the sequence again from the starting position.

---

3. Coordination: Skip, Pass, Receive, Dribble & Run

15 mins

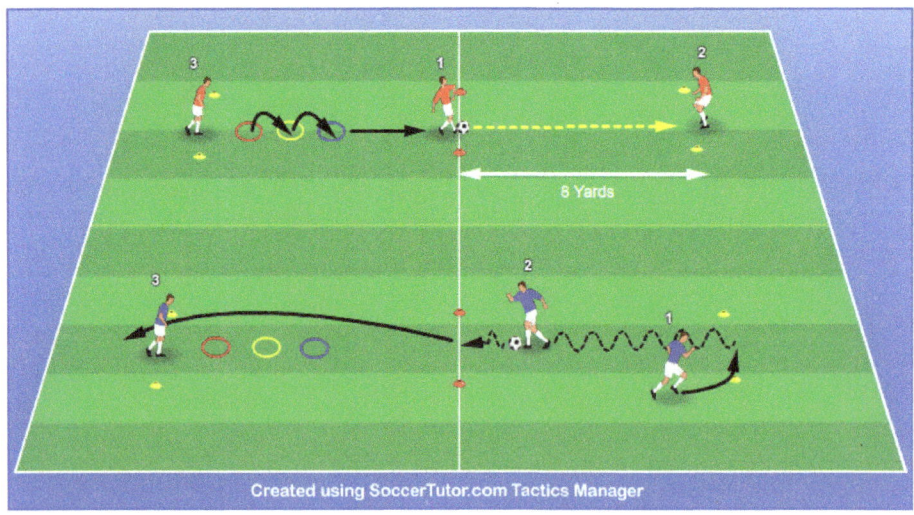

Description
PLAYER 1 hops through the rings with only the left foot and then passes to Player 2 with the right foot.

PLAYER 2 receives the ball, dribbles the ball up to the cones and runs to the starting position where player 3 is waiting.

PLAYER 3 starts the sequence again.

Variation
Substitute the rings with a foam mat and ask the players to do a forward roll.

Coaching Points
1. The pass should be weighted correctly make receiving easy.
2. When receiving, the first touch should push the ball out of their feet to dribble forwards quickly.

DAY 03: Passing and Receiving

4. Game Situation: Passing and Receiving in a 2v1 Duel   15 mins

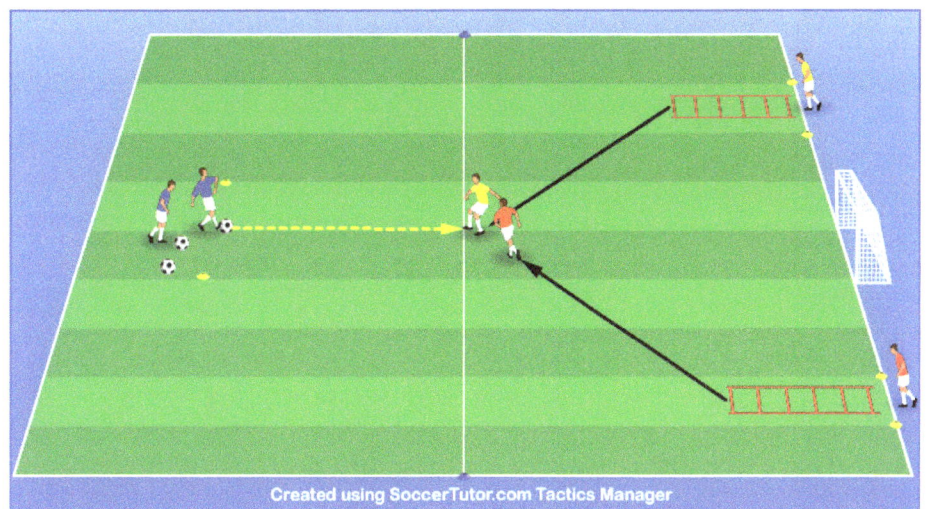

Description

The players are split into teams and the blue player passes the ball into the middle. The yellow and red players run through the ladder and then they sprint towards the ball. The first player to the ball passes back to the blue player and we have a 2v1 game.

Give 2 points if the goal is scored after a 1-2 combination.

Variations
1. Substitute the rings with poles or a forward roll.
2. Allow the defender to be able to score a goal too.

Coaching Points
1. Players need quick steps lifting the knees when running through the ladder.
2. The correct body shape when receiving is important, making sure to shield the ball from the defender.

5. Game with a Theme: 5v5 End to End Possession Game   15 mins

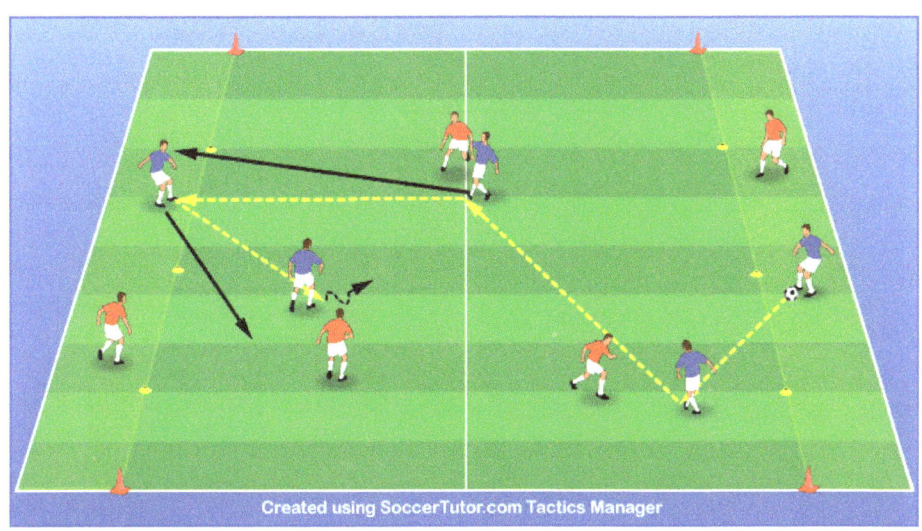

Description

In an area 40 x 25 yards we have a 5v5 game. 2 players from each team stand in the end zones (1 at each end).

A point is scored every time the ball is worked from 1 target player to the other.

When a pass is made to the target player, this player enters the middle area and the passing player takes his place. The team maintains possession to attack in the opposite direction.

Coaching Points
1. Correct body shape (open up on the half-turn) and positioning is important to view the options for where the next pass is going.
2. When the players are exchanging positions in the end zones, they need to do so quickly and provide a passing option to keep possession.

6. 5v5 Small Sided Games   30 mins

WEEK 1

Shooting

Primary Technical Objective: Shooting and finishing.

Secondary Technical Objective: Quick combination play and feints/moves to beat.

Coordination Objective: Balance, strength, explosive power, quickness, adaptation and transformation.

Tactical Objective: 1v1 Duels, attacking combination play and man marking.

Duration of Session: 2 hours 15 mins

---

1. Warm Up: Technical Block 4 — 30 mins

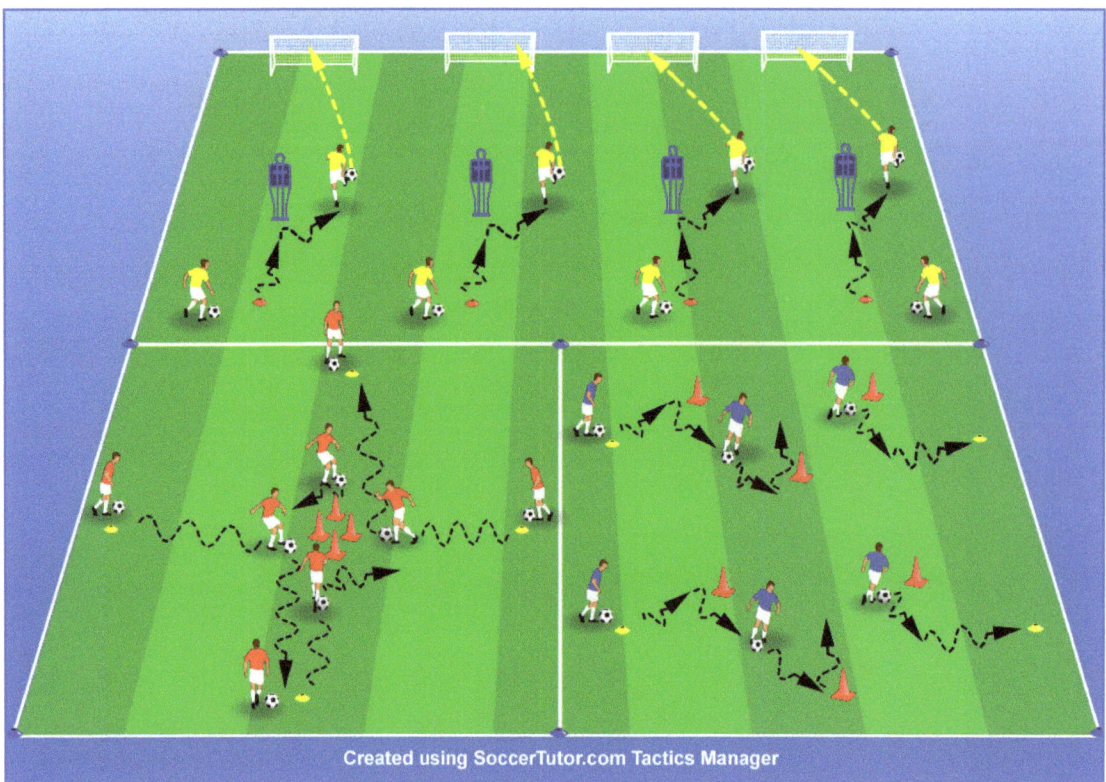

Group A

The red players line up behind the 4 cones as shown. 4 players start at the same time and dribble the ball towards the cone in front of them, perform a feint pre-determined by the coach and move to the cone to the right. Change the type of feint after every completed lap and also change the direction from anticlockwise to clockwise so the players move to the left as well.

Group B

The blue players are divided into 2 groups and practice dribbling with feints to change direction. Initially the players simply use the inside and outside of both feet to dribble and change directions. They then progress to perform a specific feint at each cone which is pre-determined by the coach. Examples of feints include the scissor, the cut back and the chop.

Group C

The yellow players are divided into teams of 3 or 4 and are in a competition to see who can score the most goals. 4 players start simultaneously with a ball, dribble towards the mannequin (or cone), perform a feint to the left or right and shoot in the mini goal. A point is awarded to the player who scores first.

You can decide the type of feint to be used or leave it to the players imagination and freedom.

DAY 04: Shooting

2. Technical: One-Two Combination and Shot — 15 mins

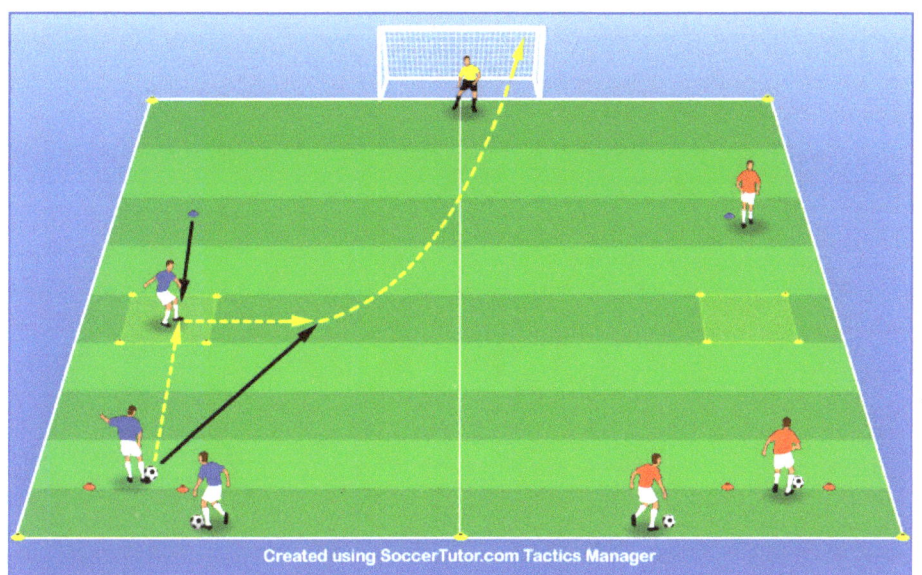

Description

2 groups (red vs blue) compete in a game of passing and shooting and take turns.

Player A passes to B who has moved into the square and he plays a first time pass into the path of A's forward run (1-2 combination).

He receives and shoots at the goal. The team that scores the most goals win.

Variations
1. Limit players to 1 touch for all aspects of the drill.
2. Use an aerial pass into the square to practice receiving ball in the air.

3. Coordination: Shooting Game with a Coordination Circuit — 15 mins

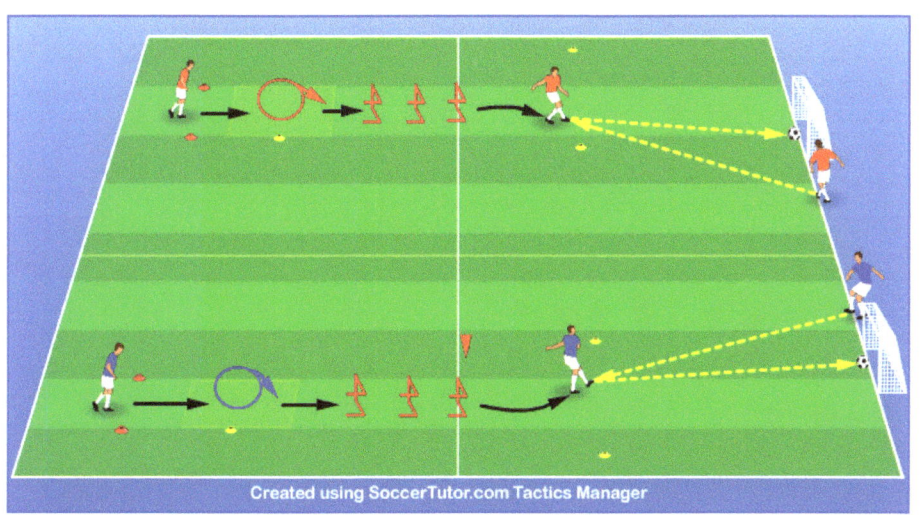

Description

Players start by doing a forward roll, then jump over the hurdles, run towards the ball and shoot with 1 touch.

This is a team game and the team with the most goals wins the competition.

Variation
Change to an aerial pass to shoot at goal with a volley.

Coaching Points
1. Good rhythm and balance is needed in the transition from the roll to jumping over the hurdles.
2. Players should use small steps up to the cones before shooting first time, for a more controlled shot.

WEEK 1

4. Game Situation: Strength, 1v1 Duels and Finishing — 15 mins

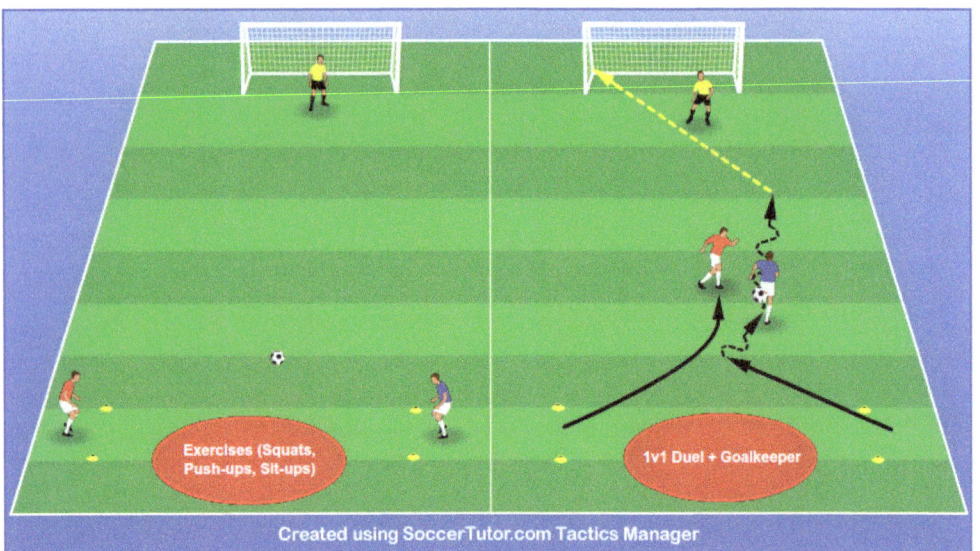

Description

2 players stand opposite each other and perform various strengthening exercises (squats, pushups, sit-ups).

Each exercise must be repeated 8-10 times and then the players race to the ball and play a 1v1 game trying to score in the goal past the goalkeeper.

5. Game with a Theme: 1v1 Marking in a 4v4 SSG — 15 mins

Description

Here we have a 4v4 tournament. Each player is assigned 1 player to mark.

If a player beats their defender then they can shoot freely as no other player can mark or tackle them.

Variation

Mark out a shooting area on the pitch.

6. 5v5 Small Sided Games — 30 mins

DAY 05: Heading

Heading

Primary Technical Objective: Heading.

Secondary Technical Objective: Throw-ins, crossing and receiving.

Coordination Objective: Quickness, motor skills (jumping), dynamic balance and reading the trajectory.

Tactical Objective: Attacking and defending aerial balls.

Duration of Session: 2 hours 15 mins

1. Warm Up: Technical Block 5 — 30 mins

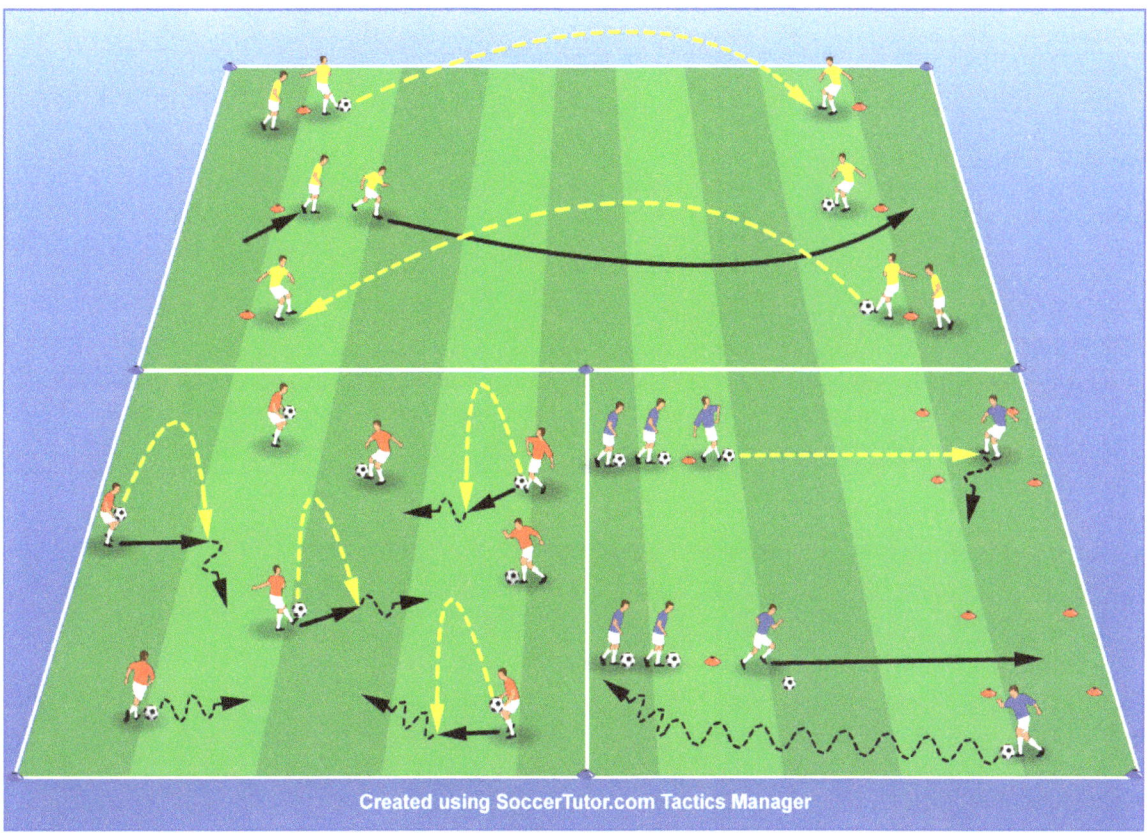

Group A

The red players move freely around the area and control the ball in different ways. The players throw (or kick) the ball up in the air, control the ball and then dribble for a few yards. Vary the type of control used - inside of foot, outside of foot, with the sole, with the laces, thigh, head etc.

Group B

Divide the blue players into 2 groups and set up 5 x 5 yard squares as shown. This is a relay competition with the 2 teams starting simultaneously. The first player passes the ball to the player in the square and then runs into the square. The player in the square take s a directional first touch out the side of the square and dribbles the ball to the next player who repeats the same sequence.

Group C

The yellow players work on passing and receiving high balls at a 25 yard distance. The first player makes an aerial pass to their teammate and then runs 25 yards to their position. The second player controls the ball and then plays the next aerial pass and runs 25 yards to the opposite cone. The same sequence continues.

Vary the type of control used - inside of foot, outside of foot, the sole, the laces, thigh, head etc.

WEEK 1

2. Technical: Heading Accuracy 'Aim for a Corner' — 15 mins

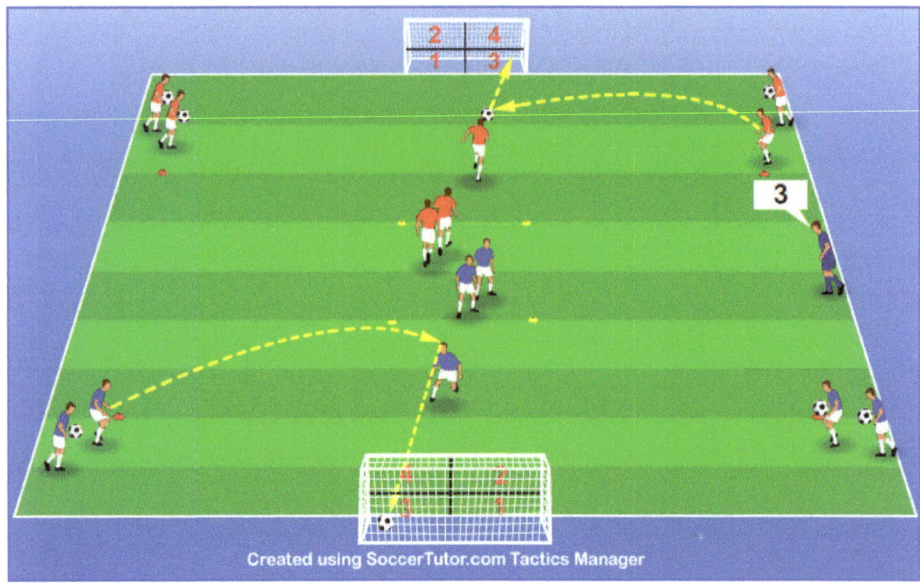

Description

Divide the goals into various sections with tape and assign a point system to each zone.

The players at the side use a throw-in to pass the ball and the central players must direct their header towards the section of the goal (1,2,3 or 4) called out by the coach.

Variation

Competitive game with 2 goals (as shown in the diagram).

Coaching Point

The players will have to use different heading techniques and different parts of the head depending on the throw and which section the coach calls out - middle, side of the head, heading down, diving header etc.

3. Coordination: Jump, Run, Change of Direction and Headed Pass — 15 mins

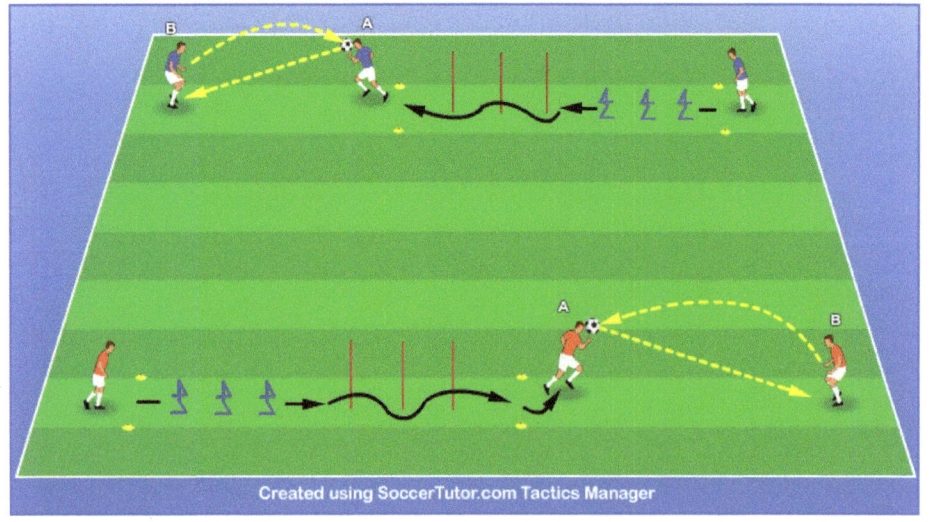

Description

Player A jumps over the hurdles, runs through the poles as shown and then runs to head the ball thrown by their teammate.

Player A then takes up Player B's position and Player B runs to the starting position at the opposite end.

Make the game a competition.

Variation

Change the agility circuit.

Coaching Points

1. Players should take small, quick side-to-side steps through the poles.
2. To head down, the player must jump higher than the ball and lean the head forwards.

DAY 05: Heading

4. Game Situation: Throw-ins, Heading, 1v1s and Finishing — 15 mins

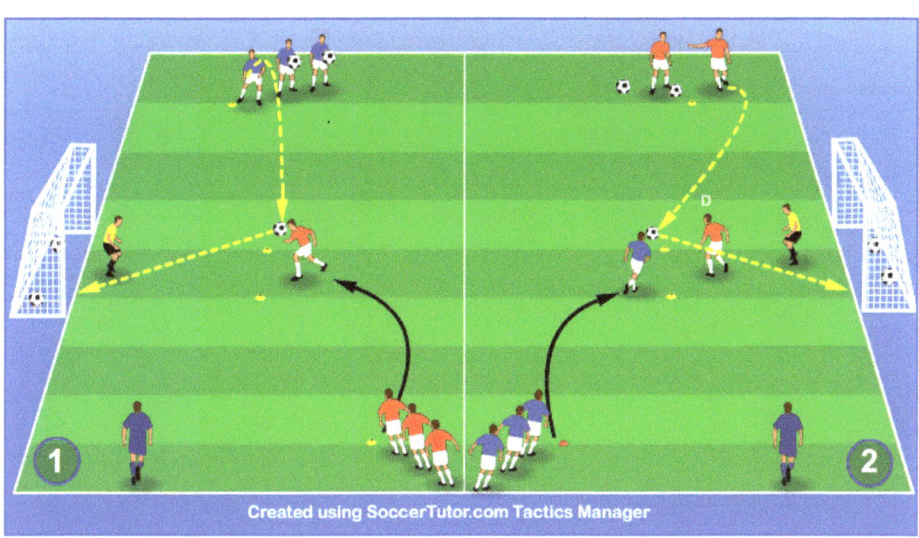

Description

GROUP 1

The red player starts from the side and runs to the middle and heads at goal from 7-8 yards away from the goal. The ball is thrown by the blue player using a throw-in.

GROUP 2

The blue player does the same as the red player in group 1, but faces a defender when trying to head at goal. The red player at the side crosses the ball instead of throwing.

The blues and reds compete and the team that scores the most goals wins.

Variations

1. Diving header.
2. Add a defender to group 1.
3. Cross with feet in group 1.

5. Game with a Theme: 6v6 Headers Game with 6 Outside Players — 15 mins

Description

In an area 25 x 20 yards we play a 6v6 handball game with 6 outside support players.

A goal is only valid if it is scored from a header with an assist by an outside player.

Progress to the outside players using their heads (as shown in diagram).

Variation

Play with hands and feet, kicking the ball out of the hands and catching to pass and receive.

6. 11v11 Matches on a Full Pitch — 30 mins

WEEK 2

DAY 01: Running with the Ball

Running with the Ball

Primary Technical Objective: Running with the ball.
Secondary Technical Objective: Dribbling and turning.
Coordination Objective: Speed, adaptation, balance and motor combinations.
Tactical Objective: 1v1 Duels and defensive marking.

Duration of Session: 2 hours 15 mins

1. Warm Up: Technical Block 1 — 30 mins

Divide the players into 3 groups with a minimum of 8 players at each station.

Group A

The red players perform different types of dribbling the ball in traffic, making sure to avoid collisions. Keep using variations, making sure that the players use only one foot and then the other when manoeuvring the ball. Vary the part of the foot used - outside, instep, the sole etc. Make sure to also perform different exercises - stretching and joint mobility exercises.

Group B

The blue players are each positioned on a cone. Every player practices different technical ball control exercises on the spot and around the cone. Start slowly and progress to increase the speed of execution. Use exercises such as making an 'L Shape' with the sole, quick outside then inside touches with 1 foot and many more. Each coach can create variants with their own imagination.

Group C

The yellow players line up opposite each other with a mannequin or cone in between them. Each player has a ball and they start simultaneously by dribbling the ball towards the centre and then perform a feint to the right (or left). The coach can determine a specific feint such as a scissor, chop or Maradona move. The players keep the same sequence going and start each time on the coach's whistle.

WEEK 2

2. Technical: Ball Control Exercises   15 mins

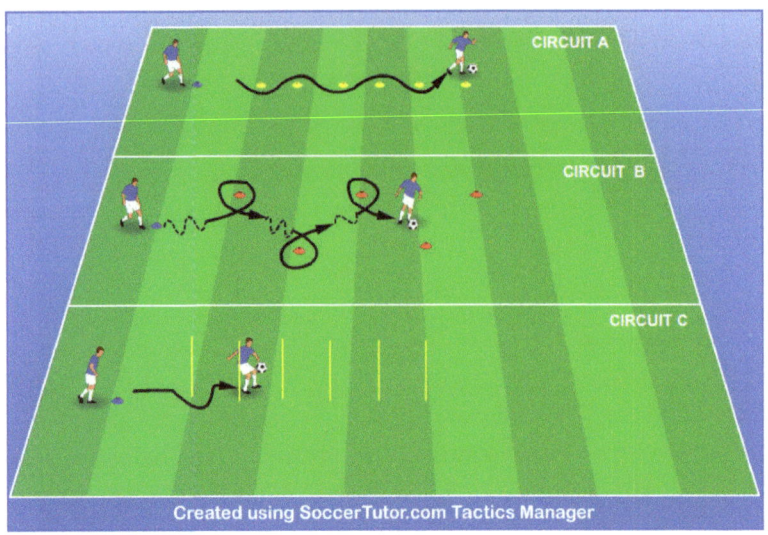

CIRCUIT A: Players dribble in and out of all the cones (distance 50 cm apart) and then pass the ball back to the next player in line.

Variations: Right foot only, left foot only, switching both feet, outside left and right, Inside outside left and right.

CIRCUIT B: Players dribble around the cones in a diagonal eight figure pattern. Players then pass the ball back to the next player in line.

Variations: Right foot only, left foot only, inside or outside of feet. Try to do it with many fast touches.

CIRCUIT C: Players must juggle the ball inside and outside of the boundary poles. Players then pass the ball back to the next player in line.

Variations
Right foot only, left foot only, both feet, 1 touch left / 1 touch right, both thighs, 2 feet / 2 thighs.

Coaching Points
1. Make many touches with the ball.
2. Soft feel with the ball.

3. Coordination: Speed & Agility Training with 1v1 Duels   15 mins

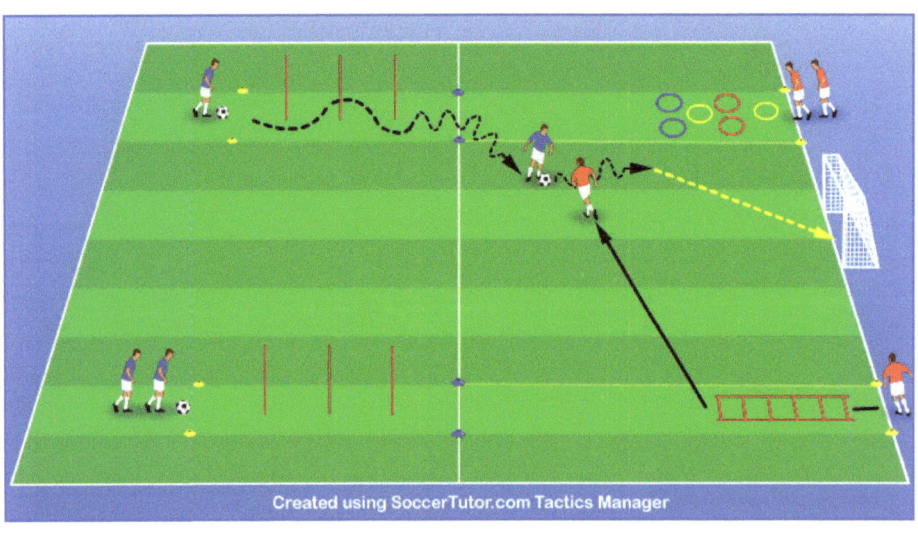

Description
The blue players dribble through the poles and then try to score a goal.

The red players work through a coordination course and then move to defend the goal.

Switch roles halfway through and the team that scores most goals wins.

Variations
1. Play with a goalkeeper.
2. Modify the coordination course.
3. Dribble using different parts of the foot.

Coaching Points
1. Players should use soft touches to dribble through the poles, keeping the ball close to their feet.
2. Encourage players to use feints/moves to beat in the 1v1 duel.

DAY 01: Running with the Ball

4. Game Situation: Frontal and Back Marking   15 mins

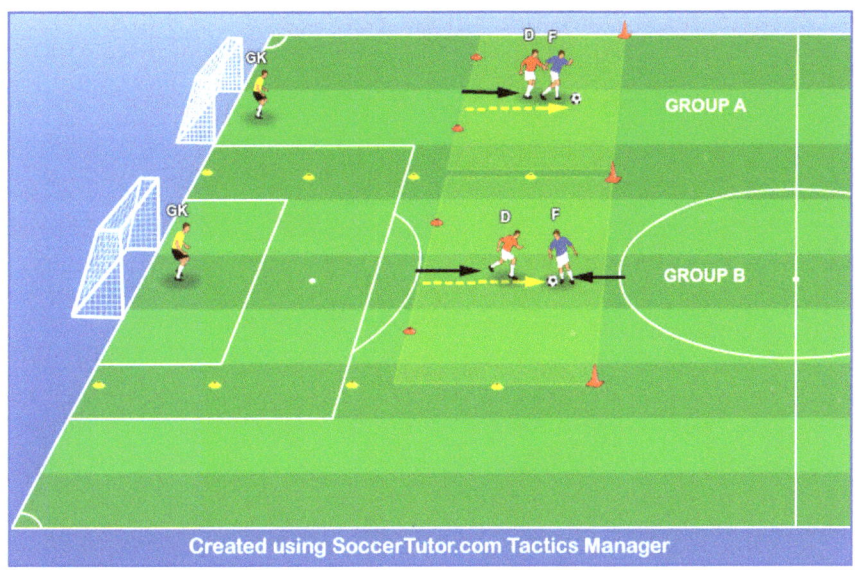

GROUP A: "Back marking"

The defender and forward start between the red disc cones. The defender passes the ball in front of the forward, who then must try to turn, advance beyond the red disc cones and shoot on goal.

The defender must try to prevent the forward from turning. The right distance for the defender is approximately 50cm. This distance allows the defender to intervene in an easy way when the forward tries to turn.

GROUP B: "Frontal marking"

The defender passes the ball to the forward in front of him, who, after receiving the ball he must try to enter the end zone (beyond the red disc cones) and shoot on goal. The defender must try to prevent the forward from entering the end zone and force the ball out of play. The coach will change both groups after 7 minutes.

Coaching Points

1. Asses the opponent's speed and try to force the opponent onto their weaker side.
2. Body shape – Be side on, known as the jockey/surfer position.

5. Game with a Theme: 5v5 'Rugby Rules' SSG   15 mins

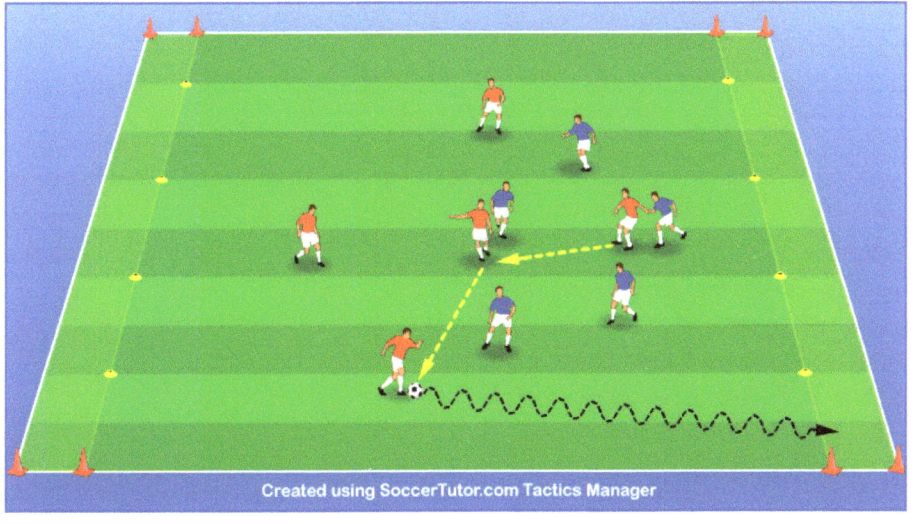

Description

In an area 30 x 30 yards we play a 5v5 game.

The objective is to score by dribbling through the end zone.

Rugby rules are adopted, therefore the players are not allowed to pass the ball forward.

Variations

1. Allow 1 forward pass.
2. If a goal is scored after a feint it is worth double.

6. 5v5 Small Sided Games   30 mins

WEEK 2

Feints / Moves to Beat

Primary Technical Objective: Dribbling with the ball and feints/moves to beat.
Secondary Technical Objective: Changing direction and shooting.
Coordination Objective: Adaptation, rhythm and balance.
Tactical Objective: 1v1 Duels and man marking.

Duration of Session: 2 hours 15 mins

1. Warm Up: Technical Block 2   30 mins

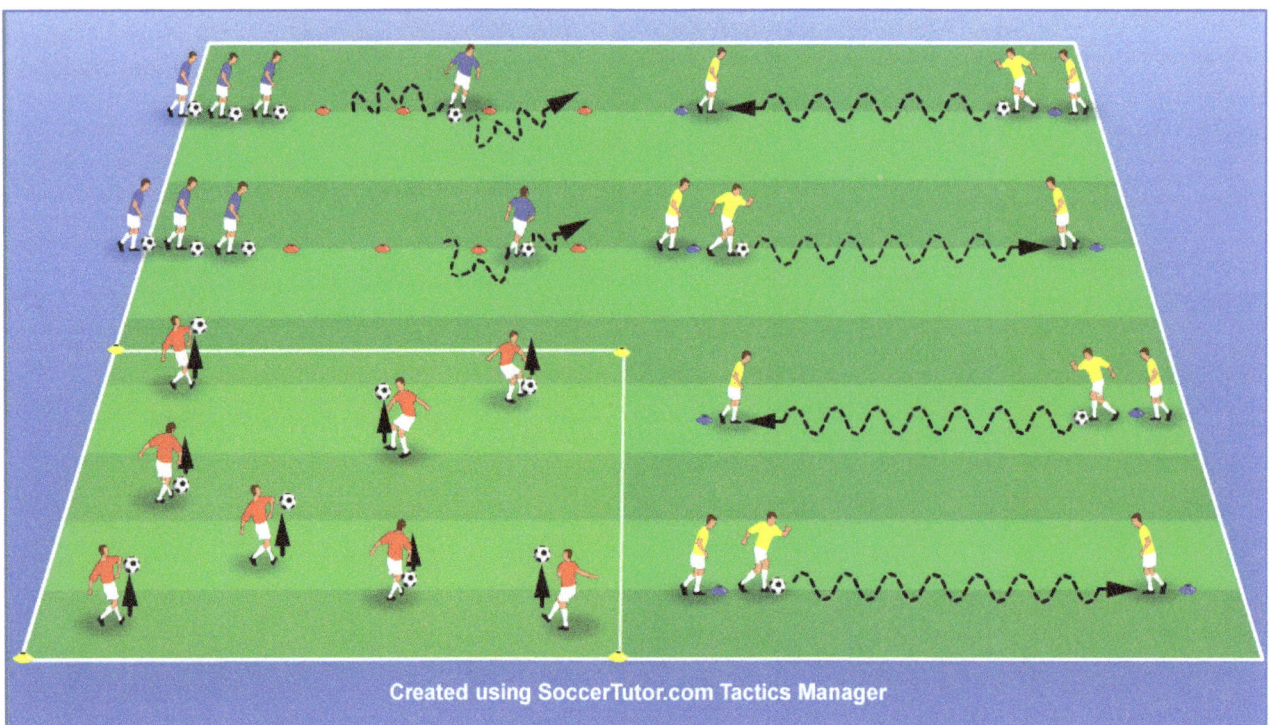

Group A

The red players use a variety of juggling techniques depending on their age/level. If the exercise is too complex for the age/level of their players they can juggle and catch using their hands.

Variations: 1 or 2 touches of the foot and then catch with the hands, juggling with either foot freely, juggle or dribble with alternating rhythm (2 right / 1 left), sequence - foot, thigh, head.

Other Exercises: Juggle at various heights (1 low / 1 high), alternate feet with bounces allowed, juggle followed by acrobatic act e.g. forward roll. You can introduce much more based on ability and propose a points race e.g. first player to complete 20 consecutive alternate touches when juggling.

Group B

The blue players are split into 2 teams and run a relay race dribbling through the cones. When each player arrives at the finish line, they wait there for their teammates to complete. The winning team is the one that finishes quickest. If any player fails to dribble the ball round one of the cones successfully the team receives a time penalty. You can assign rules such as only dribble with left foot, alternate touches etc.

Group C

The yellow players are split into teams of 3 with a ball per team. The first player must dribble the ball to his teammate who is 15 yards away. The player who receives then dribbles the ball to the third player. You can assign points based on whether the players can get the ball to their teammate without losing control of the ball. This exercise can also be done with the players having to juggle the ball.

DAY 02: Feints / Moves to Beat

2. Technical: Changing Direction Team Shooting Game

15 mins

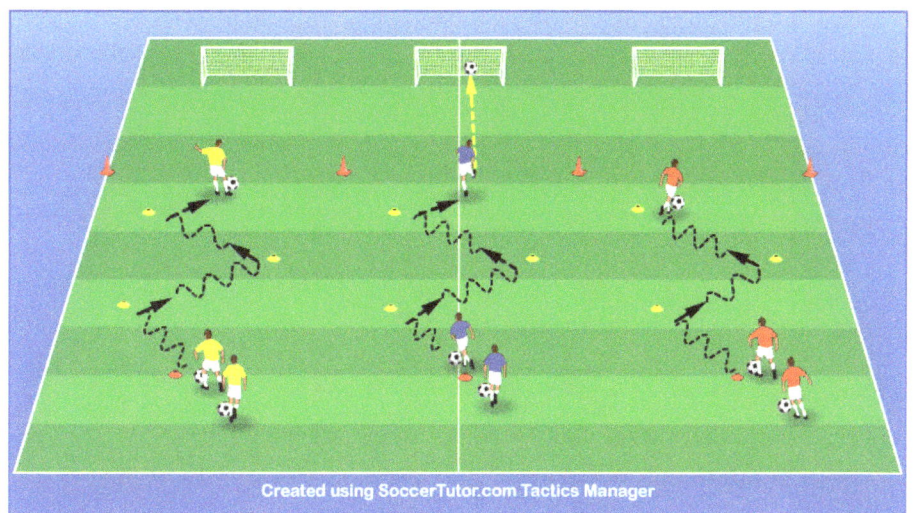

Description
Players are divided into 3 teams. A player from each team starts by dribbling to one cone and performs a predetermined feint, then dribbles to the next cone and performs another feint.

The player finishes by shooting in the small goal. The team that scores the most goals in a set time wins.

Coaching Points
1. When running with the ball and changing direction the players need to decelerate using short steps and bend the knees before accelerating in the opposite direction.
2. Although the players have to dribble the ball very quickly in this race, they need to still focus on accuracy through the cones using soft touches.

3. Coordination: Coordination Relay

15 mins

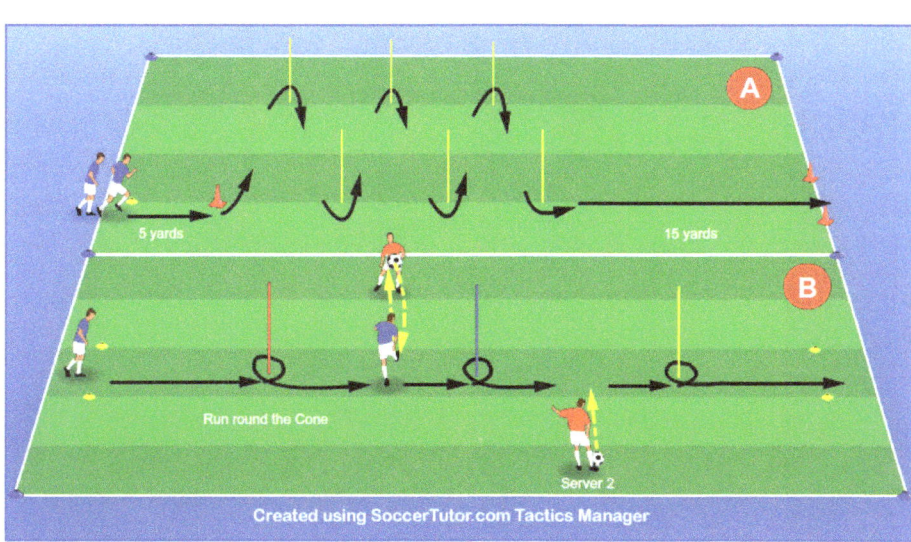

Description
Players must dribble through the cones, stop the ball (leaving it) and do a forward roll.

They then run around the pole and then repeat the exercise back to their teammates (another forward roll and dribble through the cones). The next player then goes.

Coaching Points
1. When running with the ball and changing direction the players need to decelerate using short steps and bend the knees before accelerating in the opposite direction.
2. Although the players have to dribble the ball very quickly in this race, they need to still focus on accuracy through the cones using soft touches.

WEEK 2

4. Game Situation: Frontal 1v1 Duel with Coloured Goals — 15 mins

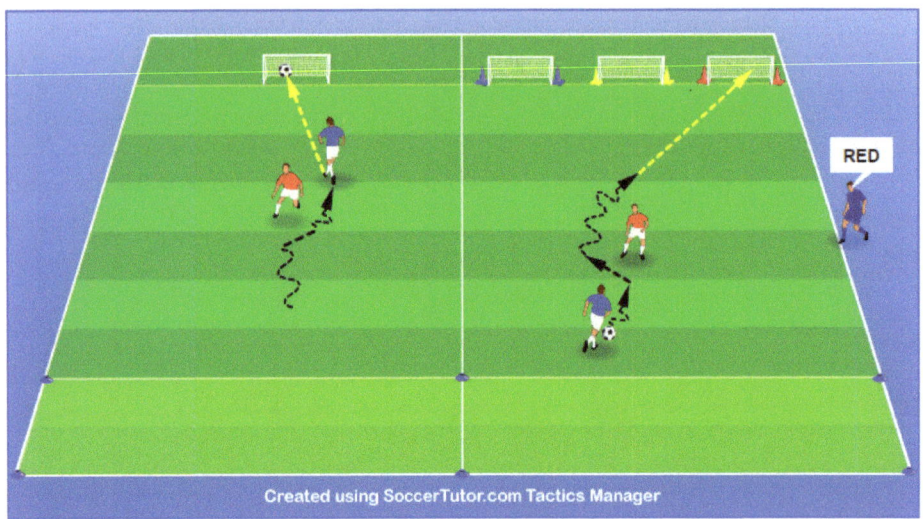

Description

SITUATION A: The attacker tries to score in the goal. If the defender wins the ball they try to dribble into the end zone to score.

SITUATION B: Each goal is assigned a colour. The coach will call out the colour of the goal the attacker must score in. If the defender wins the ball, they try to dribble into the end zone to score.

Change roles of the teams halfway through. The team with the most goals at the end wins.

Coaching Points

1. Encourage players to use feints/moves to beat in this 1v1 duel.
2. Strength and correct body shape is needed to prevent the defenders from winning the ball (getting your body in between the opponent and the ball).

5. Game with a Theme: Man to Man Marking in a 5v5 SSG — 15 mins

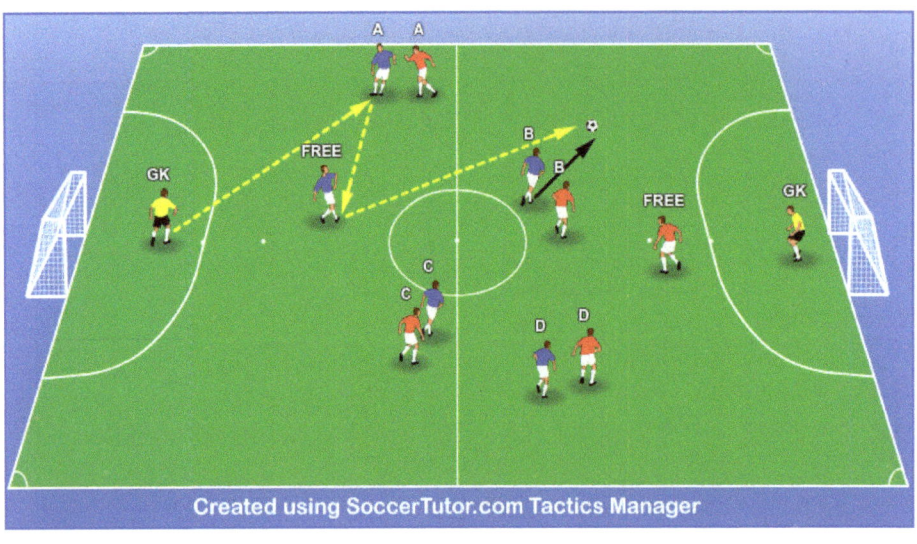

Description

In a small area, there are 2 teams of 5 players + 2 goalkeepers.

Within each team there will be:

- 1 free player, without man to man marking, that cannot shoot
- 4 players with fixed man to man marking

Every player can only intervene with his particular opponent. The player who wins the duel can shoot on goal without pressure from other opponents, except for the "free player".

If a player loses his opponent who in turn strikes on goal, he must do 10 pushups. In this special man to man marking match, the coach can reproduce many game situations. Examples of these could be a centre back against a forward, left back against right winger etc.

6. 5v5 Small Sided Games — 30 mins

DAY 03: Passing and Receiving

Passing and Receiving

Primary Technical Objective: Passing and receiving on the ground.

Secondary Technical Objective: Directional receiving of the ball, dribbling and shooting.

Coordination Objective: Quickness, balance and motor combinations.

Tactical Objective: Creating space, positioning, overlapping and attacking the space.

Duration of Session: 2 hours 15 mins

1. Warm Up: Technical Block 3   30 mins

Group A

The red players are in pairs opposite each other 15 yards apart. Both players have a ball and start simultaneously by dribbling the ball towards the centre. At the cone, the players change direction and dribble back to the starting position.

Alternate different types of turns such as turn with the sole, sole 'L' shape, internal cut etc.

Group B

The blue players all have a ball each and move around freely in a 15 x 15 yard area. 2 or more green players are added (depending on the number of players in blue) who try to win the ball from the blue players as quickly as possible. If a blue player loses the ball he is not eliminated, but instead helps the other blue players to maintain possession of the ball. Change the green players every minute.

Group C

The yellow players are divided into 4 groups and compete in a relay competition. Each player dribbles the ball towards the mannequin (or cone) which is 5 yards away, perform a specific turn pre-determined by the coach and then quickly shoot into the goal. The first team to score 10 goals wins the relay.

WEEK 2

2. Technical: Quick Passing and 1-2 Combinations

15 mins

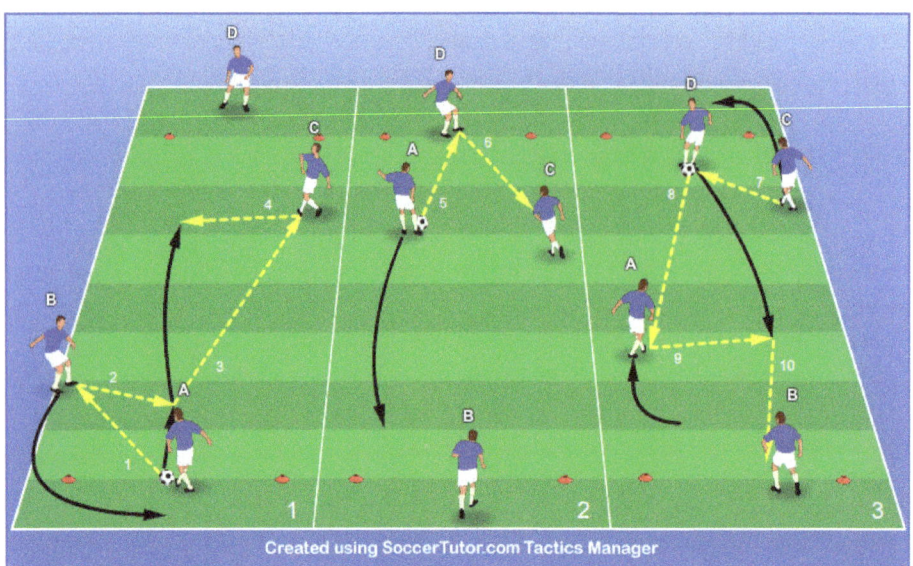

Description
Player A plays a 1-2 with B, then plays another 1-2 with Player C and finally passes to Player D.

D repeats the same combination with C and then A (who has moved back) as shown in the diagram.

Variation
Passes in the air with the players further apart.

Coaching Points
1. The rhythm of the movement together with the pass is key.
2. The side players need to display good timing of movement to meet the ball and approach it half turned.

3. Coordination: Coordination and Passing Relay

15 mins

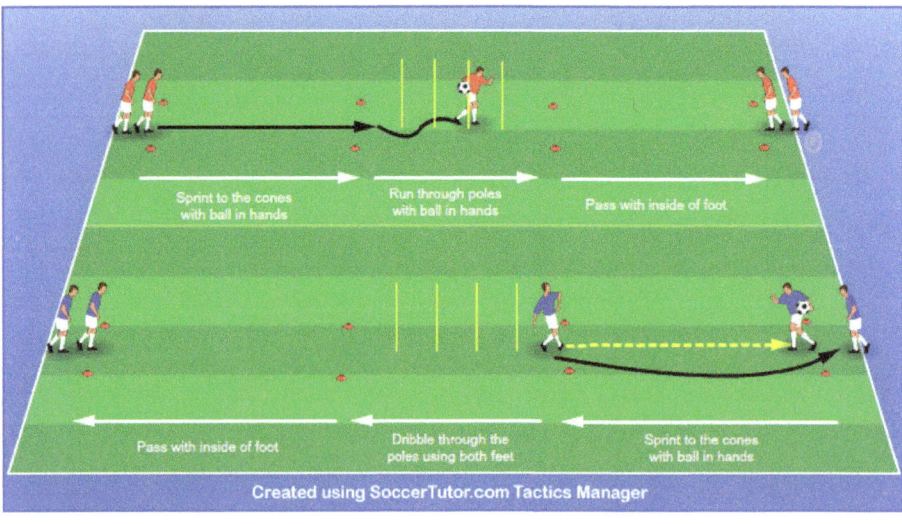

Description
The first player in each line runs up to the poles and through them with the ball in their hands. At the end, they pass the ball on the ground to the next player waiting on the opposite side.

The player that receives the ball, picks it up runs to the poles and dribbles the ball through them before passing to the player waiting on the other side.

The team that completes the most passes in a predetermined time win the relay.

Variation
Volley with the inside of the foot, the instep or half volley.

Coaching Points
1. This practice should be done at full speed.
2. The players need good rhythm in the transitions to different parts of the drill.

DAY 03: Passing and Receiving

4. Game Situation: Creating a Numerical Advantage (1v1 → 2v1) — 15 mins

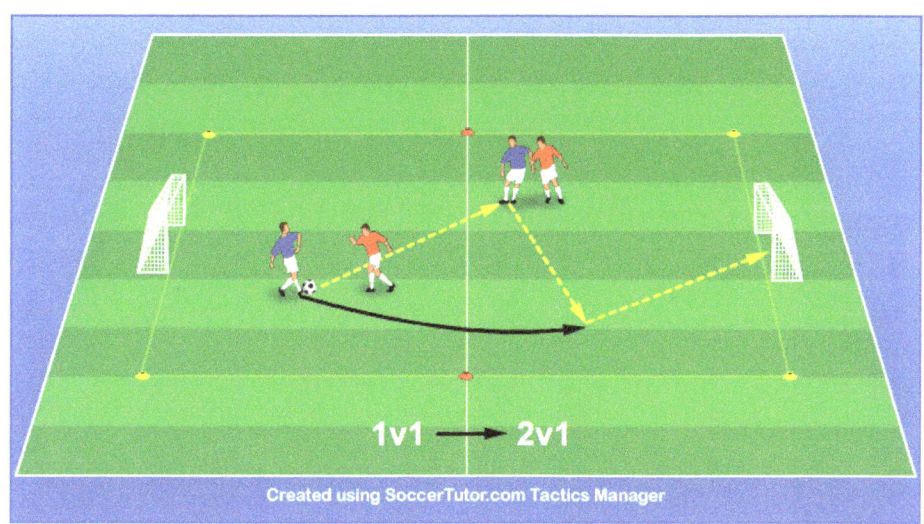

Description

Set out areas of 20 x 10 yards split into 2 equal zones. In each zone we have a 1v1.

Once the ball is passed to the teammate in the other zone, the player can join in the attack to form a 2v1 situation. The players use this advantage to score.

Variation

2v2 game.

Coaching Points

1. The pass should be made quickly forward, combined with a run into the space.
2. The player waiting in the attacking half should check away from the defender before moving into space to receive.

5. Game with a Theme: Two Small Sided Games - Rugby / 4 Goals Match — 15 mins

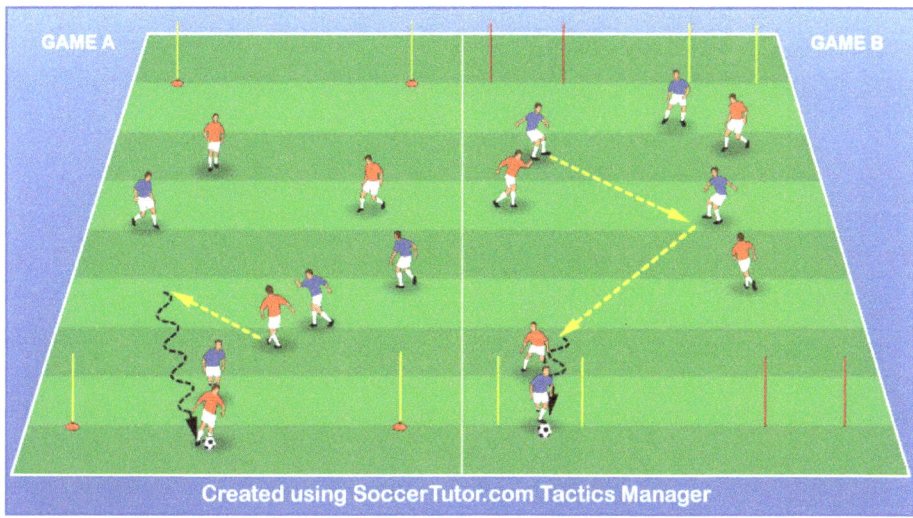

Game A: "Rugby Game"

The objective is to run with the ball between the boundary poles and score a point by stopping the ball with the sole of the foot.

The players are only allowed to pass backwards, just like in rugby.

Game B: "4 Goals Match"

This game's objective is to dribble/run with the ball through the goals (between the boundary poles) before stopping the ball within the end zone. A good variation could be if the coach changes calls out the colour of the goal to score in during the match. Stretch after 5, 10, 15 and 20 minutes.

Coaching Points

1. Play and think quickly.
2. Try to do a different feint/move every time.

6. 5v5 Small Sided Games — 30 mins

WEEK 2

Shooting

Primary Technical Objective: Shooting and finishing.
Secondary Technical Objective: Ball control and shooting first time on the move.
Coordination Objective: Balance, quickness, adaptation, reactions and explosive power.
Tactical Objective: Creating space.

Duration of Session: 2 hours 15 mins

1. Warm Up: Technical Block 4 — 30 mins

Group A

The red players line up behind the 4 cones as shown. 4 players start at the same time and dribble the ball towards the cone in front of them, perform a feint pre-determined by the coach and move to the cone to the right. Change the type of feint after every completed lap and also change the direction from anticlockwise to clockwise so the players move to the left as well.

Group B

The blue players are divided into 2 groups and practice dribbling with feints to change direction. Initially the players simply use the inside and outside of both feet to dribble and change directions. They then progress to perform a specific feint at each cone which is pre-determined by the coach. Examples of feints include the scissor, the cut back and the chop.

Group C

The yellow players are divided into teams of 3 or 4 and are in a competition to see who can score the most goals. 4 players start simultaneously with a ball, dribble towards the mannequin (or cone), perform a feint to the left or right and shoot in the mini goal. A point is awarded to the player who scores first.

You can decide the type of feint to be used or leave it to the players imagination and freedom.

DAY 04: Shooting

2. Technical: Ball Control & Shooting with 4 Goals — 15 mins

Description

Set up a large square 20 yards x 20 yards with a smaller square inside it (10 x 10 yards). Players move with the ball inside the smaller square executing different types of dribbling:

1) Use the sole of both feet. 2) Use only the right foot. 3) Only the left foot. 4) Use only the instep of both feet. 5) The coach places obstacles inside the smaller square (cones, hurdles etc) and the players must dribble the ball trying to avoid them (as shown in diagram).

At the coach's signal all the players must move towards one of the 4 goals and shoot. The last player to score in a goal loses a point. After every 2 signals to shoot at goal, change the type of dribbling.

Coaching Points

1. Players should be learning to use all parts of the foot to dribble.
2. Encourage creativity of the players to use turns and moves.
3. This is a good practice to teach awareness; to avoid the obstacles and other players.

3. Coordination: One-Two and Shoot / 20 Yard Sprints — 15 mins

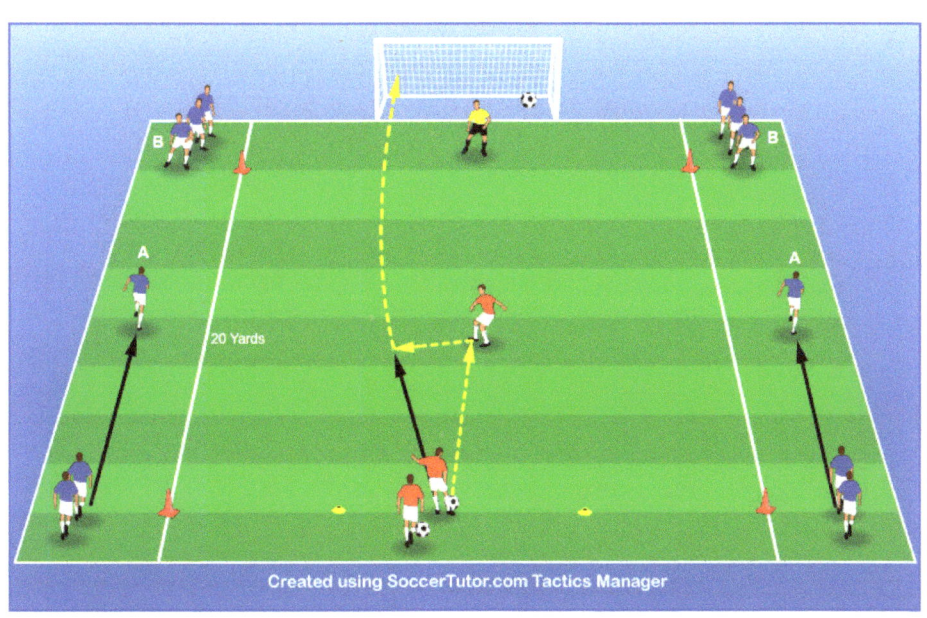

Description

Set up the drill as shown the diagram. The red players play a 1-2 and try to score as many goals as possible while the blue players perform a series of 20 yard sprints.

The blue players must complete 4 sprints of 20 yards each.

Player A sprints towards B who starts the sprint as soon as he is tagged by A.

Swap the red server player often. Also swap the roles of the reds and blues as soon as each blue player has completed 4 x 20 yard sprints.

WEEK 2

4. Game Situation: 3v2 First Time Shooting Practice   15 mins

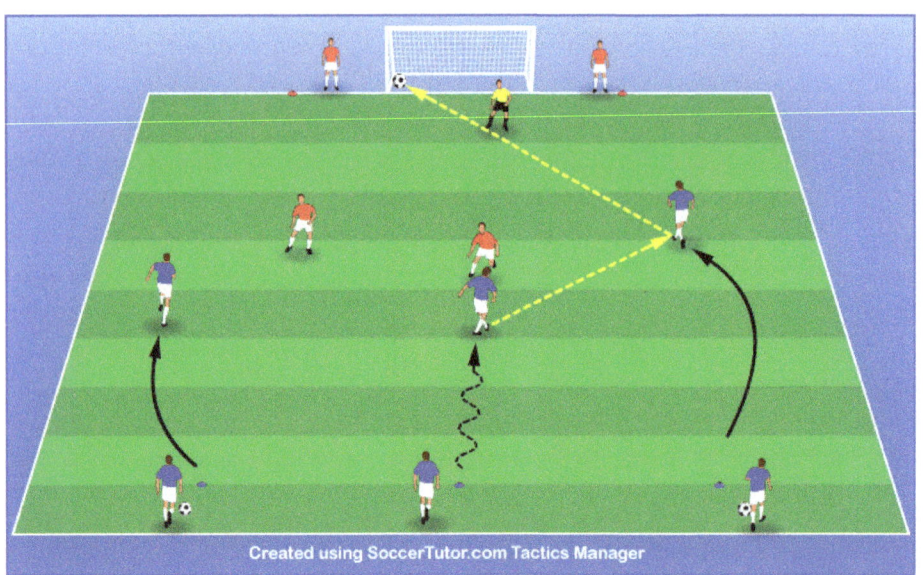

Description

3 attackers start the game with the ball against 3 defenders.

Once the 2nd defender decides to close down one of the players without the ball, the player in possession must pass to the player free in space, who must receive and shoot on goal.

Variation

Modify the starting position of the 3 attackers; 1 with their back to goal and 2 facing the goal.

---

5. Game with a Theme: 2v2 Zones in a 4v4 SSG   15 mins

Description

In this free game we have a 4v4 situation. In each half we have 2 players from both teams. The players must stay in their half.

The aim is to pass the ball from the defensive half to the attacking half and score a goal. Switch the positions of the players often.

Coaching Points

1. Push the players to be creative and demonstrate what they have learned to try and beat their opponents.
2. Players should dribble the ball with different parts of the foot.
3. Encourage players to use feints/moves to beat they have learnt.

6. 5v5 Small Sided Games   30 mins

DAY 05: Heading

Heading

Primary Technical Objective: Heading.

Secondary Technical Objective: Crossing and timing of movement.

Coordination Objective: Quickness, motor skills (jumping), dynamic balance and reading the trajectory.

Tactical Objective: Attacking and defending aerial balls.

Duration of Session: 2 hours 15 mins

1. Warm Up: Technical Block 5 — 30 mins

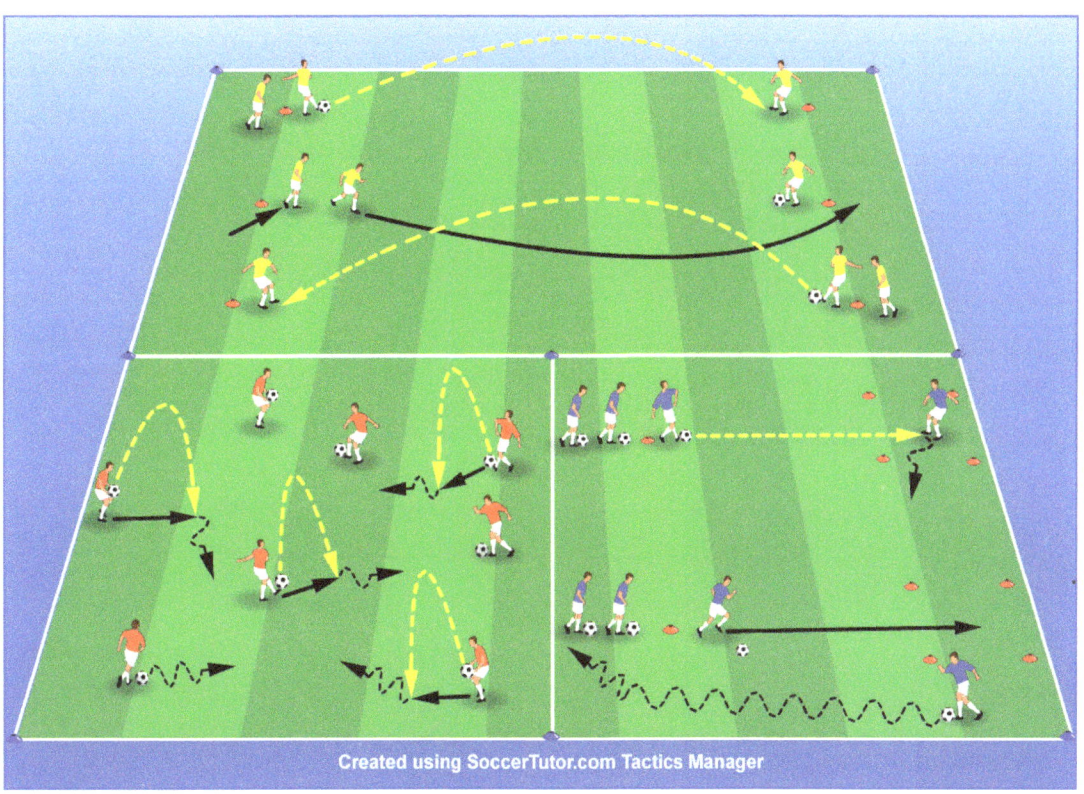

Group A

The red players move freely around the area and control the ball in different ways. The players throw (or kick) the ball up in the air, control the ball and then dribble for a few yards.

Vary the type of control used - inside of foot, outside of foot, with the sole, with the laces, thigh, head etc.

Group B

Divide the blue players into 2 groups and set up 5 x 5 yard squares as shown. This is a relay competition with the 2 teams starting simultaneously. The first player passes the ball to the player in the square and then runs into the square. The player in the square takes a directional first touch out the side of the square and dribbles the ball to the next player who repeats the same sequence.

Group C

The yellow players work on passing and receiving high balls at a 25 yard distance. The first player makes an aerial pass to their teammate and then runs 25 yards to their position. The second player controls the ball and then plays the next aerial pass and runs 25 yards to the opposite cone. The same sequence continues.

Vary the type of control used - inside of foot, outside of foot, the sole, the laces, thigh, head etc.

WEEK 2

2. Technical: Heading in Pairs

15 mins

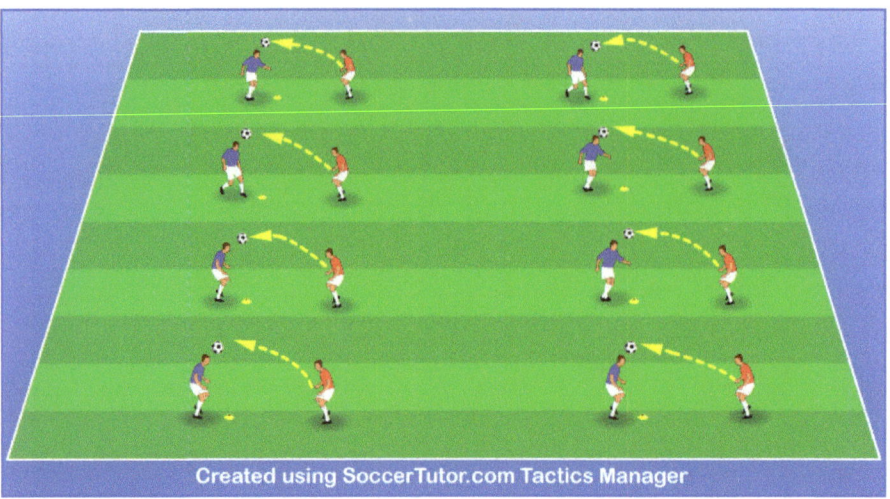

Coaching Points

1. Control the correct use of both arms (before connecting with the ball, during connection with the ball and after).
2. Control the jump before connecting with the ball (using the right leg to take off).
3. Establish the right way to run before connecting with the ball.

Description

Players are divided into pairs with one ball and named Player "A" and Player "B".

The players have to perform one of the following sequences:

- 30 Headers - without jumping
- 30 Headers - jumping with both feet at the same time
- 30 Headers - jumping to the left and to the right (simulating a pendulum)
- 30 Headers - lunging at the ball
- 30 Headers - running in the opposite direction of the ball

3. Coordination: Jump, Criss-Cross and Heading

15 mins

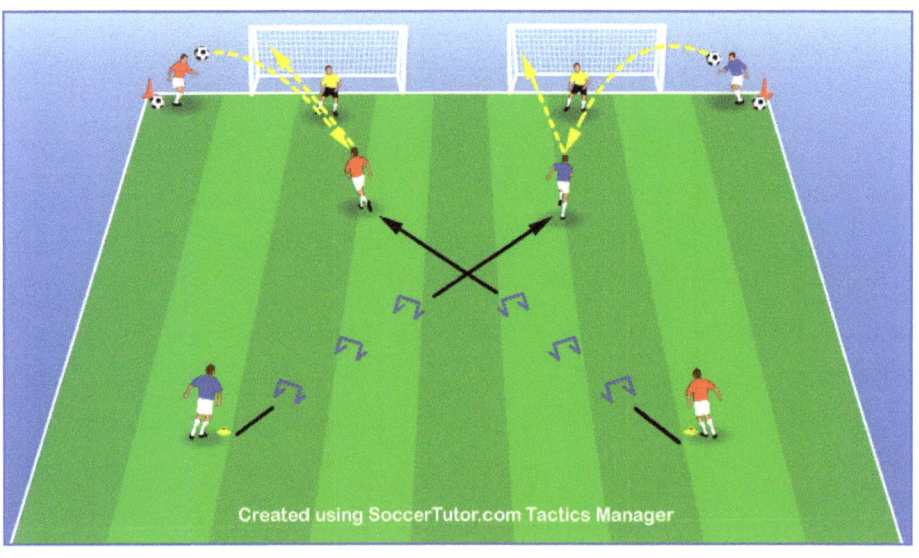

Description

2 teams compete in this game.

One player stands next to the goal and throws-in for their teammate to head the ball in the goal.

The heading player first jumps over the hurdles and sprints diagonally to meet the throw.

The team that scores the most goals win.

©SoccerTutor.com | Football Camp Training Program

DAY 05: Heading

4. Game Situation: 1v1 Heading in the Penalty Area — 15 mins

Description

The blue players cross the ball from the side of the penalty area.

There is a 1v1 situation in the penalty area with 1 attacker vs 1 defender. The aim is to score with a header.

A headed goal counts double.

Variation

The defender is passive.

Coaching Points

1. The cross and the run need to be well coordinated.
2. When under pressure from a defender, the attacker needs to check away/change direction to create space.

5. Game with a Theme: Heading with Target Players SSG — 15 mins

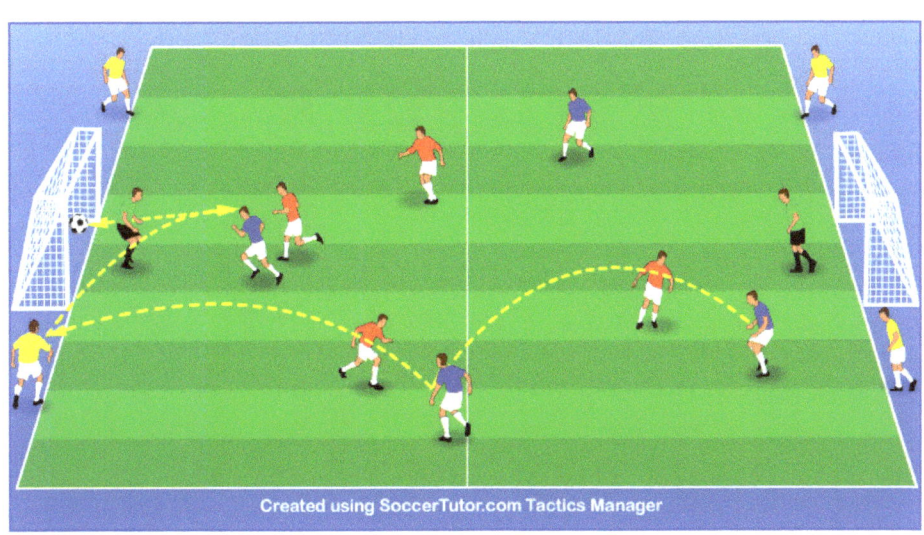

Description

In an area 20 x 25 yards we have a 4v4 (+2 GKs) game.

There are also 4 target players who stand either side of the goal (2 at each end).

The objective is to score with a header with an assist from a target player.

The game is played with the hands and head. Change the target players often.

Variations

1. Hands and feet game.
2. Game with only feet.

6. 11v11 Matches on a Full Pitch — 30 mins

WEEK 3

DAY 01: Running with the Ball

Running with the Ball

Primary Technical Objective: Running with the ball.

Secondary Technical Objective: Dribbling, turning and shooting.

Coordination Objective: Quickness, adaptation, rhythm and motor combinations.

Tactical Objective: 1v1 Duels.

Duration of Session: 2 hours 15 mins

1. Warm Up: Technical Block 1 — 30 mins

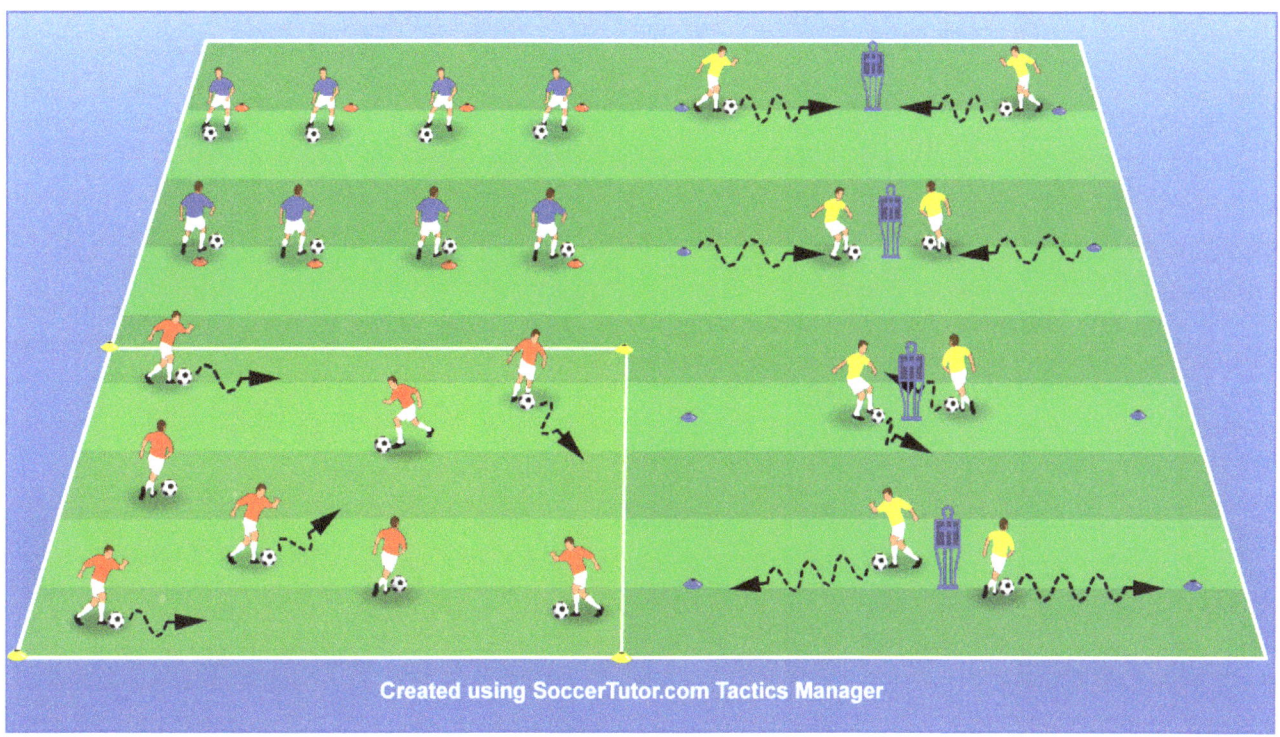

Divide the players into 3 groups with a minimum of 8 players at each station.

Group A

The red players perform different types of dribbling the ball in traffic, making sure to avoid collisions. Keep using variations, making sure that the players use only one foot and then the other when manoeuvring the ball. Vary the part of the foot used - outside, instep, the sole etc. Make sure to also perform different exercises -stretching and joint mobility exercises.

Group B

The blue players are each positioned on a cone. Every player practices different technical ball control exercises on the spot and around the cone. Start slowly and progress to increase the speed of execution. Use exercises such as making an 'L Shape' with the sole, quick outside then inside touches with 1 foot and many more. Each coach can create variants with their own imagination.

Group C

The yellow players line up opposite each other with a mannequin or cone in between them. Each player has a ball and they start simultaneously by dribbling the ball towards the centre and then perform a feint to the right (or left). The coach can determine a specific feint such as a scissor, chop or Maradona move. The players keep the same sequence going and start each time on the coach's whistle.

WEEK 3

2. Technical: **Dribbling with Different Obstacles**   **15 mins**

Description

In a marked out area we place various objects (cones, poles, hurdles etc) in a square.

Players dribble the ball and work around the obstacles, first without conditions, then based on the coach's command:

1. Using only the inside or outside of the feet.
2. Using only the left or right foot.
3. Juggling the ball.

Coaching Points

1. Awareness is key to perform different techniques with the various obstacles and avoid collisions.
2. Players should use soft touches, keeping close control of the ball.

3. Coordination: **Ball Control and Coordination Relay**   **15 mins**

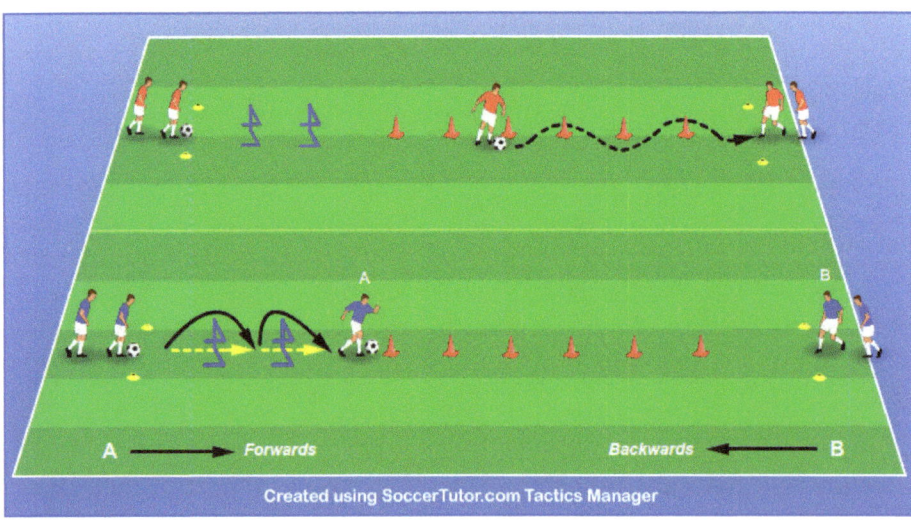

Description

The first player must pass the ball under the hurdles and jump over them, dribble through the cones and finally give/pass the ball to the teammate opposite them (B).

Player B must do the same while going backwards (cones first, hurdles second).

Make this a competition.

Variations

1. Dribbling only with the right or left foot.
2. Vary the distances between the cones.

Coaching Points

1. Close control is important here so the players should use many touches.
2. There should be a soft feel with the ball.

©SoccerTutor.com   Football Camp Training Program

DAY 01: Running with the Ball

4. Game Situation: Dribble, Turn & Shoot - 'The 1v1 Duel'   **15 mins**

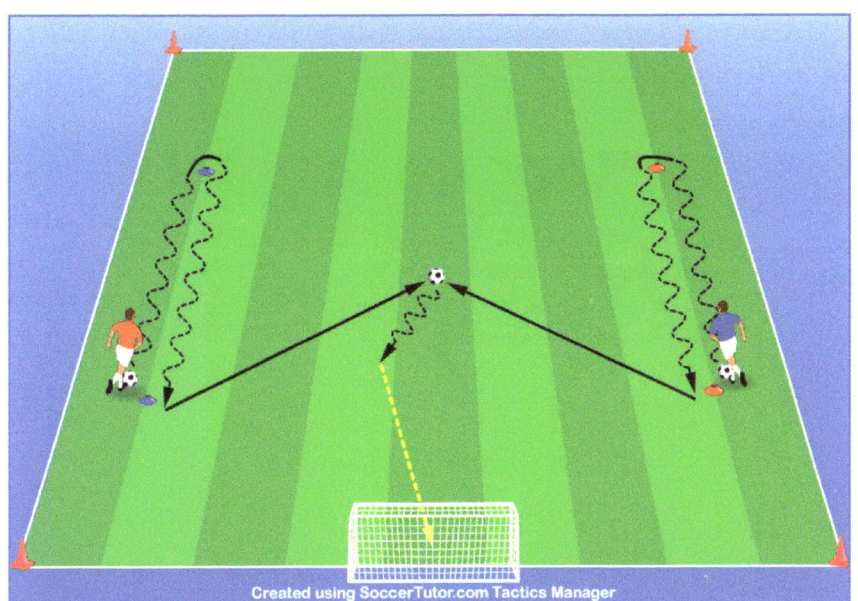

Description

In an area 10 yards x 15 yards, 2 players start from the cone nearest the goal.

They dribble round the opposite cone and back to the starting point where they leave their ball.

They then run towards the ball in the centre and the first to arrive to the ball becomes the attacker and tires to score in the goal.

The player that is second to the ball becomes the goalkeeper.

Variation
You can start the first 5 minutes of the drill with the players carrying the ball in their hands for the first phase around the cones.

Coaching Points
1. Create a positive environment to stimulate the competitiveness and speed.
2. During the dribbling phase, the players should first run quickly with the ball before slowing down, using soft touches to turn around the cone.

---

5. Game with a Theme: 4v4 (+GK) Attacking Combinations & Incisive Dribbling in and Around the Penalty Area   **15 mins**

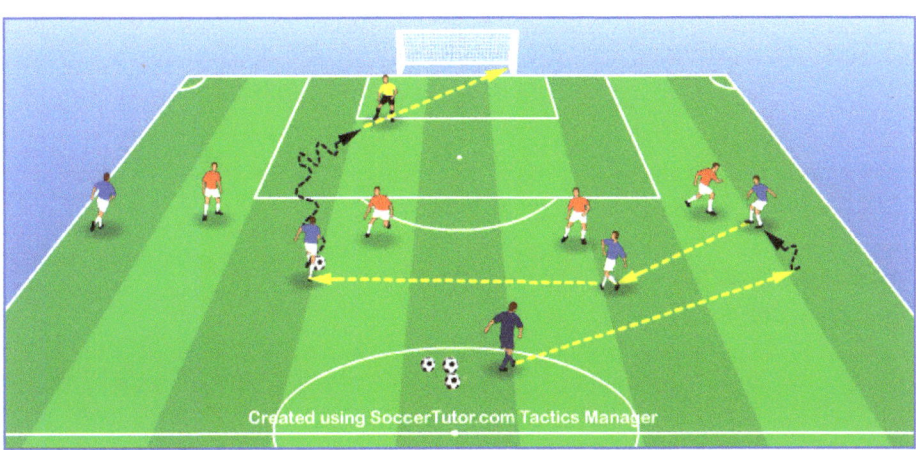

Description

The blue players outside the penalty area pass the ball around looking to find a channel/space to enter and attack the box trying to shoot and score a goal.

The 4 red players defend the goal. Change the roles often.

Coaching Points
1. Awareness and good decision making is required to judge the right time to dribble into the box.
2. Players need to check away from their marker before moving to create space and receive the ball.

6. 5v5 Small Sided Games   **30 mins**

WEEK 3

Feints / Moves to Beat

Primary Technical Objective: Dribbling with the ball and feints/moves to beat.

Secondary Technical Objective: Protecting the ball, receiving, turning and shooting.

Coordination Objective: Quickness, adaptation, transformation and reactions.

Tactical Objective: 1v1 Duels, collective shape/reactions and transition play.

Duration of Session: 2 hours 15 mins

1. Warm Up: Technical Block 2   30 mins

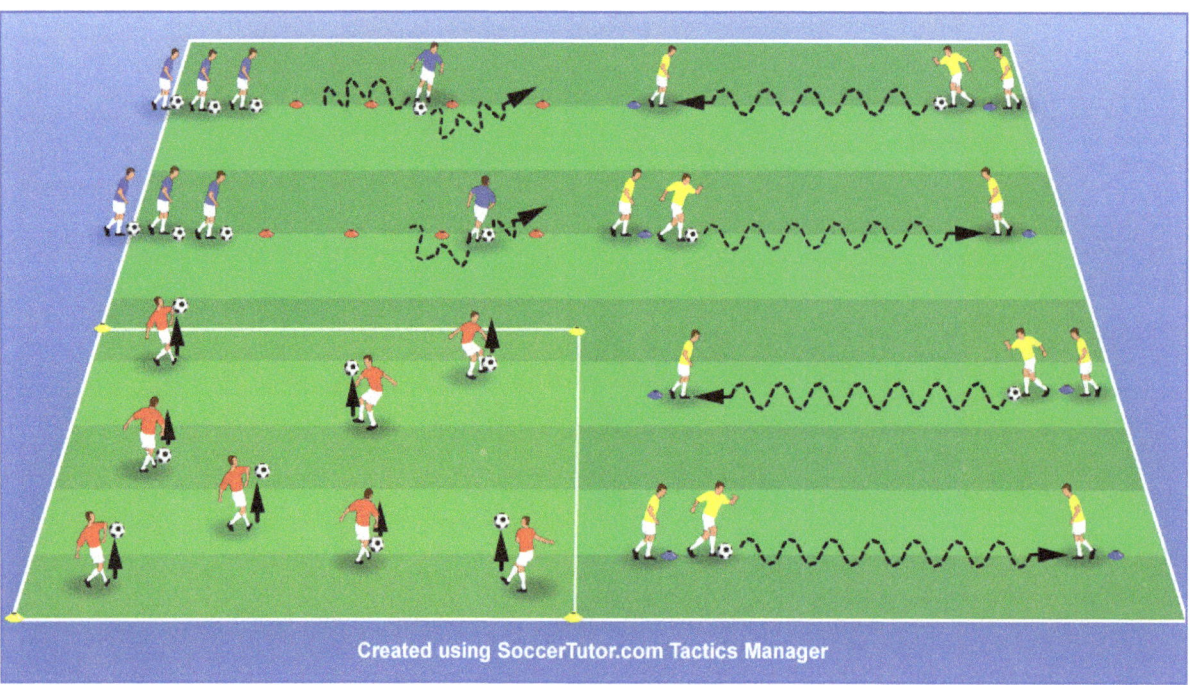

Group A

The red players use a variety of juggling techniques depending on their age/level. If the exercise is too complex for the age/level of their players they can juggle and catch using their hands.

Variations: 1 or 2 touches of the foot and then catch with the hands, juggling with either foot freely, juggle or dribble with alternating rhythm (2 right / 1 left), sequence - foot, thigh, head.

Other Exercises: Juggle at various heights (1 low / 1 high), alternate feet with bounces allowed, juggle followed by acrobatic act e.g. forward roll. You can introduce much more based on ability and propose a points race e.g. first player to complete 20 consecutive alternate touches when juggling.

Group B

The blue players are split into 2 teams and run a relay race dribbling through the cones. When each player arrives at the finish line, they wait there for their teammates to complete. The winning team is the one that finishes quickest. If any player fails to dribble the ball round one of the cones successfully the team receives a time penalty. You can assign rules such as only dribble with left foot, alternate touches etc.

Group C

The yellow players are split into teams of 3 with a ball per team. The first player must dribble the ball to his teammate who is 15 yards away. The player who receives then dribbles the ball to the third player. You can assign points based on whether the players can get the ball to their teammate without losing control of the ball. This exercise can also be done with the players having to juggle the ball.

DAY 02: Feints / Moves to Beat

2. Technical: Running with the Ball, Feints and Shooting 15 mins

Description

SITUATION A: Running with the ball and shooting into the goal with the same colour called out by the coach.

SITUATION B: Players run with the ball performing a feint to the left then a feint to the right, followed by a shot.

SITUATION C: Players run with the ball, pass around the pole, run around it and shoot first time.

Coaching Points

1. Players need to keep close control of the ball for all aspects of this exercise.
2. The accuracy of the shot is important, and not the power.

3. Coordination: 1v1 RWTB Race - 'Quickest Player Shoots' 15 mins

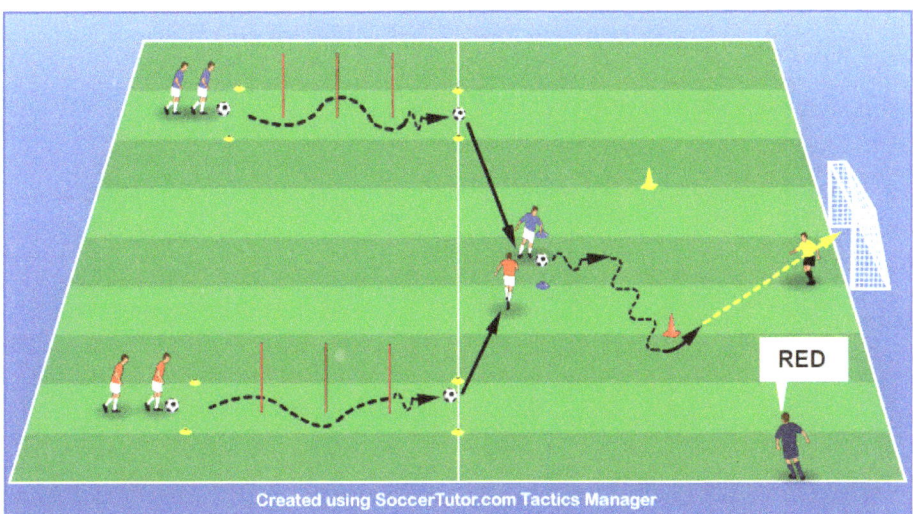

Description

2 players start with a ball and dribble through the poles as shown and leave the ball in between the 2 cones.

The players race to the ball in the centre. The first one there aims to dribble the ball round one of the cones and score past the goalkeeper.

The other player becomes the defender so we have a 1v1 situation.

The next 2 players start at the same time. There are 2 teams and the team with the most goals at the end wins.

Variations

1. Free choice of feints.
2. Assign specific feints e.g. scissors, double scissors, cut back, chop etc.

Coaching Points

1. The feints should be performed at pace, as if moving away from a defender sharply in a game.
2. When assigning specific feints, demonstrate the correct execution if necessary.

WEEK 3

4. Game Situation: 1v1 Back to Goal Duel with Goalkeepers   15 mins

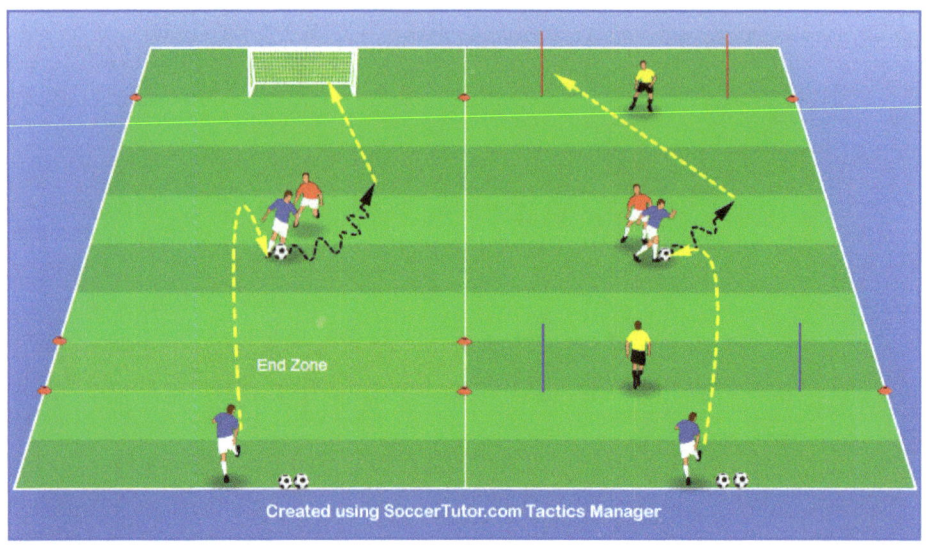

Description

In the first part we have a 1v1 with the attacking player receiving a high ball with his back to goal and the aim is to beat the defender and score in the small goal. If the defender wins the ball, he must dribble through the end zone to get a point.

In the second part we have a 1v1 with 2 goals and 2 goalkeepers.

We have the same practice as in A, but this time if the defender wins the ball he must shoot in the other goal.

Coaching Points

1. Players need to check away before moving to receive the pass.
2. When receiving a high pass, the player needs to put their body in between the defender and the ball.

5. Game with a Theme: Transition Play / Collective Reactions in a SSG   15 mins

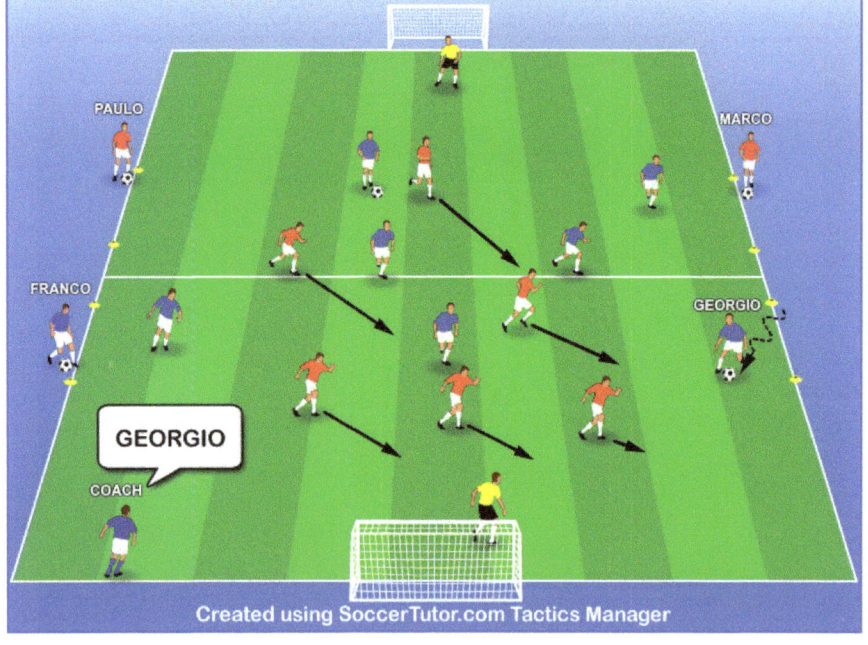

Description

In a large area (the area in between the 2 penalty boxes on a full pitch) 2 teams play 7v7. Each team has 2 additional side players in the opposition's half.

Everyone should be set up in their positions until the coach calls out a name of one of the side players. The player who is called out quickly reacts by dribbling the ball at the opposition defence creating a breakaway for his team to attack and score.

The defending team has to adapt immediately, dropping back to cover the space as a team to defend the goal.

Coaching Points

1. We work on quick transition play and coping with numerical disadvantages.
2. The attackers must advance quickly at a high pace to make use of the numerical advantage and create a chance on goal.

6. 5v5 Small Sided Games   30 mins

DAY 03: Passing and Receiving

Passing and Receiving

Primary Technical Objective: Passing and receiving on the move.
Secondary Technical Objective: Protecting the ball, shooting and ball control.
Coordination Objective: Quickness, motor reactions and reading the ball's trajectory.
Tactical Objective: Creating space, support angles and judging the right time to play.

Duration of Session: 2 hours 15 mins

1. Warm Up: Technical Block 3 — 30 mins

Group A

The red players are in pairs opposite each other 15 yards apart. Both players have a ball and start simultaneously by dribbling the ball towards the centre. At the cone, the players change direction and dribble back to the starting position.

Alternate different types of turns such as turn with the sole, sole 'L' shape, internal cut etc.

Group B

The blue players all have a ball each and move around freely in a 15 x 15 yard area. 2 or more green players are added (depending on the number of players in blue) who try to win the ball from the blue players as quickly as possible. If a blue player loses the ball he is not eliminated, but instead helps the other blue players to maintain possession of the ball. Change the green players every minute.

Group C

The yellow players are divided into 4 groups and compete in a relay competition. Each player dribbles the ball towards the mannequin (or cone) which is 5 yards away, perform a specific turn pre-determined by the coach and then quickly shoot into the goal. The first team to score 10 goals wins the relay.

WEEK 3

2. Technical: Passing Practice for the Right Time of Play   15 mins

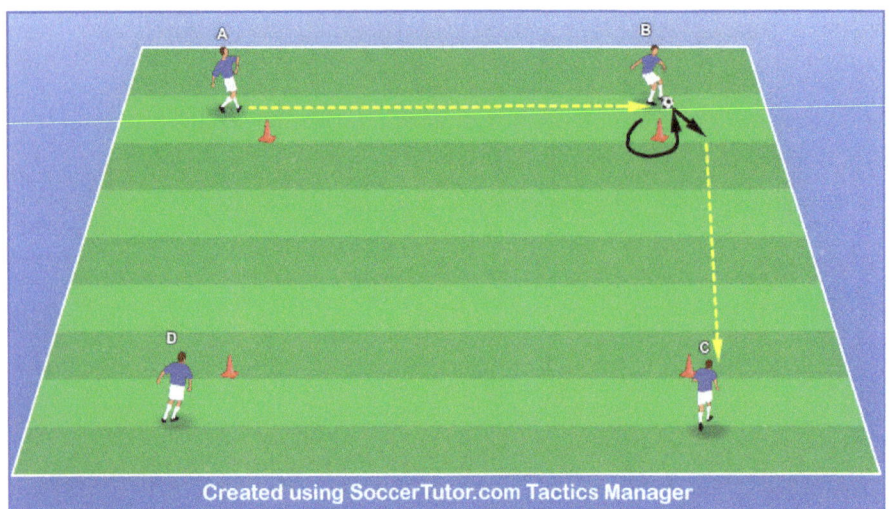

Description

In football, passing at the right time and in the right way is very, very important. With this simple drill, we are going to work on both aspects:

4 players are positioned on all 4 corners of a square 1 yard away from the cones. The ball must always be out of the square moving in a circular way.

Before the player receives the ball, he must go round on his cone clockwise, then pass the ball to the next player.

Coaching Points

1. The crucial aspect of this drill is that all of the players time their run around the cone at the right time. If they delay, they will not receive the ball, if they do it in advance, they will wait for the ball and therefore the movement will not be timed correctly.
2. When timing the run around the cone, keep the body open to see both the ball and the player.
3. The players must meet the ball and receive it with the back foot (the foot furthest away from the ball) so they are automatically on the half-turn.

3. Coordination: Ball Control, Agility, Passing and Receiving with Shooting   15 mins

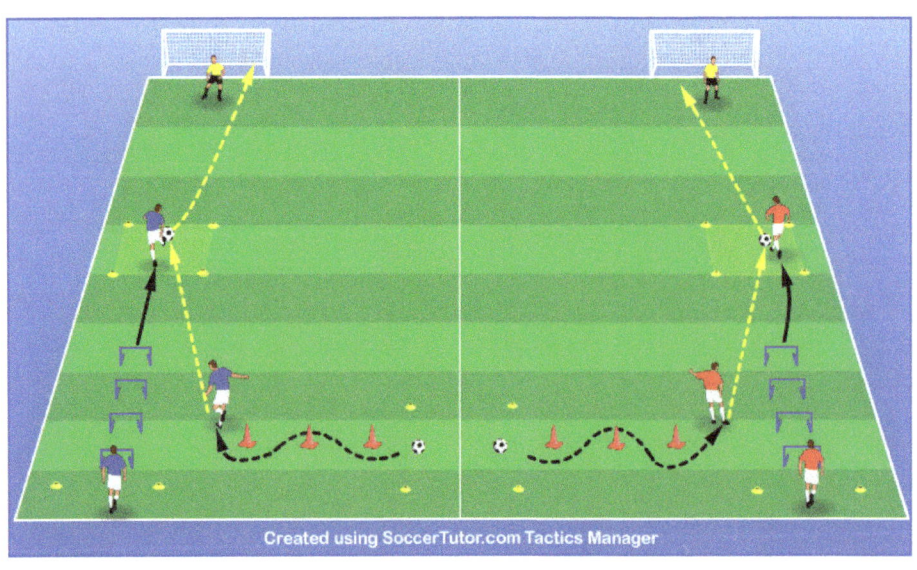

Description

The first player dribbles the ball around the cones and passes the ball into the square for their teammate.

The other player has jumped over the 4 hurdles and sprints into the square to receive the pass and shoot at goal.

The team that scores the most goals wins the game.

Coaching Points

1. The pass from player A and the run from player B must be done at maximum speed.
2. The pass should be accurate and weighted correctly to be out in front of the player who can run onto the ball and shoot quickly.

©SoccerTutor.com   Football Camp Training Program

DAY 03: Passing and Receiving

4. Game Situation: Back to Goal 2v1 Dynamic Practice

15 mins

Description

The orange player passes the ball into the middle with the inside of the foot. The other players are turned away from the orange player.

When they hear the sound of the ball being passed they turn and run to the ball trying to play the ball back to the orange player.

Whoever arrives first to the ball plays with the orange player and they try to score in the big goal with the goalkeeper.

If the defender wins the ball, they can score in one of the 2 smaller goals.

Variations
1. The orange player uses an aerial pass into the middle.
2. Introduce the offside rule.

---

5. Game with a Theme: 5v5 Passing Gate Game

15 mins

Description

In an area 30 x 20 yards, 2 teams of 5 players play a game trying to score by passing the ball through one of the small goals (cone gates).

To score, the ball must be passed through the cones to a teammate, who must successfully control the ball.

Set out 1 goal more than the players in each team. In this example we have a 5v5, so have 6 goals.

Coaching Points
1. The timing of the movement with the pass is key to score 'goals' in this game.
2. Encourage players to mark 1 player each, aiming to prevent them passing or receiving the ball.

6. 5v5 Small Sided Games

30 mins

WEEK 3

Shooting

Primary Technical Objective: Accurate shooting and volleying.

Secondary Technical Objective: Running with the ball and directional receiving of the ball.

Coordination Objective: Balancing on one foot, quickness, planting the foot and reading the trajectory of the ball.

Tactical Objective: Defend the goal and feints/moves to beat.

Duration of Session: 2 hours 15 mins

---

1. Warm Up: Technical Block 4   30 mins

Group A

The red players line up behind the 4 cones as shown. 4 players start at the same time and dribble the ball towards the cone in front of them, perform a feint pre-determined by the coach and move to the cone to the right. Change the type of feint after every completed lap and also change the direction from anticlockwise to clockwise so the players move to the left as well.

Group B

The blue players are divided into 2 groups and practice dribbling with feints to change direction. Initially the players simply use the inside and outside of both feet to dribble and change directions. They then progress to perform a specific feint at each cone which is pre-determined by the coach. Examples of feints include the scissor, the cut back and the chop.

Group C

The yellow players are divided into teams of 3 or 4 and are in a competition to see who can score the most goals. 4 players start simultaneously with a ball, dribble towards the mannequin (or cone), perform a feint to the left or right and shoot in the mini goal. A point is awarded to the player who scores first.

You can decide the type of feint to be used or leave it to the players imagination and freedom.

DAY 04: Shooting

2. Technical: Volleying Accuracy - 'Aim for a Corner'

15 mins

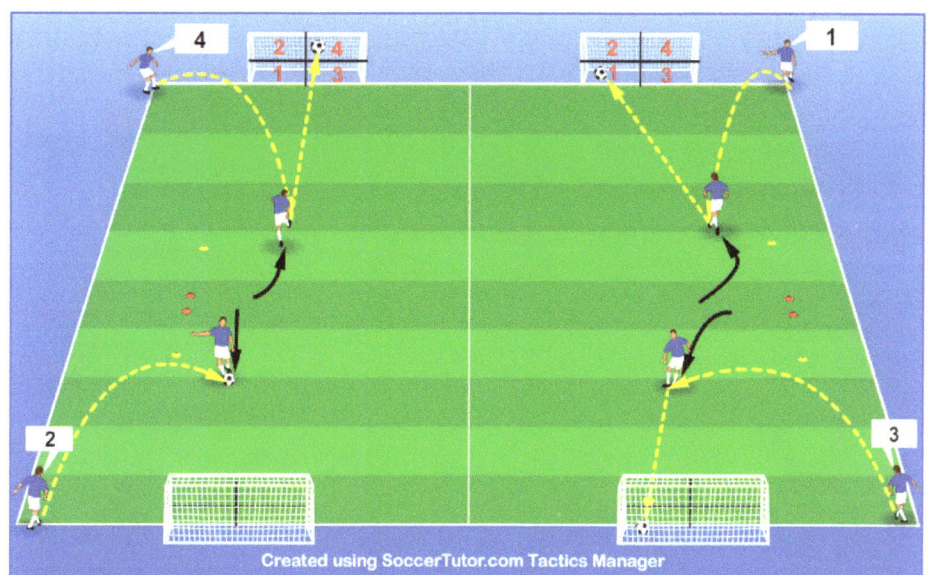

Description

The players are divided into 4 groups. Each group of players stand in front of a goal. The first player runs toward the ball and volleys the ball chipped by the player on the side.

The goal is divided into 4 zones with tape. The player chipping the ball from the side calls out a number and the player shooting must aim for the zone called out by the teammate.

Variations

1. Heading. 2. Receive with the chest and volley. 3. Volley with inside of foot. 4. Volley with instep.

Coaching Points

1. The accuracy and flight of the pass is key for the players to be able to move forward and volley the ball.
2. When volleying, the players heads should be over the ball and their back should be straight.

---

3. Coordination: Dribble, Shoot, Roll and Save

15 mins

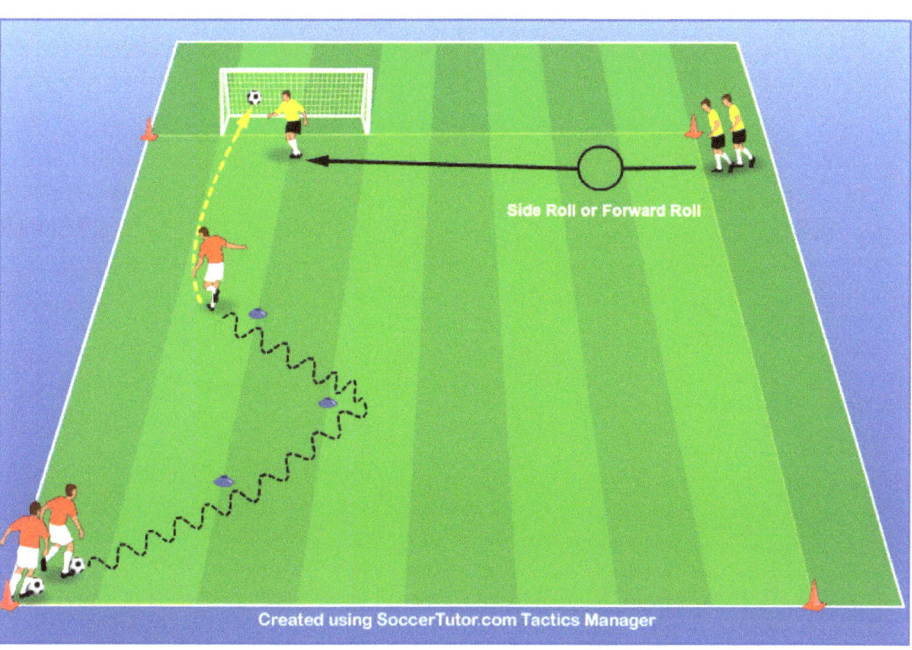

Description

In an area 10 x 15 yards, we split the players into 2 teams. Both teams start at the same point and go one at a time.

One team will run with the ball round and through the cones as shown and then shoot at goal.

The other team are the goalkeepers and after they do a roll as shown in the diagram, they try to save the shot. After each shot the 2 players change positions (they run to the end of the other queue).

Coaching Points

1. Monitor the correct execution of running with the ball round the cones.
2. Players need to keep the ball close to their feet using soft touches.
3. The speed of play should be high for the player and the goalkeeper to get into position.

WEEK 3

4. Game Situation: 1v1 Dribbling and Shooting Duel   15 mins

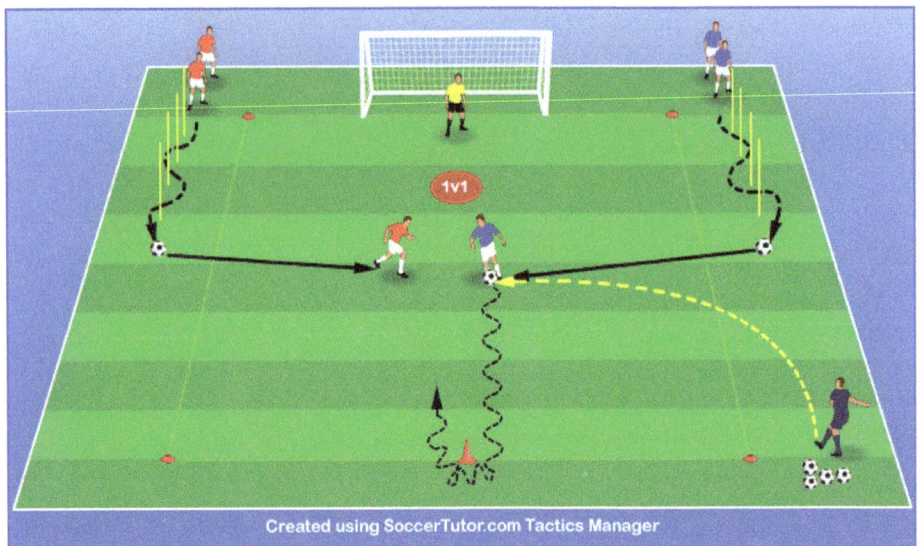

Description

2 players dribble the ball around the poles and at the end they leave the ball and sprint inside to win the ball played in by the coach.

The first player to the ball must dribble to the cone outside the area and turn around it. The other player must run and touch a cone beside the goal.

The defender then moves quickly to apply pressure to the player with the ball as he dribbles forwards.

The attacker tries to work space to shoot by beating the defender with a dribbling move (feint).

5. Game with a Theme: Shooting Accuracy in a 6v6 SSG   15 mins

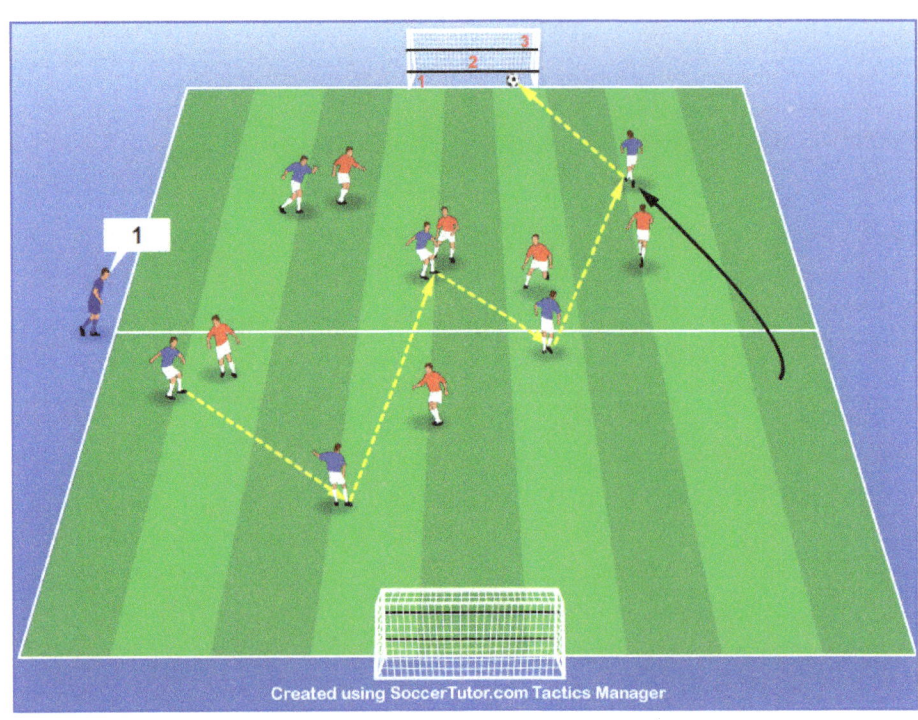

Description

Players play a regular 6v6 small sided game but without goalkeepers.

The goal is marked with tape and separated into 3 zones horizontally. A goal is only valid if it is scored in the zone called out by the coach.

The coach will constantly change the zone the players are aiming for.

Variations

1. Assign different points to the different areas.
2. Introduce a penalty or a point for the opposing team if the goal is scored in the wrong zone.

6. 5v5 Small Sided Games   30 mins

DAY 05: Receiving in the Air & Finishing

Receiving in the Air & Finishing

Primary Technical Objective: Receiving in the air, heading and volleying.
Secondary Technical Objective: Shielding the ball, turning and dribbling.
Coordination Objective: Quickness, motor skills (jumping), dynamic balance and reading the trajectory.
Tactical Objective: Possession, transition play and defending the area.

Duration of Session: 2 hours 15 mins

1. Warm Up: Technical Block 5 — 30 mins

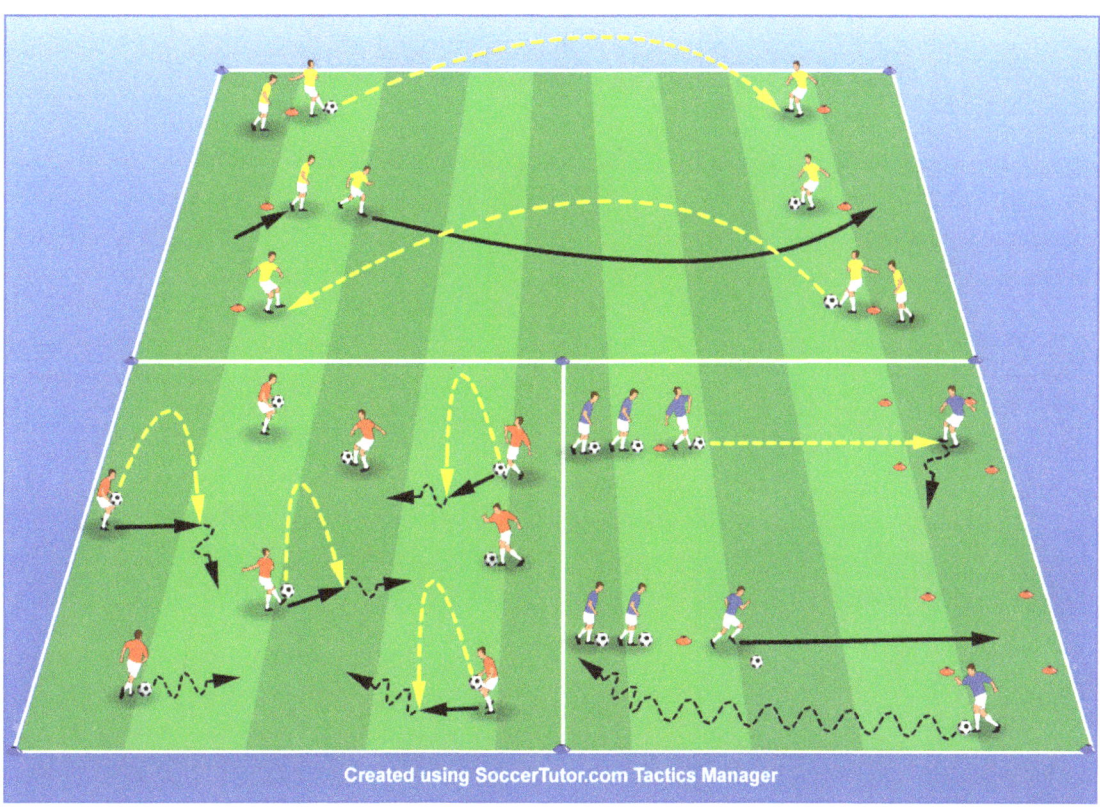

Group A

The red players move freely around the area and control the ball in different ways. The players throw (or kick) the ball up in the air, control the ball and then dribble for a few yards. Vary the type of control used inside of foot, outside of foot, with the sole, with the laces, thigh, head etc.

Group B

Divide the blue players into 2 groups and set up 5 x 5 yard squares as shown. This is a relay competition with the 2 teams starting simultaneously. The first player passes the ball to the player in the square and then runs into the square. The player in the square takes a directional first touch out the side of the square and dribbles the ball to the next player who repeats the same sequence.

Group C

The yellow players work on passing and receiving high balls at a 25 yard distance. The first player makes an aerial pass to their teammate and then runs 25 yards to their position. The second player controls the ball and then plays the next aerial pass and runs 25 yards to the opposite cone. The same sequence continues.

Vary the type of control used - inside of foot, outside of foot, the sole, the laces, thigh, head etc.

WEEK 3

2. Technical: Heading Accuracy 'Against the Crossbar' — 15 mins

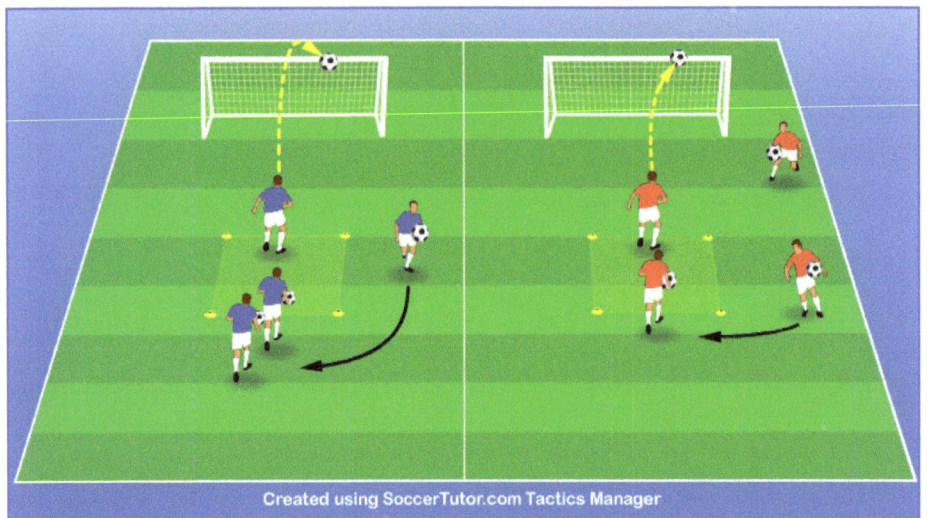

Description
2 teams of 4-5 players compete in a game where the players throw the ball in the air and head the ball trying to hit the crossbar.

Variation
Substitute a header for a goal with a volley or with an acrobatic shot.

Coaching Points
1. To head the ball up onto the crossbar, the players need to get under the flight of the ball and use the middle of the forehead.
2. For older or more developed players have them juggle the ball and then kick it up in the air for the header against the crossbar.

3. Coordination: Roll, Run, Volley Pass and Sprint — 15 mins

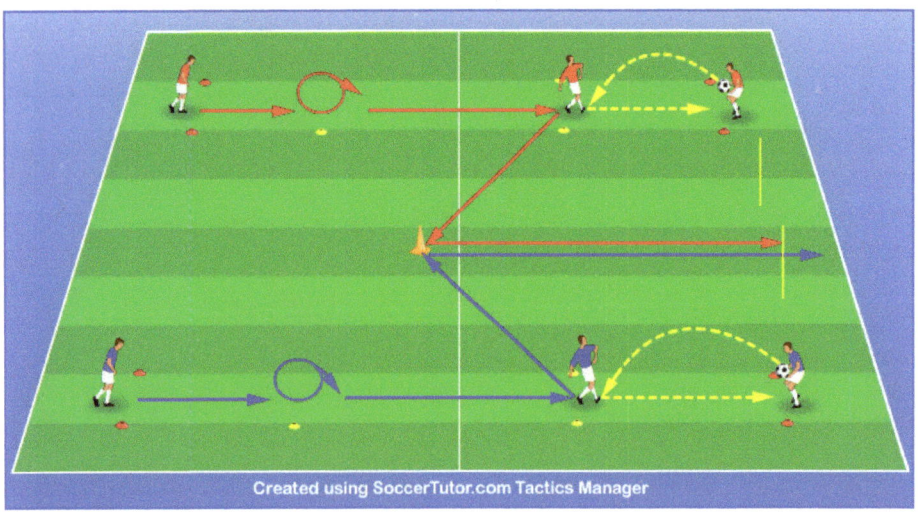

Description
Players are divided into 2 teams. The first player does a forward roll and runs to control the ball in the air thrown by a teammate and passes it back to him.

After controlling the ball, they run to touch the cone in the middle and sprint though the poles. The first player to cross the line wins a point for their team.

Variations
1. Pass the ball with a header.
2. Volley pass using inside of the foot.
3. Control with chest and pass.

Coaching Points
1. Players should be at full speed and change direction by slowing down while slightly bending their knees.
2. The accuracy and technique of the throw and the pass should be monitored.

DAY 05: Receiving in the Air & Finishing

4. Game Situation: Receiving a Long pass & Shielding the Ball   15 mins

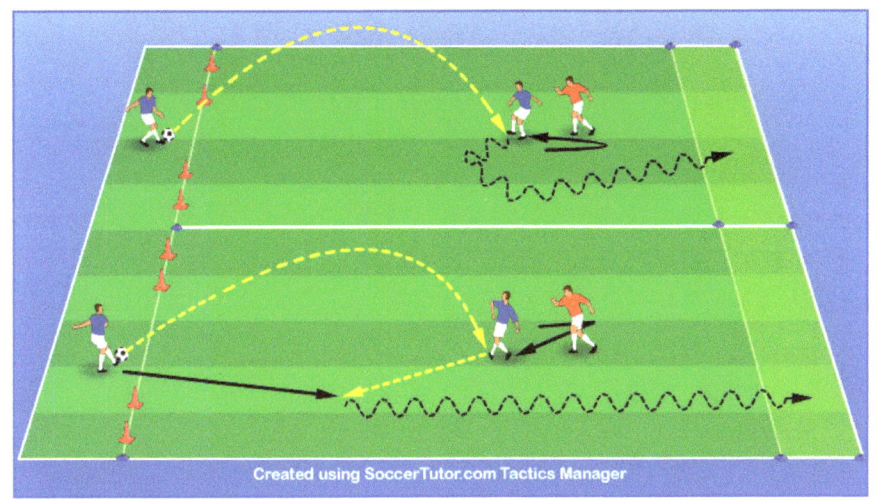

Description

The first player makes a long pass to his teammate who can receive the ball and shield it for 5 seconds or play a first time pass back to his teammate.

The player receiving the ball must check away from their marker, making a short movement followed by a longer movement to receive (as shown).

The attacking players must score by dribbling into the end zone. If the defender intercepts the ball, they can score in one of the 2 mini goals at the other end.

5. Game with a Theme: Quick Possession and Transition Play to the Striker   15 mins

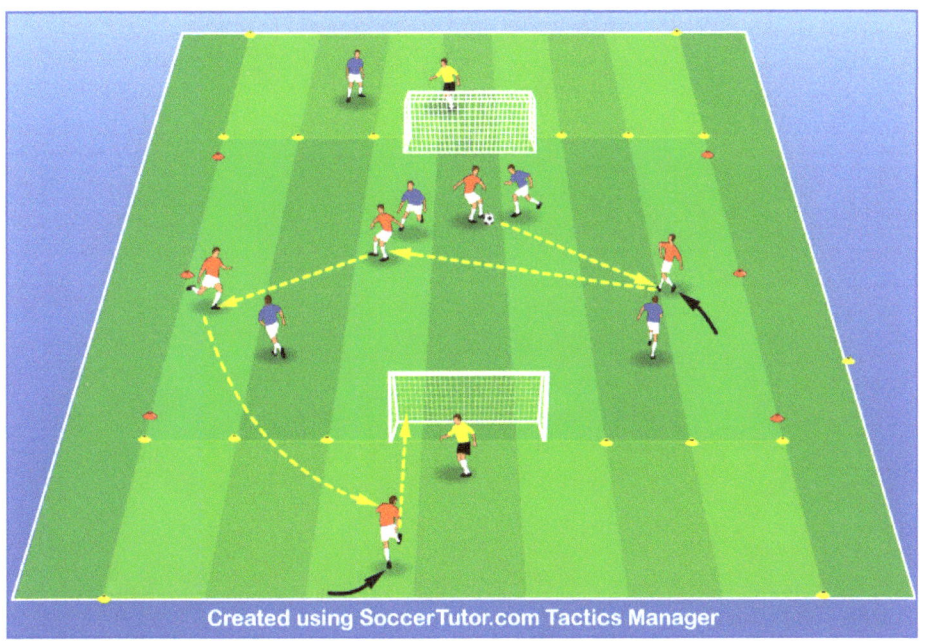

Description

In a 50 x 30 yard area we play 4 v 4 with each side having 1 player in a neutral end zone with a goal and goalkeeper.

The teams must complete 5 successful passes before playing a lofted pass to their teammate (forward/striker) in the neutral zone.

The forward has a maximum of 2 touches to take a shot on goal. If a goal is scored from 1 touch it will count as 2 goals.

Coaching Points

1. Body shape should be open on half-turn to see all players and must play quickly with 1 or 2 touches.
2. If marked, create space to get away from marker.
3. The players should have their heads up and be aware of the position of their forward player.
4. If volleying, head should be over the ball to keep the shot down.

6. 11v11 Matches on a Full Pitch   30 mins

WEEK 4

DAY 01: Running with the Ball

Running with the Ball

Primary Technical Objective: Running with the ball.
Secondary Technical Objective: Receiving, body shape, turning and shooting.
Coordination Objective: Quickness, adaptation, transformation and reactions.
Tactical Objective: 1v1 Duels.

Duration of Session: 2 hours 15 mins

1. Warm Up: Technical Block 1 — 30 mins

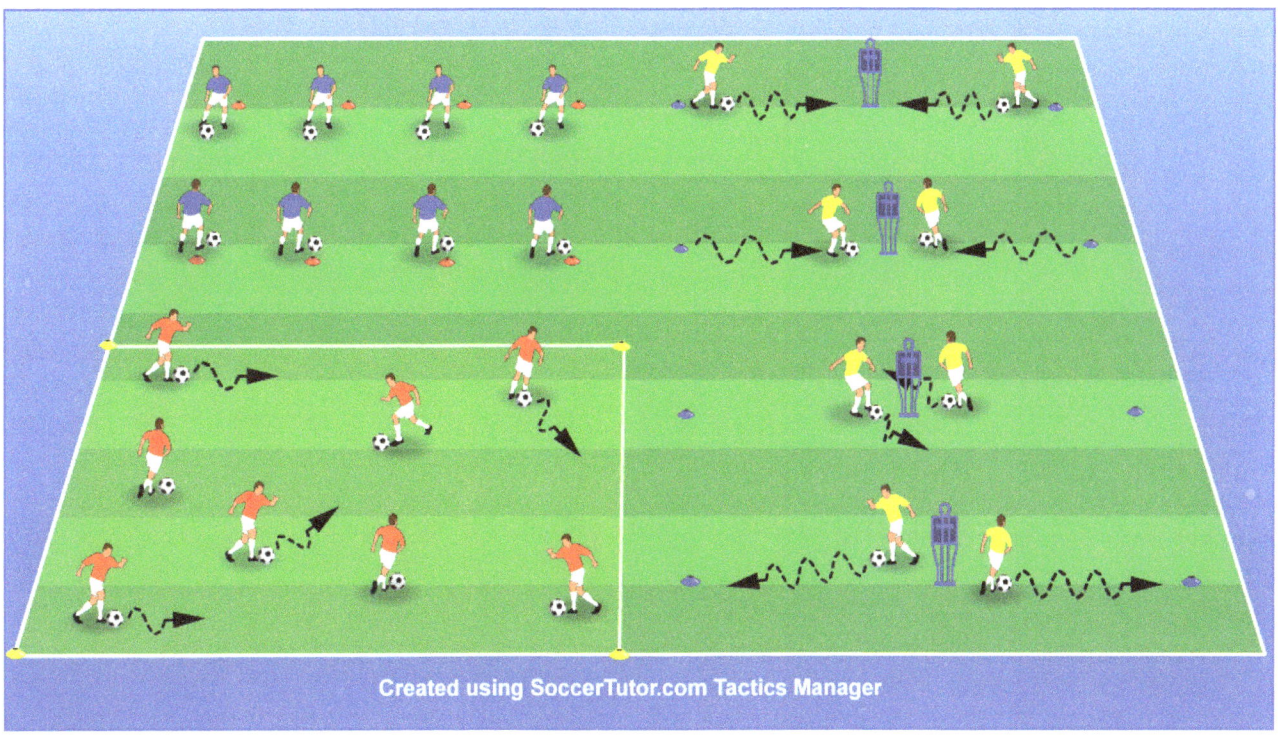

Divide the players into 3 groups with a minimum of 8 players at each station.

Group A

The red players perform different types of dribbling the ball in traffic, making sure to avoid collisions. Keep using variations, making sure that the players use only one foot and then the other when manoeuvring the ball. Vary the part of the foot used - outside, instep, the sole etc. Make sure to also perform different exercises - stretching and joint mobility exercises.

Group B

The blue players are each positioned on a cone. Every player practices different technical ball control exercises on the spot and around the cone. Start slowly and progress to increase the speed of execution. Use exercises such as making an 'L Shape' with the sole, quick outside then inside touches with 1 foot and many more. Each coach can create variants with their own imagination.

Group C

The yellow players line up opposite each other with a mannequin or cone in between them. Each player has a ball and they start simultaneously by dribbling the ball towards the centre and then perform a feint to the right (or left). The coach can determine a specific feint such as a scissor, chop or Maradona move. The players keep the same sequence going and start each time on the coach's whistle.

WEEK 4

2. Technical: Receiving, Turning and Dribbling with the Back to Goal 15 mins

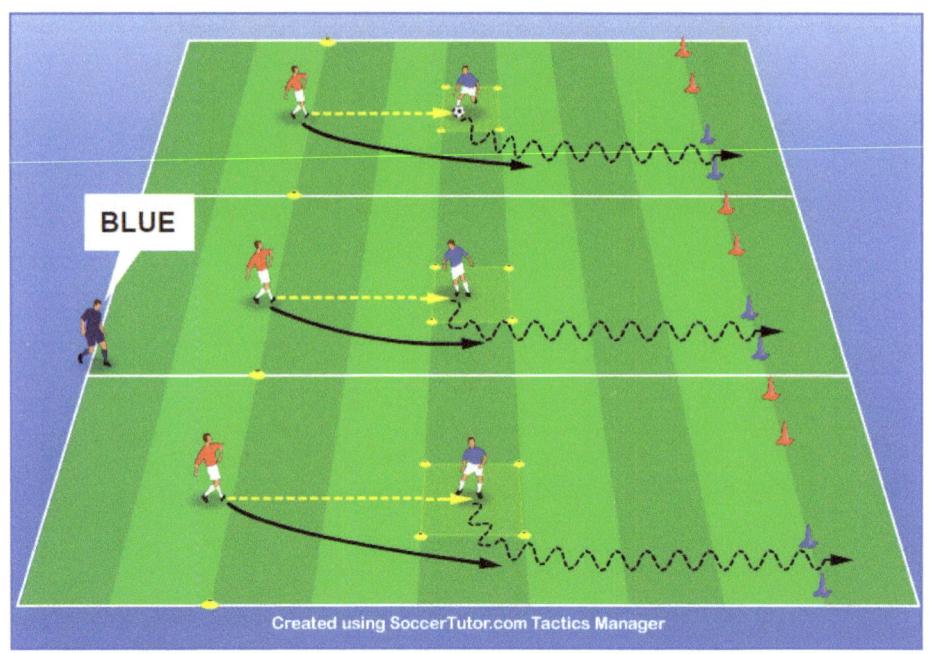

Description

Players stand in the yellow square zones as shown in the diagram.

They receive a pass from their teammate, turn and dribble towards the coloured goal called out by the coach.

They must dribble through the cone goal while the teammate who passed the ball applies pressure from behind.

Coaching Points

1. The player should receive the ball on the half turn to make a quick transition to dribble the ball towards the cones.
2. A directional first touch is very important to quickly move towards the cone before the defender is able to close them down.

3. Coordination: Dribbling Race with Turning and Shooting 15 mins

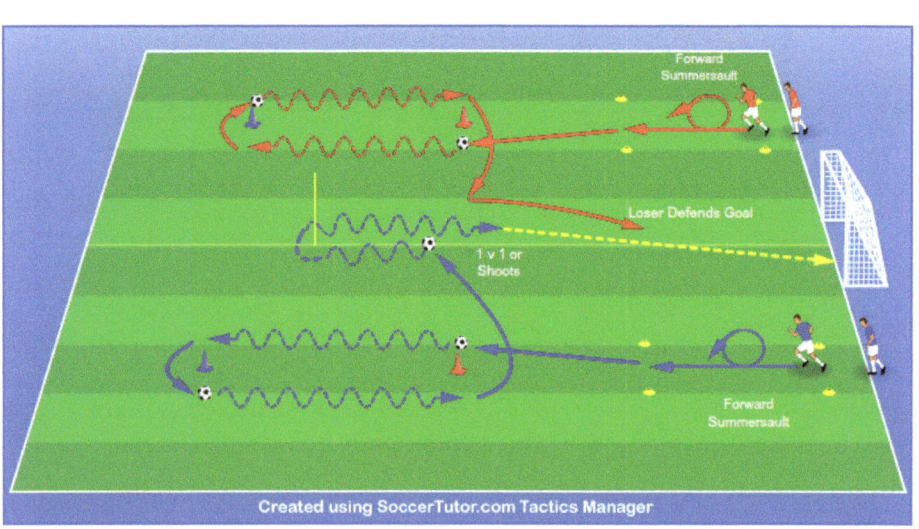

Description

In this practice, 2 teams are racing. The red and blue players start at the same time and must do a forward roll, collect the ball and dribble round the blue cone as shown and then dribble back, stopping the ball with their sole.

The 2 players then both try to run and get to the ball in the middle first.

The first player to get to the ball in the middle dribbles around the pole and shoots at goal, while the other player becomes the goalkeeper.

Variations

1. Dribbling with outside of the feet.
2. Dribble with only right or left foot.

Coaching Point

Quick reactions and rhythm are required for the transitions to the different sections of the practice (Roll -> Dribble -> Turn -> Sprint -> 1v1 -> Shoot).

DAY 01: Running with the Ball

4. Game Situation: **Dribbling Team Game with Numbers**   **15 mins**

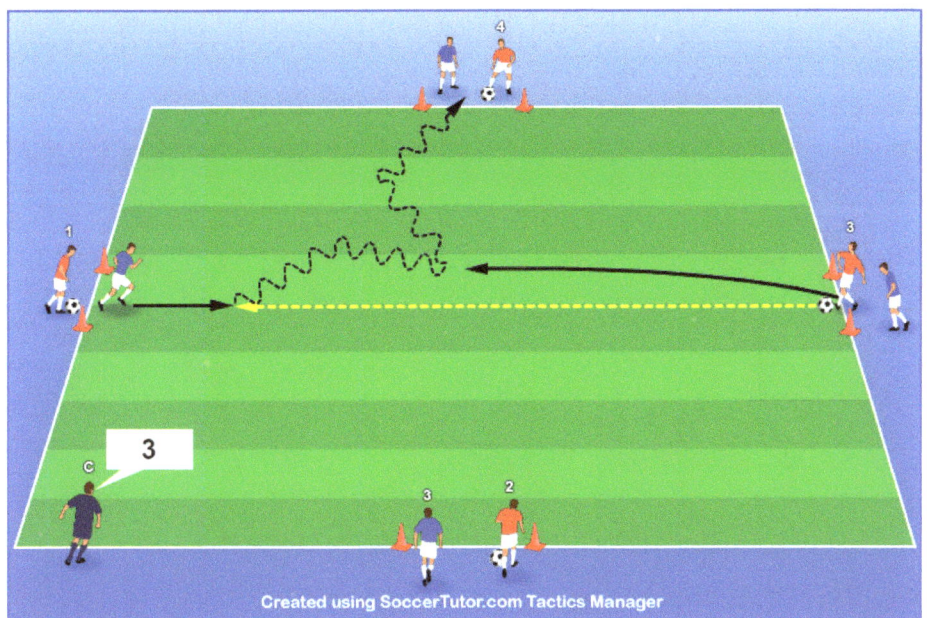

Description
The players wait for the coach to call out a number which relates to a player.

Here, red no.3 passes the ball to a blue player and then moves towards them to become the defender.

The blue player who receives the ball tries to score in one of the other 3 goals by dribbling through the cones.

Variation
If the goal is scored in the opposite goal it is worth double.

Coaching Points
1. This exercise requires many different changes of directions and turns.
2. Use a directional first touch when receiving the pass to quickly dribble through one of the cone gates.

---

5. Game with a Theme: **4v4 with 'Scoring Zones' in a SSG**   **15 mins**

Description
This is a free game of 4v4. There are 2 End Zones in which the defending team are not allowed to enter. The team in possession aim to dribble in or pass to a teammate in the End Zone.

If the player successfully receives and controls the ball in the zone, they are free to shoot on goal unopposed.

Coaching Points
1. Push the players to be creative and demonstrate what they have learned to try and beat their opponents.
2. Players should dribble the ball with different parts of the foot.

6. **5v5 Small Sided Games**   **30 mins**

WEEK 4

Feints / Moves to Beat

Primary Technical Objective: Dribbling with the ball and feints/moves to beat.
Secondary Technical Objective: Changing direction and finishing (accurate shooting).
Coordination Objective: Quickness, adaptation, transformation and reactions.
Tactical Objective: 1v1 / 1v2 duels and tactical play - positioning and movement.

Duration of Session: 2 hours 15 mins

---

1. Warm Up: Technical Block 2 — 30 mins

Group A
The red players use a variety of juggling techniques depending on their age/level. If the exercise is too complex for the age/level of their players they can juggle and catch using their hands.

Variations: 1 or 2 touches of the foot and then catch with the hands, juggling with either foot freely, juggle or dribble with alternating rhythm (2 right / 1 left), sequence - foot, thigh, head.

Other Exercises: Juggle at various heights (1 low / 1 high), alternate feet with bounces allowed, juggle followed by acrobatic act e.g. forward roll. You can introduce much more based on ability and propose a points race e.g. first player to complete 20 consecutive alternate touches when juggling.

Group B
The blue players are split into 2 teams and run a relay race dribbling through the cones. When each player arrives at the finish line, they wait there for their teammates to complete. The winning team is the one that finishes quickest. If any player fails to dribble the ball round one of the cones successfully the team receives a time penalty. You can assign rules such as only dribble with left foot, alternate touches etc.

Group C
The yellow players are split into teams of 3 with a ball per team. The first player must dribble the ball to his teammate who is 15 yards away. The player who receives then dribbles the ball to the third player. You can assign points based on whether the players can get the ball to their teammate without losing control of the ball. This exercise can also be done with the players having to juggle the ball.

DAY 02: Feints / Moves to Beat

2. Technical: Feints, Changes of Direction & Accurate Shot   15 mins

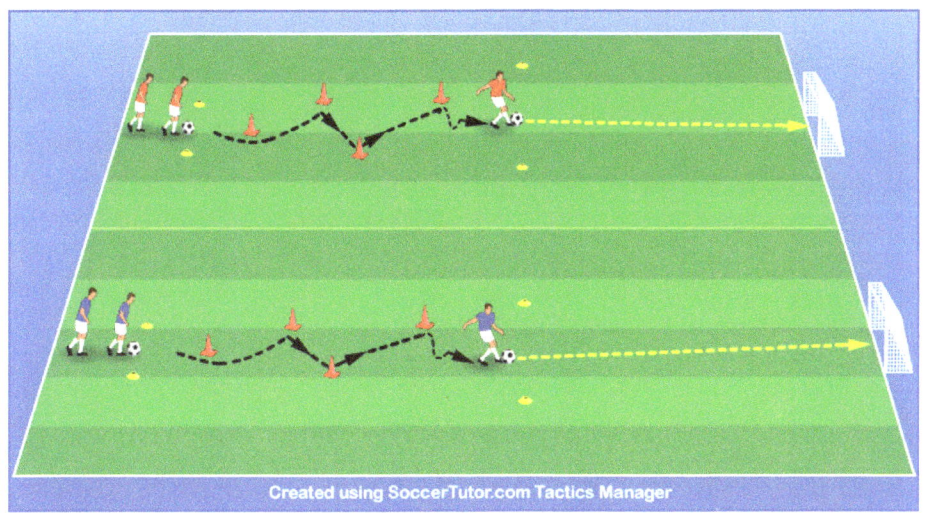

Description

Players are in 2 groups dribbling as shown in the diagram, making various types of feints and then shooting in the small goals.

The second player begins as soon as the first one shoots.

This is a competition of which team can score the most goals.

Variations

1. Free choice of feints.
2. Assign specific feints e.g. scissors, double scissors, cut back, chop etc.

Coaching Points

1. The feints should be performed at pace, as if moving away from a defender sharply in a game.
2. When assigning specific feints, demonstrate the correct execution if necessary.

---

3. Coordination: Dribbling Coordination and 1v2 Duel   15 mins

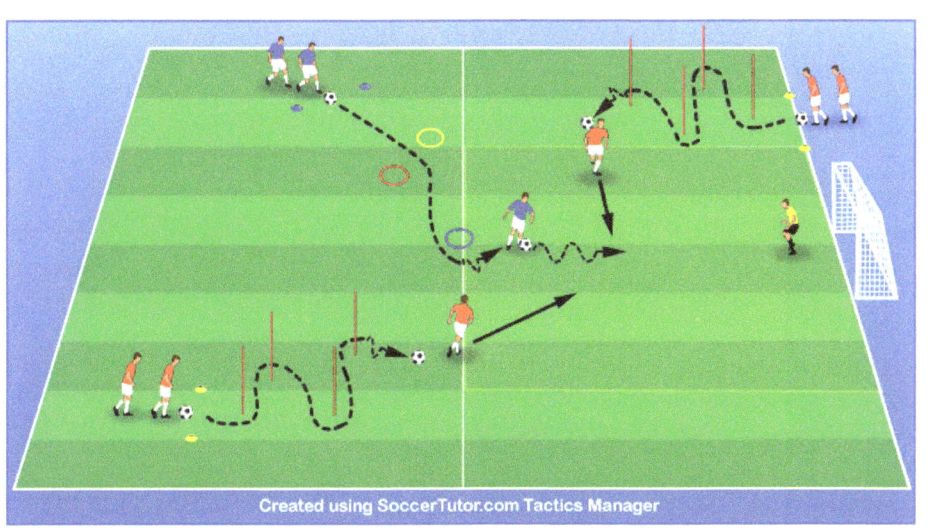

Description

2 defenders (red) dribble the ball around the poles, leave the ball at the end of the course and run to defend the goal.

The blue player dribbles round the rings, and then quickly dribbles towards the goal trying to score past the goalkeeper in a 2v1 situation.

Variations

1. Dribbling with the outside/inside of the foot. 2. Switch sides. 3. Dribble with left/right foot only.

Coaching Points

1. Again, there needs to be soft touches and close control when dribbling through the obstacles.
2. Start with passive defenders and progress to them being fully active.

©SoccerTutor.com   Football Camp Training Program

WEEK 4

4. Game Situation: 1v1 Play with Feints / Moves to Beat   15 mins

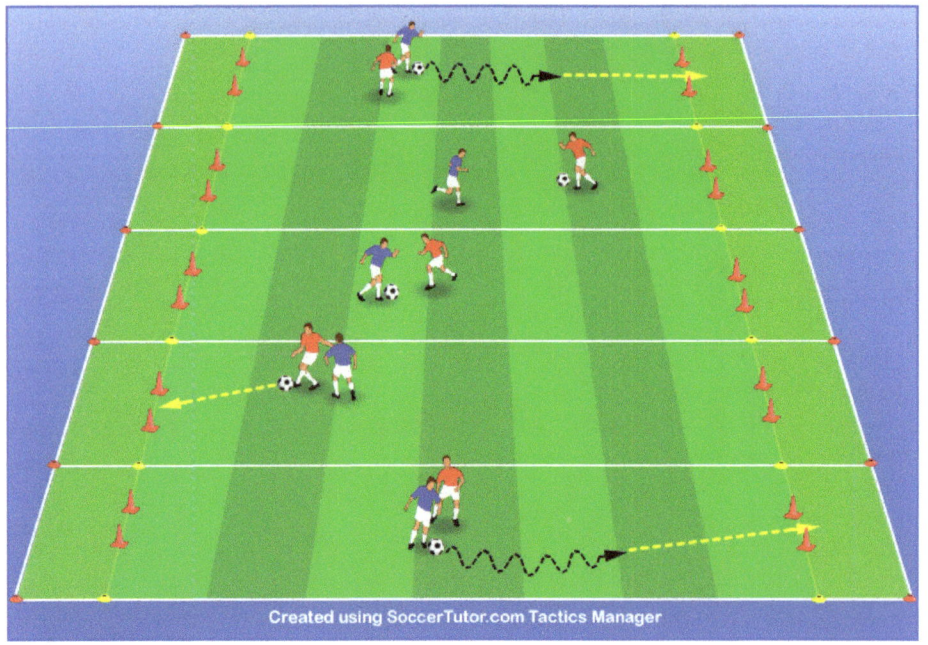

Description

Set out 1v1 channels 5 x 10 yards in size. Place 2 small goals (cones) 1 yard wide at the ends.

Players can score by dribbling past their opponent and scoring in the small goal.

If a goal is scored or the ball goes out of play, the defending player becomes the attacker.

Coaching Points

1. The attacking player needs to keep the ball close to their feet using feints and quick changes of direction to get past the defender and score.
2. Players need to have explosive acceleration to continuously beat the defender.

5. Game with a Theme: Collective Tactical Movement in a SSG   15 mins

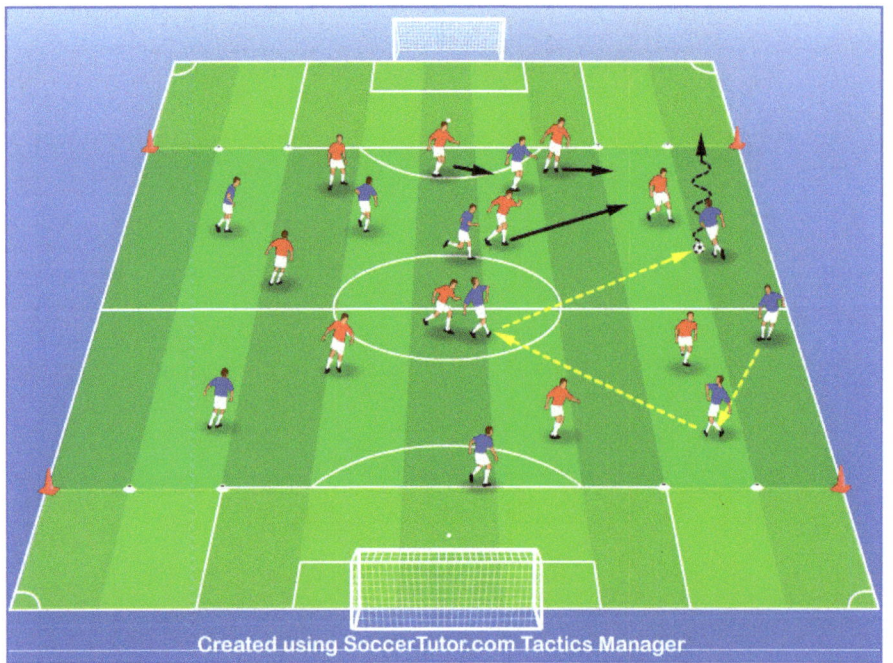

Description

In the area shown we play a 10v10 game. If you haven't got that many players, then simply play with the numbers you have, e.g. 7v7 etc.

The aim for the team in possession is to advance the ball past the last line of defence and the line of cones at the end of the pitch.

Variation

Shorten the area of play to put the players under more pressure.

Coaching Point

As play develops observe the positioning and movements. Stop the play and correct the mistakes.

6. 5v5 Small Sided Games   30 mins

DAY 03: Passing and Receiving

Passing and Receiving

Primary Technical Objective: Passing and receiving.

Secondary Technical Objective: Receiving the ball in the air, dribbling and feints/moves to beat.

Coordination Objective: Quickness, adaptation, transformation, balance and reading the path of the ball.

Tactical Objective: Creating space, support angles and possession play.

Duration of Session: 2 hours 15 mins.

1. Warm Up: Technical Block 3 — 30 mins

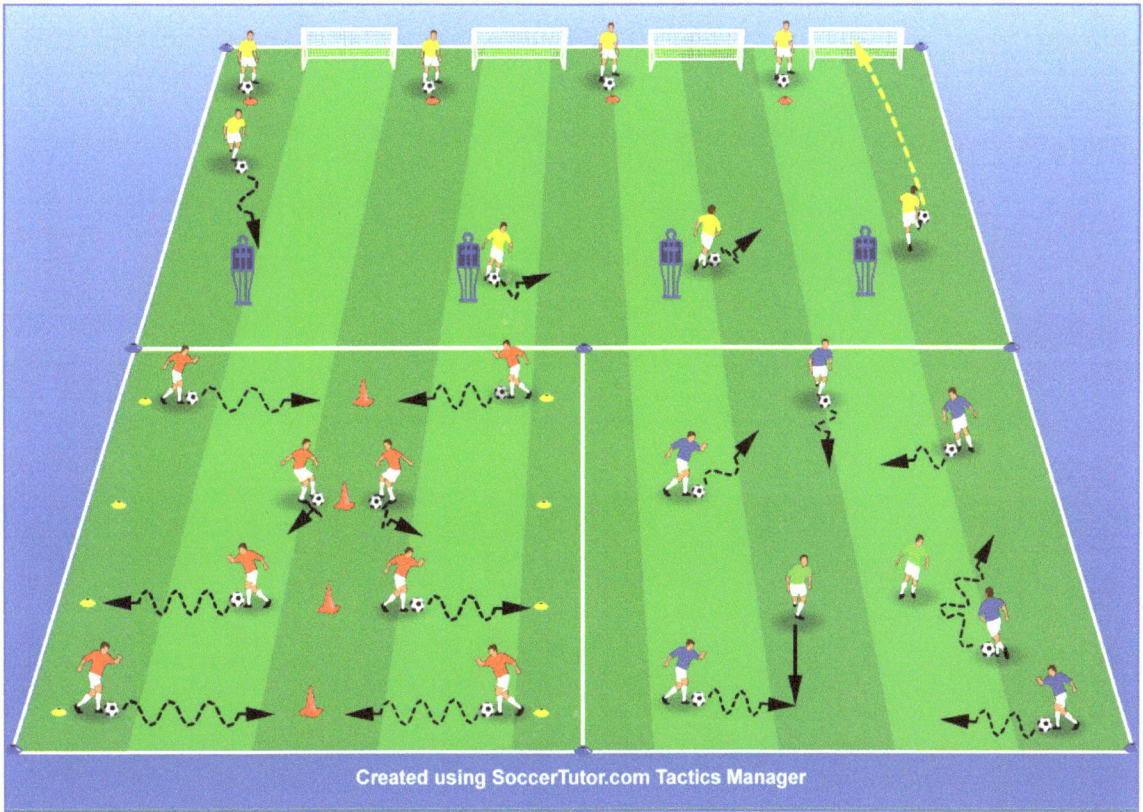

Group A

The red players are in pairs opposite each other 15 yards apart. Both players have a ball and start simultaneously by dribbling the ball towards the centre. At the cone, the players change direction and dribble back to the starting position.

Alternate different types of turns such as turn with the sole, sole 'L' shape, internal cut etc.

Group B

The blue players all have a ball each and move around freely in a 15 x 15 yard area. 2 or more green players are added (depending on the number of players in blue) who try to win the ball from the blue players as quickly as possible. If a blue player loses the ball he is not eliminated, but instead helps the other blue players to maintain possession of the ball. Change the green players every minute.

Group C

The yellow players are divided into 4 groups and compete in a relay competition. Each player dribbles the ball towards the mannequin (or cone) which is 5 yards away, perform a specific turn pre-determined by the coach and then quickly shoot into the goal. The first team to score 10 goals wins the relay.

WEEK 4

2. Technical: Passing, Receiving and 1v1 Play

15 mins

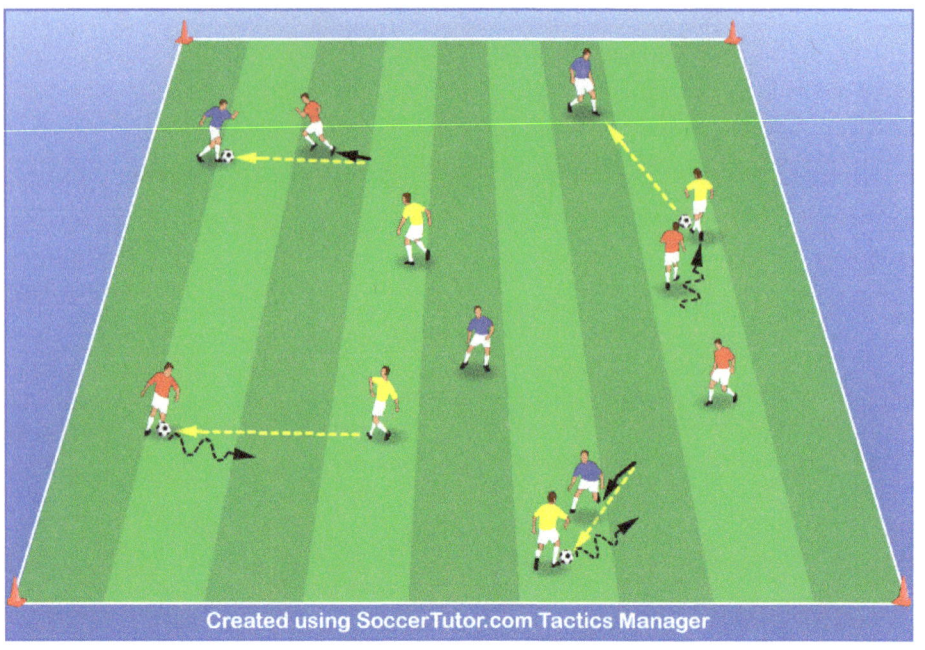

Description

In a 20 x 20 yard square there are 3 teams of at least 4 players and 4 balls.

The players with possession of the ball pass to other players of a different colour who automatically become passive defenders.

The player who receives the ball becomes the attacker and has to beat the defender before searching for a player that is available with a different colour to pass the ball to. The sequence continues.

Coaching Points

1. An advancement from using mannequins/cones; the players practice their feints on a passive defender.
2. The players should vary the feints outlined by the coach.
3. The defender simply uses frontal marking without touching the player.

3. Coordination: 'Psycho-Kinetics' Passing in Pairs

15 mins

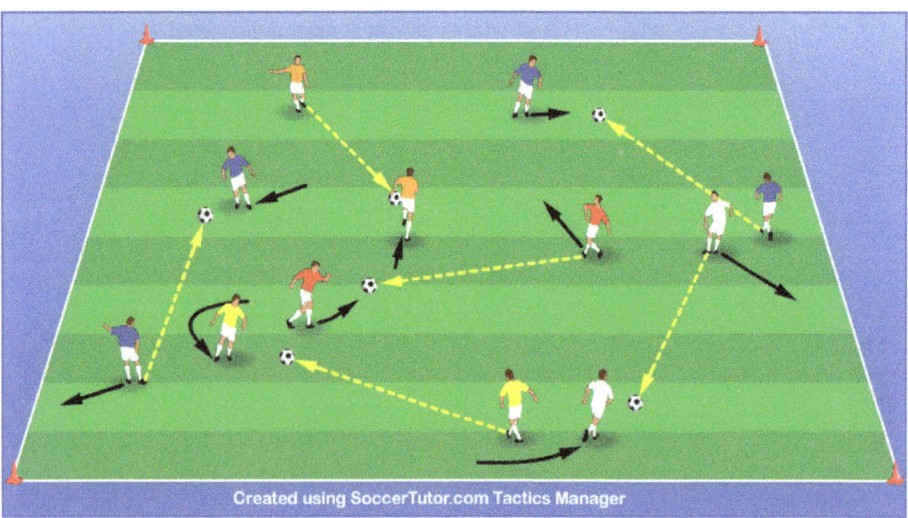

Description

Players are in pairs and try to complete the highest possible number of passes in a preset time.

They must avoid the other pairs and show good awareness to be able to successfully pass to each other amongst all the 'traffic.' The pair that complete the most passes in the allocated time win.

Variations

1. Volley pass with inside of foot or instep.
2. Headed pass.
3. Receive the ball with chest and volley pass with inside of the foot.

Coaching Points

1. Accuracy of pass, weight of pass and good communication are all key elements for this practice.
2. Players need to play with their heads up and have good awareness to avoid collisions and make successful passes to their teammate.
3. Close control is needed with directional first touches, especially if receiving with the chest.

DAY 03: Passing and Receiving

4. Game Situation: Passing Combinations with a 3v2 Advantage   **15 mins**

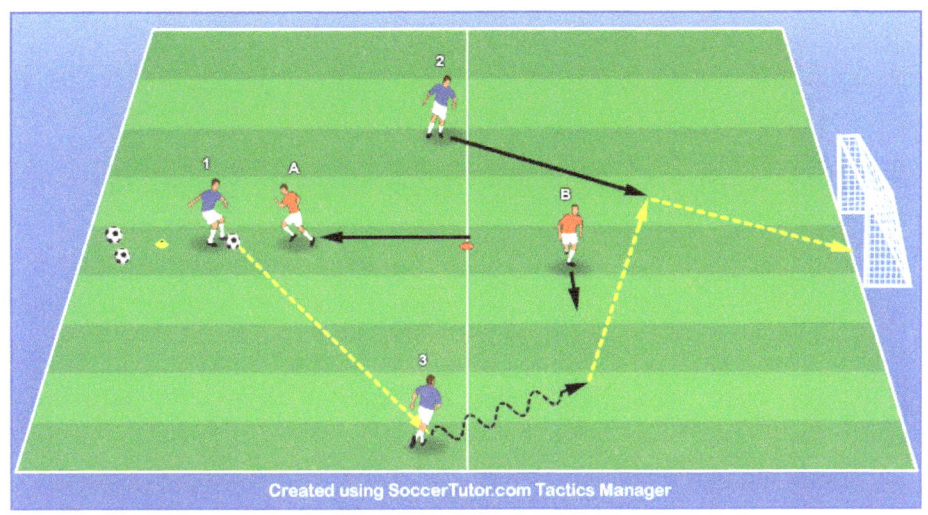

Description

Player 1 starts with the ball and as player A applies pressure he makes a pass to player 2 or 3 based on which opponent player B marks.

Player 1 must use the inside of his left foot to pass to player 3 and the inside of his right foot to pass to player 2.

Player B's starting position is behind player A and the blues have a 3v2 situation with the aim to score in the goal.

Change defenders often.

Variation
Pass with the outside of the foot.

Coaching Points
1. Awareness is needed to choose which side to pass to.
2. Move the ball quickly to exploit the numerical advantage.

5. Game with a Theme: 4v4v4 Dynamic 3 Zone Possession Game   **15 mins**

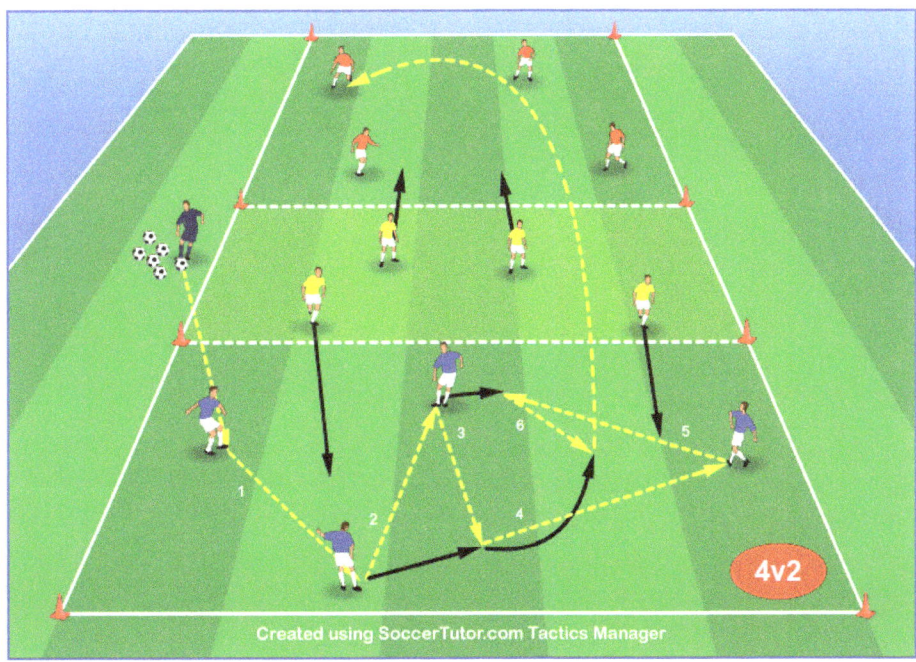

Description

Set up a long and narrow area divided into 3 zones (smaller middle zone). There are 3 teams of 4 and the objective is to make a lofted pass to the team in the opposite end zone after successfully completing 6 passes.

The coach passes to a team in an end zone and the defending team move 2 players to apply pressure on the team in possession (4v2 as shown).

If a team loses possession or does not complete the lofted pass to the other team, they become the defending team who must apply pressure and try to intercept the ball.

Coaching Points
1. This practice requires all types of passes (short, medium, long, to feet and into space).
2. The defending players need to apply collective pressure to close off the passing angles.

6. 5v5 Small Sided Games   **30 mins**

WEEK 4

Shooting

Primary Technical Objective: Shooting and finishing.

Secondary Technical Objective: Ball control, dribbling and receiving.

Coordination Objective: Balance, quickness, differentiation, adaptation and transformation.

Tactical Objective: Attacking combination play and quick finishing.

Duration of Session: 2 hours 15 mins.

1. Warm Up: Technical Block 4   30 mins

Group A

The red players line up behind the 4 cones as shown. 4 players start at the same time and dribble the ball towards the cone in front of them, perform a feint pre-determined by the coach and move to the cone to the right. Change the type of feint after every completed lap and also change the direction from anticlockwise to clockwise so the players move to the left as well.

Group B

The blue players are divided into 2 groups and practice dribbling with feints to change direction. Initially the players simply use the inside and outside of both feet to dribble and change directions. They then progress to perform a specific feint at each cone which is pre-determined by the coach. Examples of feints include the scissor, the cut back and the chop.

Group C

The yellow players are divided into teams of 3 or 4 and are in a competition to see who can score the most goals. 4 players start simultaneously with a ball, dribble towards the mannequin (or cone), perform a feint to the left or right and shoot in the mini goal. A point is awarded to the player who scores first.

You can decide the type of feint to be used or leave it to the players imagination and freedom.

DAY 04: Shooting

2. Technical: Ball Control, Dribbling & Shooting Circuits   15 mins

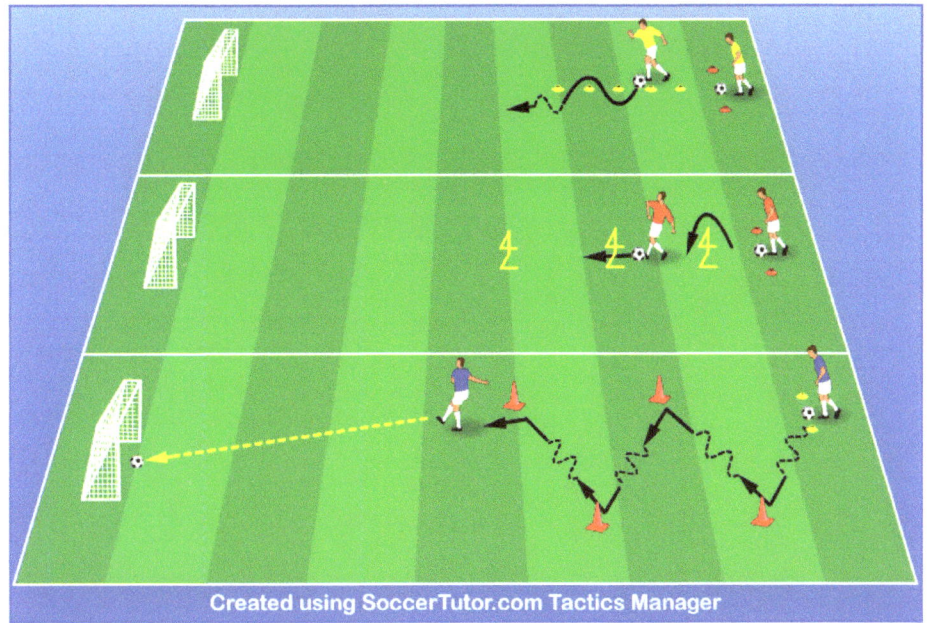

Description

The team works in 3 groups and will rotate.

Circuit 1: In the first section the players dribble the ball through the cones using two touches with alternative feet; right, then left. The player then takes a shot at the goal.

Variations: Dribble with one foot. Outside of feet only.

Circuit 2: In the second section the player guides the ball through the hurdles and jumps over them. The player then takes a shot at goal.

Circuit 3: In the third section the players dribble the ball towards the cones and quickly change direction with a feint at a 45 degree angle to the next cone and does this twice more before taking a shot at goal.

3. Coordination: Speed & Agility Shooting Competition   15 mins

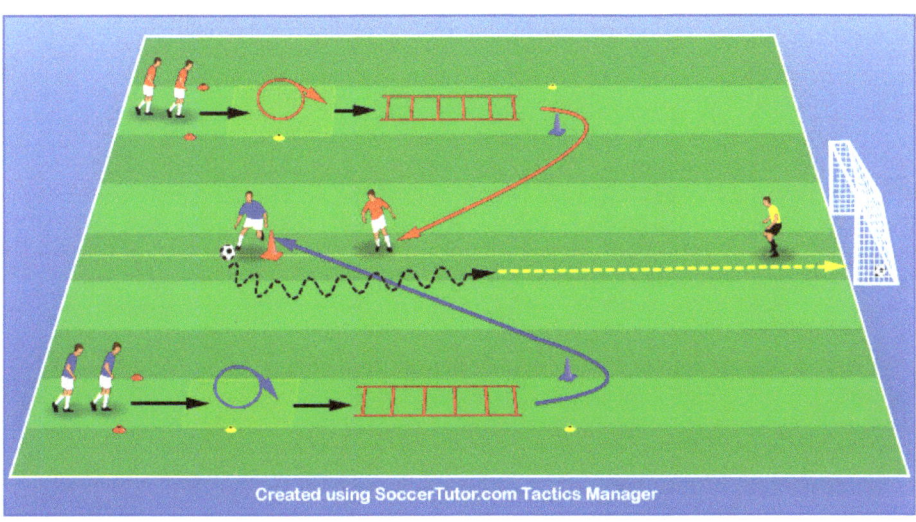

Description

The first player from each group performs a forward roll, and runs through the ladder using diagonal steps (left foot step on the right and right foot step on the left).

Both players run around the cone and race to the ball.

The first player to the ball aims to score in the goal, as the other player becomes the defender.

Variations

1. Introduce a second ball.
2. Use speed rings instead of ladders.
3. Substitute the forward roll with a side roll.

WEEK 4

4. Game Situation: 2v2 with 4 Goals: 10 Ball Competition in a SSG   15 mins

Description

The coach has 10 balls in the corner or outside the area and he passes them 1 at a time into the centre.

When a goal is scored or the ball goes out, the coach passes the next ball in.

There are 4 goals and both teams can score in any of them. The team that scores the most goals using these 10 balls wins.

Coaching Points

1. This is a free game which should stimulate expression, initiative and the creativity of the players.
2. Encourage the players to take each other on and run into space to score.
3. The aim is to develop their technique and individual tactical play.

5. Game with a Theme: 3v3 Quick Combinations and Finishing in the Box   15 mins

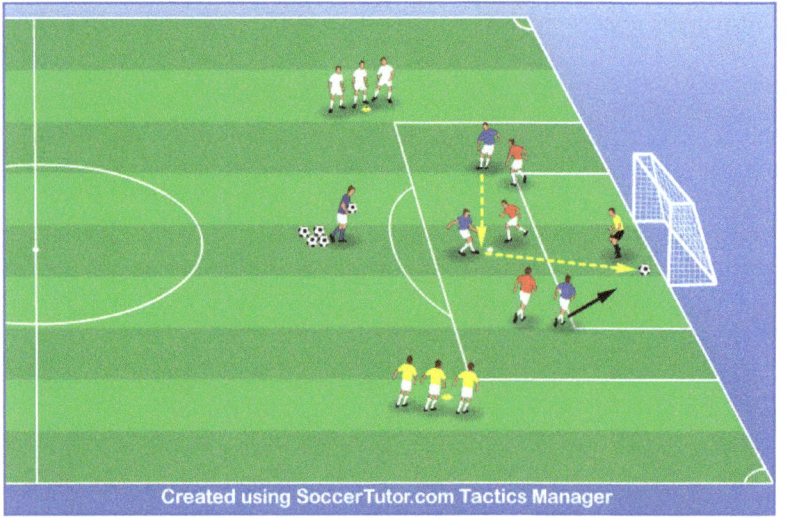

Description

Inside the penalty area we play 3v3. The team that scores a goal remains in the field of play while the other team swaps with another team waiting at the edge of the box.

The coach throws the ball in every time the ball leaves the box and every time there is a missed shot or goalkeeper's save.

The players should aim to use quick combinations to create space for an attempt on goal.

Coaching Points

1. Players must try to use 1 touch as often as possible making sure to have fast positive movement.
2. A shot on goal should be realised when half a yard of space is achieved.
3. The play should be of intense speed as the players have time to rest when they are not playing.

6. 5v5 Small Sided Games   30 mins

DAY 05: Receiving in the Air & Finishing

Receiving in the Air & Finishing

Primary Technical Objective: Receiving in the air, heading and shooting.

Secondary Technical Objective: Shielding the ball (correct body shape) and turning.

Coordination Objective: Quickness, motor skills (jumping), strength, dynamic balance and reading the trajectory.

Tactical Objective: 2v1 play and attacking/defending in the air.

Duration of Session: 2 hours 15 mins.

1. Warm Up: Technical Block 5   30 mins

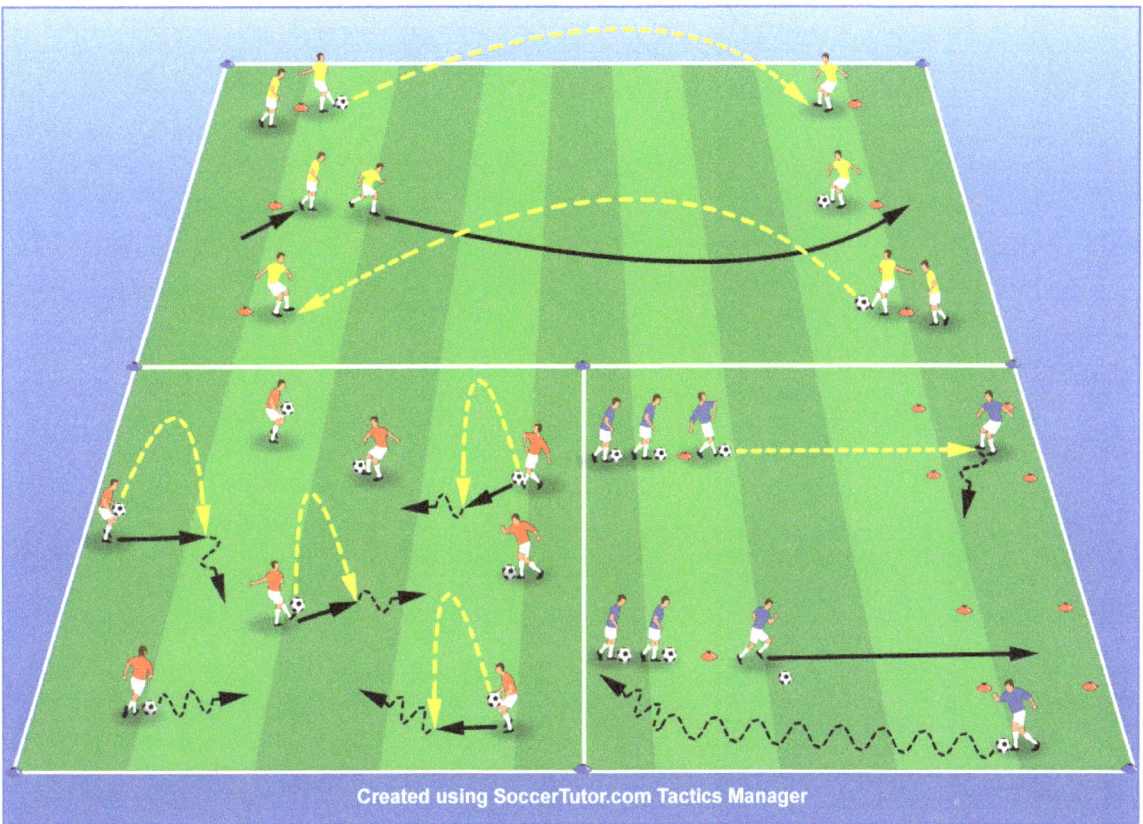

Group A

The red players move freely around the area and control the ball in different ways. The players throw (or kick) the ball up in the air, control the ball and then dribble for a few yards. Vary the type of control used inside of foot, outside of foot, with the sole, with the laces, thigh, head etc.

Group B

Divide the blue players into 2 groups and set up 5 x 5 yard squares as shown. This is a relay competition with the 2 teams starting simultaneously. The first player passes the ball to the player in the square and then runs into the square. The player in the square takes a directional first touch out the side of the square and dribbles the ball to the next player who repeats the same sequence.

Group C

The yellow players work on passing and receiving high balls at a 25 yard distance. The first player makes an aerial pass to their teammate and then runs 25 yards to their position. The second player controls the ball and then plays the next aerial pass and runs 25 yards to the opposite cone. The same sequence continues.

Vary the type of control used - inside of foot, outside of foot, the sole, the laces, thigh, head etc.

WEEK 4

2. Technical: Heading Accuracy - 'Aim for the Ring'

15 mins

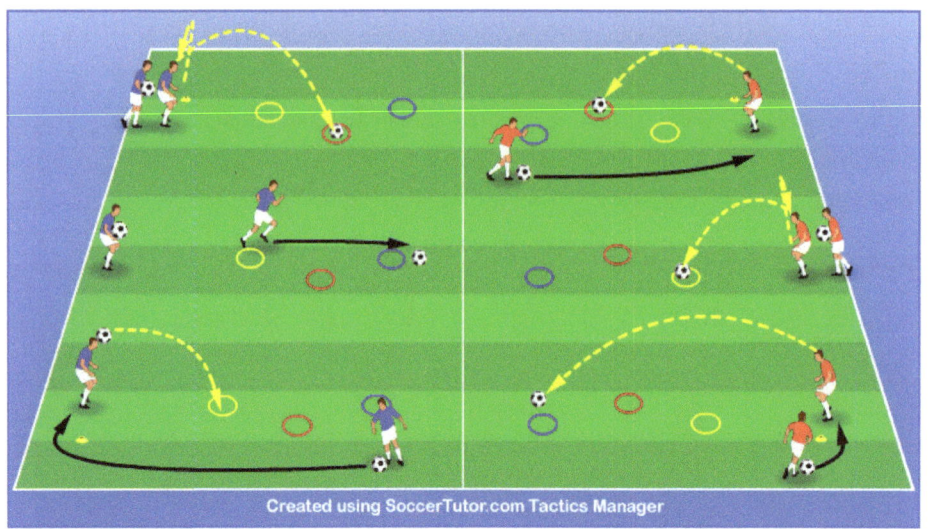

Description
Each player throws the ball in the air and heads it towards one of the rings positioned at various distances (3 yards, 5 yards, 7 yards).

Assign a point to the rings based on the distance and colour.

The team with the most points win the game.

Variation
The ball is kicked up in the air and then headed (instead of thrown).

Coaching Points
1. Players should get good height on their throws/kicks so that they are able to jump up and head the ball.
2. These headers should be made with the middle of the forehead.

3. Coordination: Roll, Receive and Shoot

15 mins

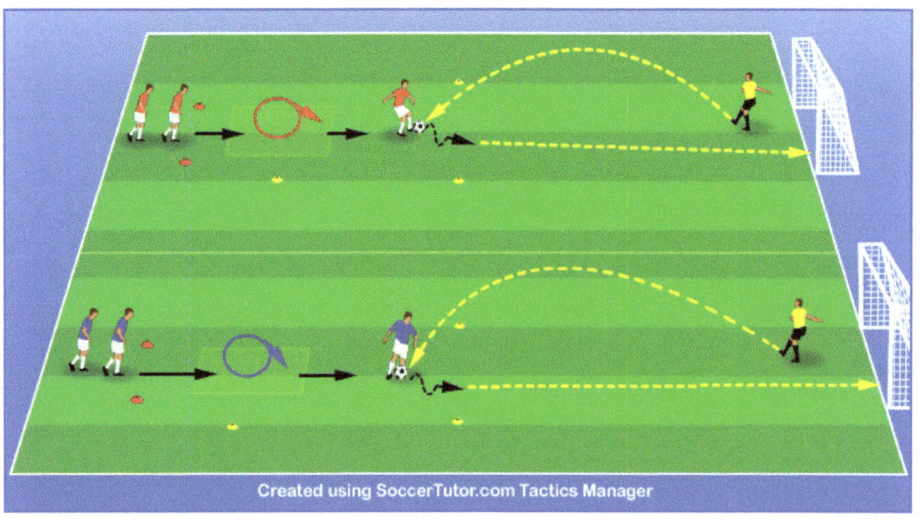

Description
Every player does a forward roll and moves to receive the ball chipped by the goalkeeper.

Once the ball is controlled the player shoots at goal.

The team with the most goals win the game (red v blue).

Variations
1. The pass from the goalkeeper is along the ground.
2. Receive the ball with a different part of the body.

Coaching Point
Receive the ball using a directional first touch to move forward and shoot at goal.

DAY 05: Receiving in the Air & Finishing

4. Game Situation: Passing and Receiving with Good Communication 15 mins

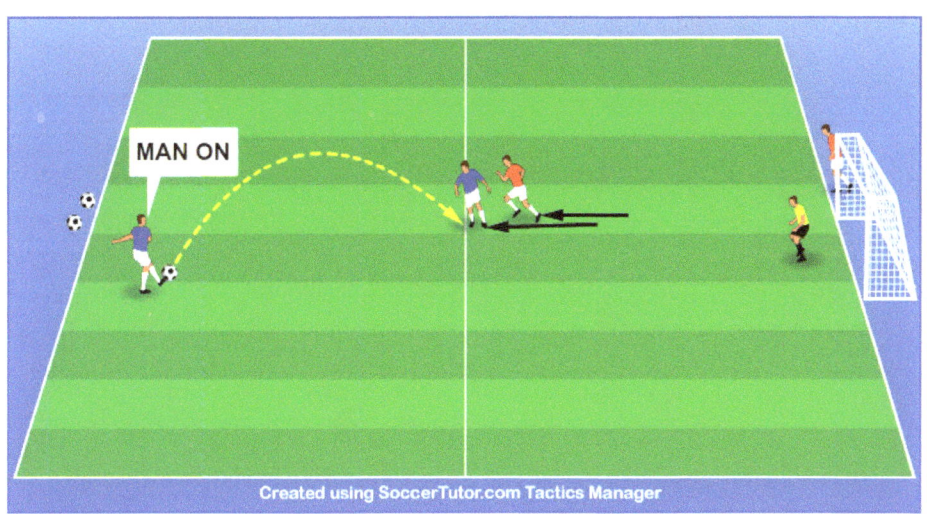

Description

The blue player passes the ball in the air to his teammate and depending on the defenders positioning, calls "man on" and receives the ball back.

We then have a 2v1 situation with the aim to score.

Alternatively, he can call "turn" then a frontal 2v1 situation is created.

Variations

1. Introduce the offside rule.
2. The player passes the ball back with a header.

Coaching Points

1. The player needs to use their body as a barrier between the ball and the defender (shielding).
2. In a 2v1 situation, the player with the ball can wait for the defender to commit, then pass into the space.

5. Game with a Theme: Heading with Target Players SSG (2) 15 mins

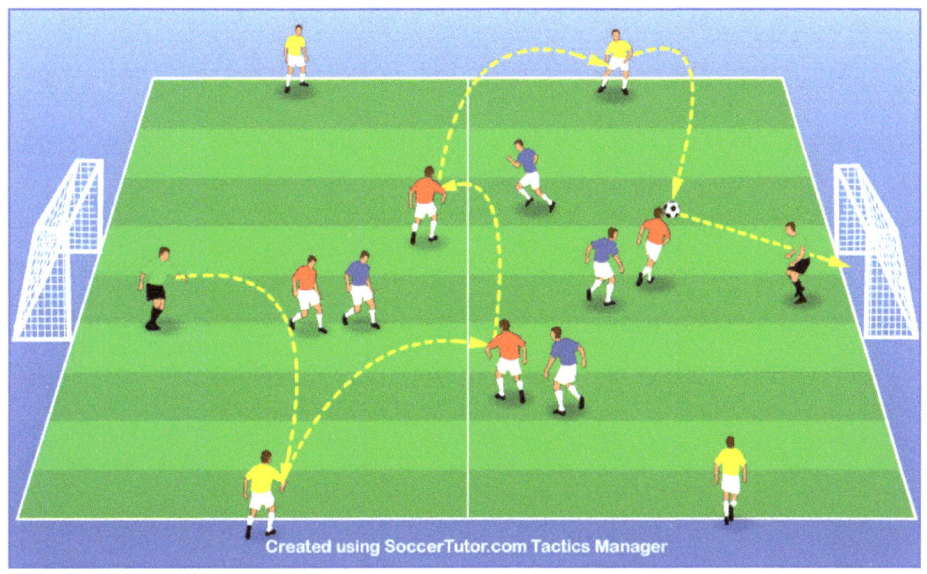

Description

In an area 20 x 25 yards we have a 4v4 (+2 GKs) game.

There are 4 target players who stand either side of the goal (2 on each side).

The objective is to score with a header with an assist from a target player.

The game is played with the hands and heads. Change the target players.

Variations

1. Hands and feet game.
2. Game with just feet.
3. Headed goal after a headed assist counts as 5 points.

6. 11v11 Matches on a Full Pitch 30 mins

WEEK 5

DAY 01: Running with the Ball

Running with the Ball

Primary Technical Objective: Running with the ball.
Secondary Technical Objective: Dribbling, turning and changes of direction.
Coordination Objective: Quickness, adaptation, transformation and reactions.
Tactical Objective: Creating space and 1v1 Duels.

Duration of Session: 2 hours 15 mins

---

1. Warm Up: Technical Block 1   30 mins

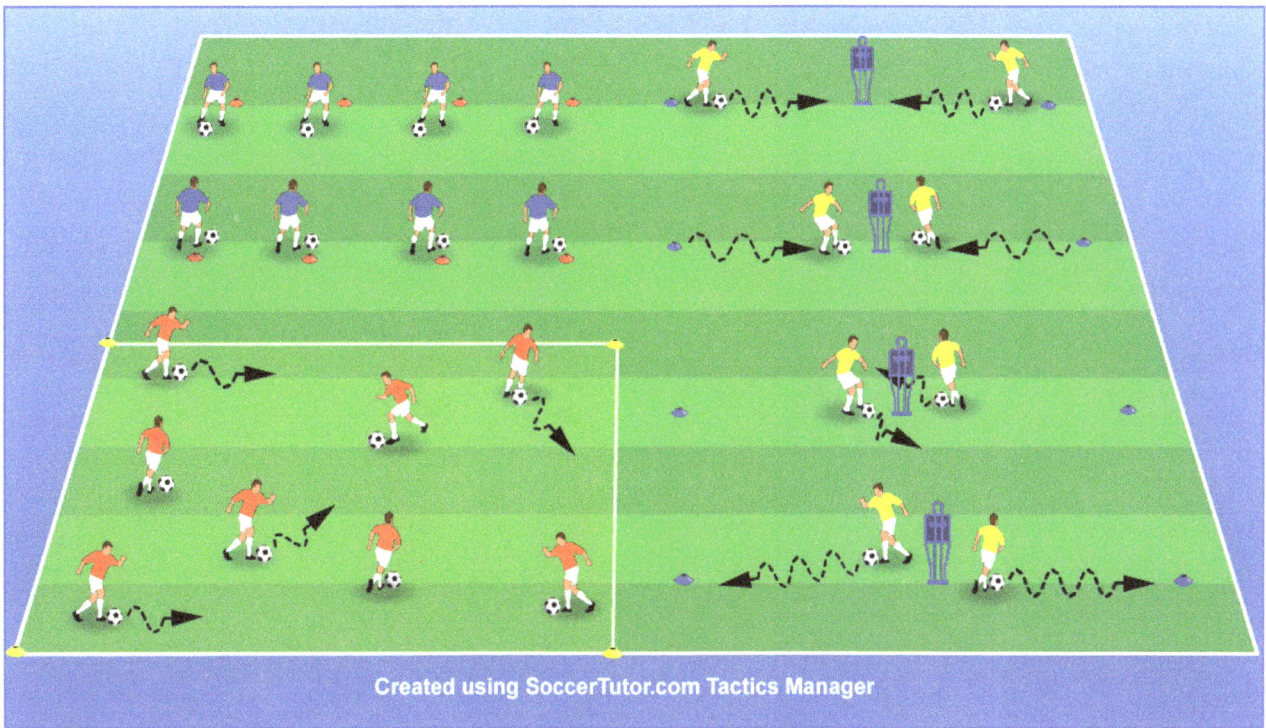

Divide the players into 3 groups with a minimum of 8 players at each station.

Group A

The red players perform different types of dribbling the ball in traffic, making sure to avoid collisions. Keep using variations, making sure that the players use only one foot and then the other when manoeuvring the ball. Vary the part of the foot used - outside, instep, the sole etc. Make sure to also perform different exercises stretching and joint mobility exercises.

Group B

The blue players are each positioned on a cone. Every player practices different technical ball control exercises on the spot and around the cone. Start slowly and progress to increase the speed of execution. Use exercises such as making an 'L Shape' with the sole, quick outside then inside touches with 1 foot and many more. Each coach can create variants with their own imagination.

Group C

The yellow players line up opposite each other with a mannequin or cone in between them. Each player has a ball and they start simultaneously by dribbling the ball towards the centre and then perform a feint to the right (or left). The coach can determine a specific feint such as a scissor, chop or Maradona move. The players keep the same sequence going and start each time on the coach's whistle.

WEEK 5

2. Technical: Quick Reactions Man Marking Dribbling Game   15 mins

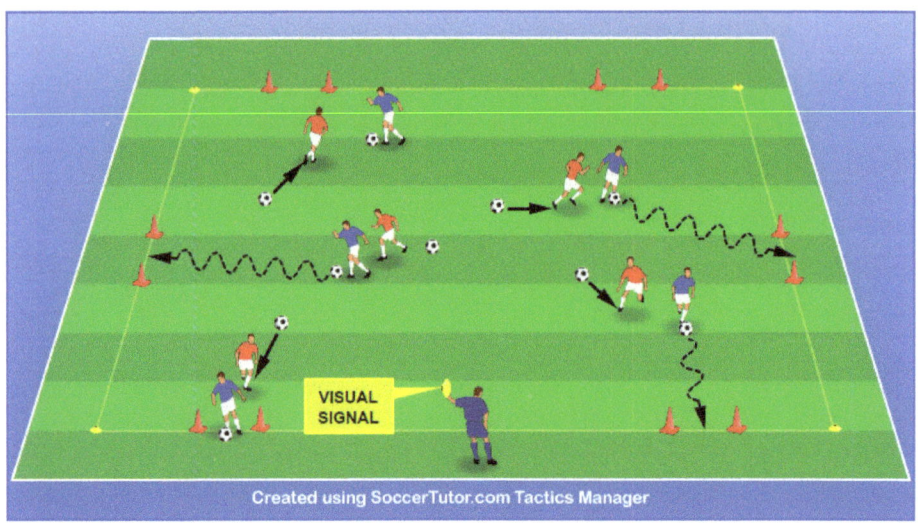

Variation
Change the type of dribbling.

Coaching Points
1. Quick reactions are essential to get in front of the defender and score quickly.
2. The correct body shape is required to shield the ball, making sure their body is a barrier between the opponent and the ball.

Description
Players are divided into 2 teams, with 1 attacking team and 1 defending team. Every player starts the drill with a ball as they all dribble the ball around the area avoiding each other. We also have 6 different cone gates (goals) positioned on the sides of the area.

On the coach's whistle (or visual signal as shown in diagram), the attacking players try to score by dribbling through the small goals. The defending players leave their ball to defend and tackle the attacking players.

Players are put into pairs and assigned 1 player to mark. They are not allowed to tackle the other players.

---

3. Coordination: Quick Reactions Colours Game   15 mins

Description
10 minutes

We have 4 teams all wearing different colours. 2 teams play against the other 2 teams.

Goals are scored in the goals with the colours of the opposition.

Change the alliances during the game to prompt quick reactions to a changing situation.

2 minutes
Active recovery juggling.

3 minutes
Stretching.

DAY 01: Running with the Ball

4. Game Situation: Dribbling and Turning - '1v1 Pursuit'   15 mins

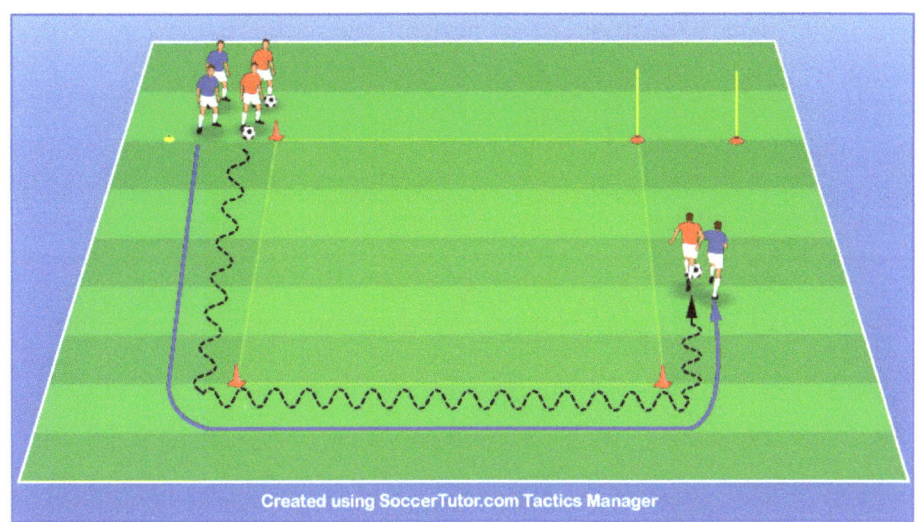

Description

The player must dribble the ball around the cones as shown and get to the small goal/gate at the end.

The other player (blue) chases the red player without a ball and tries to prevent him from going through the goal/gate.

Progress from a passive defender to active defender.

Variation
1. Dribbling with the outside of the foot.
2. With the inside of the foot.
3. With just the left or right foot.

Coaching Points
1. When running with the ball round corners, you need to slow down and bend the knees to change direction.
2. Players should use both feet and all parts of the feet when dribbling the ball.

5. Game with a Theme: Dribbling and RWTB in a SSG   15 mins

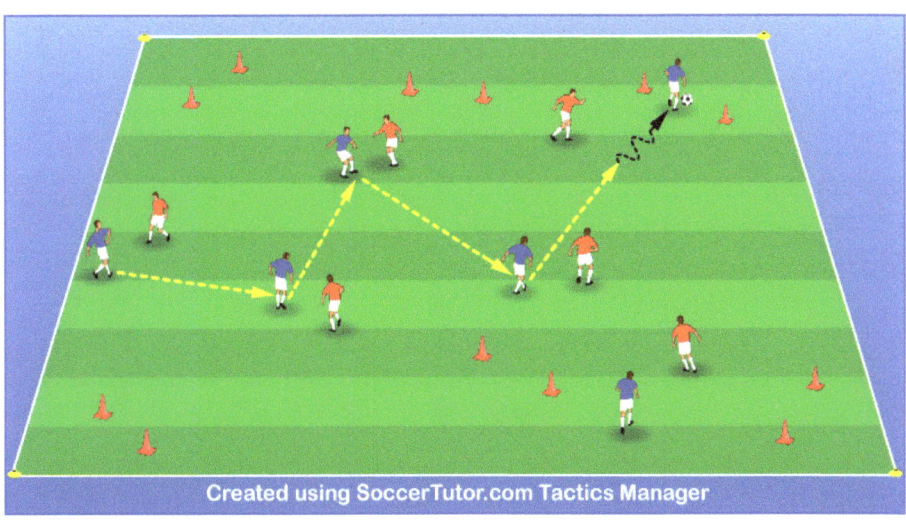

Description

Six goals (2 yards apart) are positioned randomly within the area.

The objective is to run with the ball/dribble through the cone goals. When a player scores, they maintain possession and look to score in another goal.

Stretch after 5, 10, and 15 minutes.

Coaching Points
1. All players must always be moving, so no walking for the duration of the exercise.
2. Encourage receiving passes half-turned. This enables players to develop their awareness, which allows for quicker and better decision making.
3. Encourage players to look up and ahead so they can see the ball, the other players and the goals.

6. 5v5 Small Sided Games   30 mins

WEEK 5

Feints / Moves to Beat

Primary Technical Objective: Dribbling with the ball and feints/moves to beat.

Secondary Technical Objective: Ball control.

Coordination Objective: Quickness, adaptation, transformation, differentiation, motor combinations and balance.

Tactical Objective: 1v1 Duels and possession play.

Duration of Session: 2 hours 15 mins

---

1. Warm Up: Technical Block 2 — 30 mins

Group A

The red players use a variety of juggling techniques depending on their age/level. If the exercise is too complex for the age/level of their players they can juggle and catch using their hands.

Variations: 1 or 2 touches of the foot and then catch with the hands, juggling with either foot freely, juggle or dribble with alternating rhythm (2 right / 1 left), sequence - foot, thigh, head.

Other Exercises: Juggle at various heights (1 low / 1 high), alternate feet with bounces allowed, juggle followed by acrobatic act e.g. forward roll. You can introduce much more based on ability and propose a points race e.g. first player to complete 20 consecutive alternate touches when juggling.

Group B

The blue players are split into 2 teams and run a relay race dribbling through the cones. When each player arrives at the finish line, they wait there for their teammates to complete. The winning team is the one that finishes quickest. If any player fails to dribble the ball round one of the cones successfully the team receives a time penalty. You can assign rules such as only dribble with left foot, alternate touches etc.

Group C

The yellow players are split into teams of 3 with a ball per team. The first player must dribble the ball to his teammate who is 15 yards away. The player who receives then dribbles the ball to the third player. You can assign points based on whether the players can get the ball to their teammate without losing control of the ball. This exercise can also be done with the players having to juggle the ball.

DAY 02: Feints / Moves to Beat

2. Technical: Dribbling with Feints / Moves to Beat   15 mins

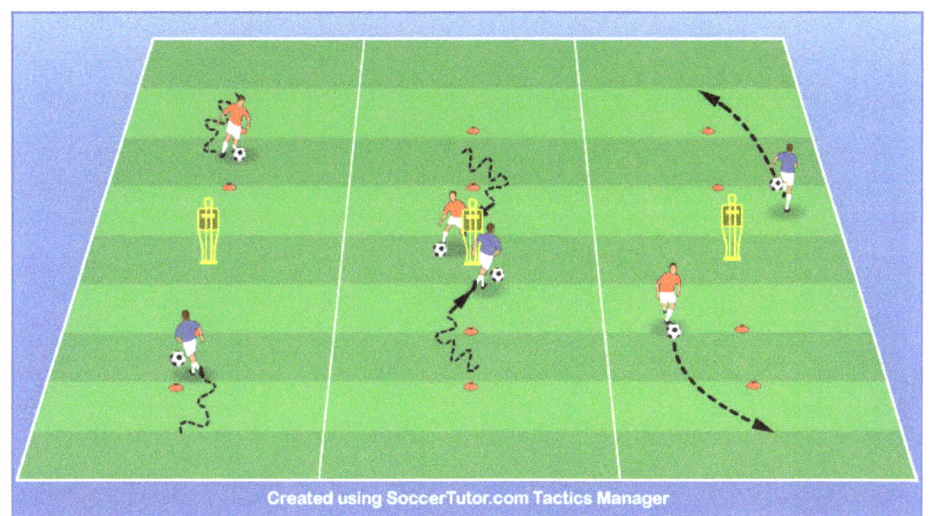

Description
2 players have a ball each and dribble through the cones (as shown).

When they reach the mannequin, they make a feint and move the ball to the right side and then continue running with the ball to the end of the line (switching places).

Variations
Use different feints (possibly specified by the coach).

Coaching Points
1. Players need to keep the ball close to their feet, so they can quickly change direction.
2. Use both feet and all parts of the foot for this practice, performing different dribbling techniques and feints/moves to beat.

3. Coordination: Motor Aerobic Exercise - 'Fantasy Track'   15 mins

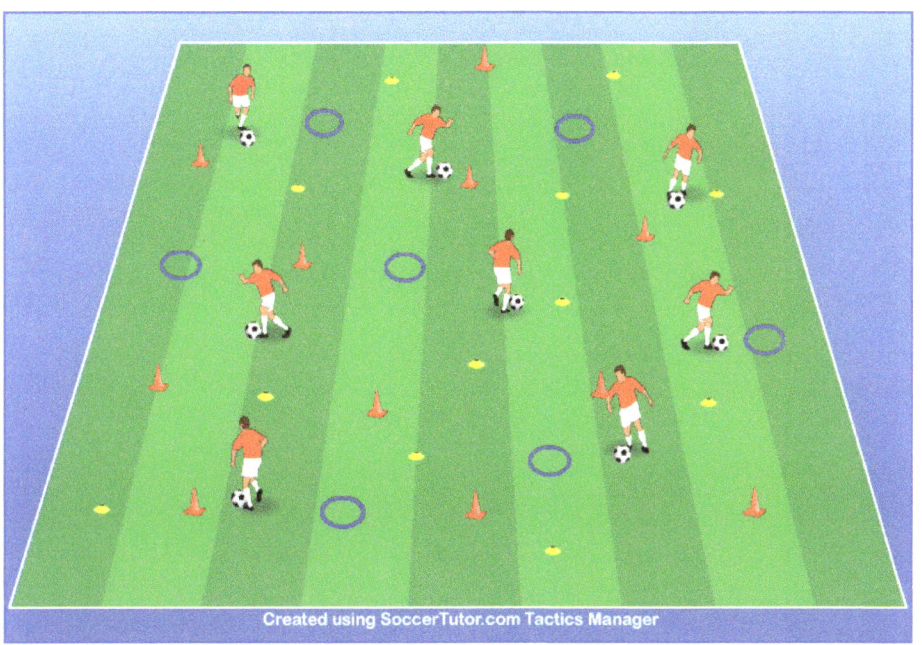

Description
Various obstacles are placed in an area 20 x 20 yards, such as cones, traffic cones, speed rings etc.

The players are asked to run freely around the field and around the obstacles.

We then introduce the balls and ask the players to do everything they want on the field allowing them to dribble, play with their hands, roll, crawl, jump, etc.

Coaching Points
1. Encourage the players to use different parts of the feet when dribbling.
2. Use this exercise to observe the creativity of the players when they are free.

WEEK 5

4. Game Situation: 1v1 Situations — 15 mins

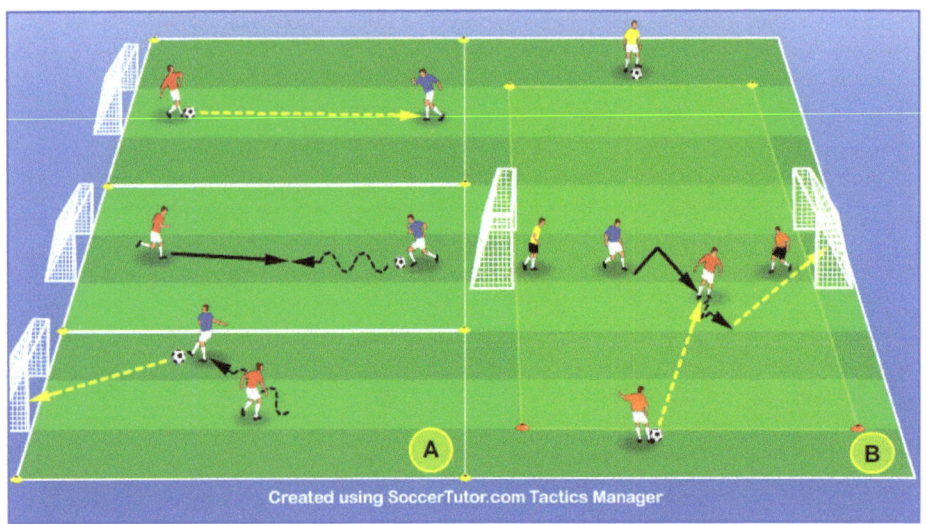

Description

EXERCISE A: The defender passes the ball to the attacker and we start the 1v1. The aim for the attacker is to beat the defender and score in the goal.

Use different ways to pass the ball, like along the ground or in the air.

EXERCISE B: We have a 1v1 situation with 2 goals and 2 goalkeepers. The ball is passed in by the 2 players on the outside. The attacking player must free himself from the defender and call for the ball from one of the outside players.

The colour of the player who passes the ball (orange in diagram) is which goal they must shoot in (orange goalkeeper). If the defender wins the ball he becomes the attacker.

5. Game with a Theme: 5v5 'Nutmeg' Possession Game — 15 mins

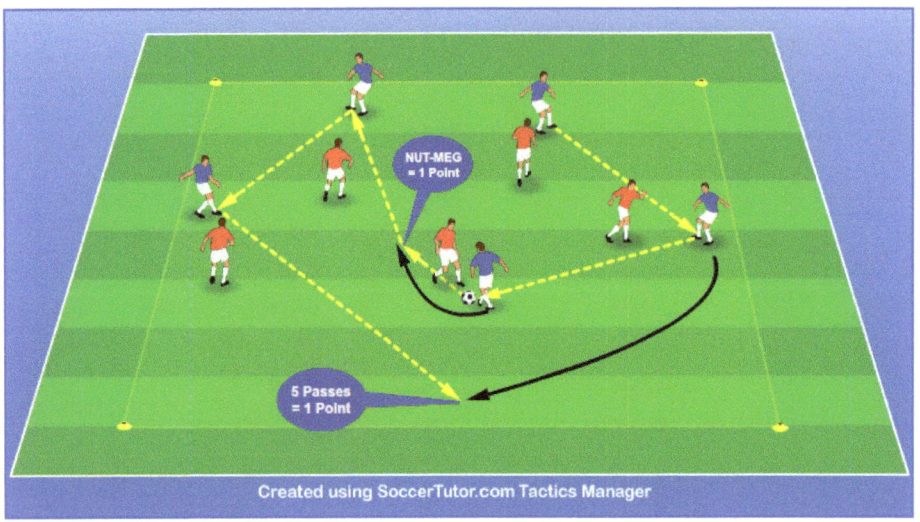

Description

In an area 20 x 20 yards we play a 5v5 game.

A team scores 2 points if an opponent is beaten with a 'nutmeg' and the team maintain possession. A team can also win 1 point if an opponent is beaten with a feint and every time 5 consecutive team passes are completed.

Play for 5 minutes, stretch for minutes, play for 5 minutes and stretch for 2 minutes.

Coaching Point

1. The nutmeg needs to be weighted so that the player can receive the ball again without pressure.
2. Correct body shape (open up on the half turn) and positioning is important to view where the next pass is going.

6. 5v5 Small Sided Games — 30 mins

DAY 03: Passing and Receiving

Passing and Receiving

Primary Technical Objective: Passing and receiving on the ground.

Secondary Technical Objective: Moving to receive, dribbling and feints/moves to beat.

Coordination Objective: Quickness, adaptation, reactions, agility, balance and motor combinations.

Tactical Objective: Speed of play, 2v2 play, attacking the space and possession play.

Duration of Session: 2 hours 15 mins

1. Warm Up: Technical Block 3   30 mins

Group A

The red players are in pairs opposite each other 15 yards apart. Both players have a ball and start simultaneously by dribbling the ball towards the centre. At the cone, the players change direction and dribble back to the starting position.

Alternate different types of turns such as turn with the sole, sole 'L' shape, internal cut etc.

Group B

The blue players all have a ball each and move around freely in a 15 x 15 yard area. 2 or more green players are added (depending on the number of players in blue) who try to win the ball from the blue players as quickly as possible. If a blue player loses the ball he is not eliminated, but instead helps the other blue players to maintain possession of the ball. Change the green players every minute.

Group C

The yellow players are divided into 4 groups and compete in a relay competition. Each player dribbles the ball towards the mannequin (or cone) which is 5 yards away, perform a specific turn pre-determined by the coach and then quickly shoot into the goal. The first team to score 10 goals wins the relay.

WEEK 5

2. Technical: Diagonal Passing Square   15 mins

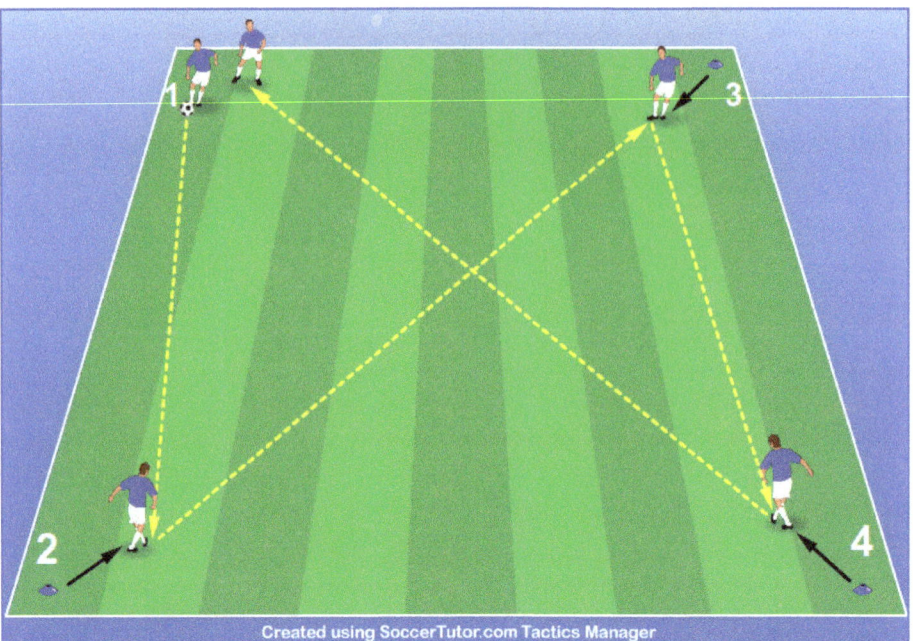

Description
5 players in a 10 x 10 yard square pass the ball in a diagonal pattern as shown.

Player 1 plays a straight pass to Player 2, who plays a diagonal pass to 3. Player 3 plays a straight pass to 4 and Player 4 plays a diagonal pass to 5 and the sequence starts again.

Each player moves to the next position after their pass.

Variations
1. Change the direction of the passes.
2. One touch passing.

Coaching Points
1. Make sure the players communicate and heads are up.
2. Start the drill with 2 touches and quickly progress to 1 touch to speed up play.

3. Coordination: Coordination, Agility and Balance Exercise   15 mins

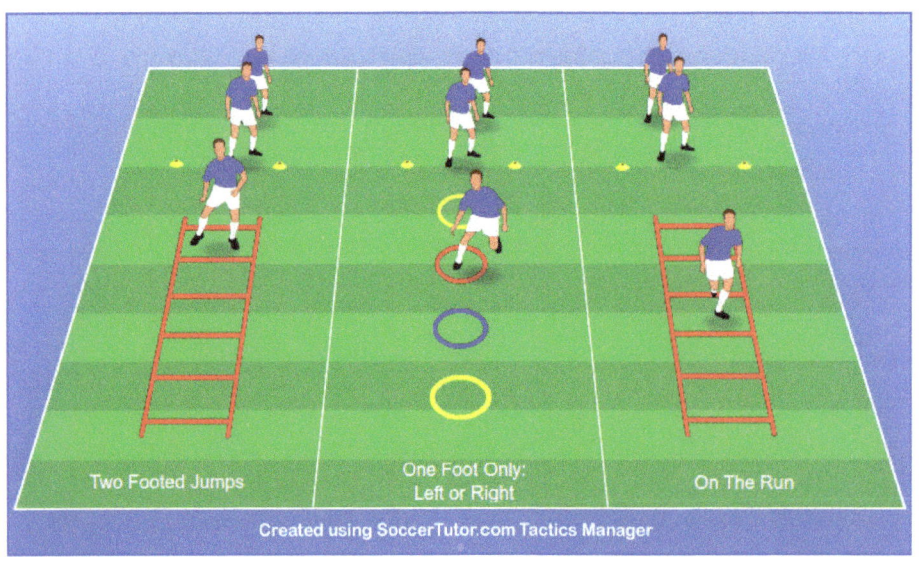

Description
In this exercise players perform various types of jumping, hopping and running in the speed rings and ladders.

They perform 2 footed jumps with the first ladder, hop on 1 foot through the speed rings and run through the last ladder.

Variation
Make it a relay competition.

DAY 03: Passing and Receiving

4. Game Situation: 2v2 (+2) Game / Double 2v2 Game

15 mins

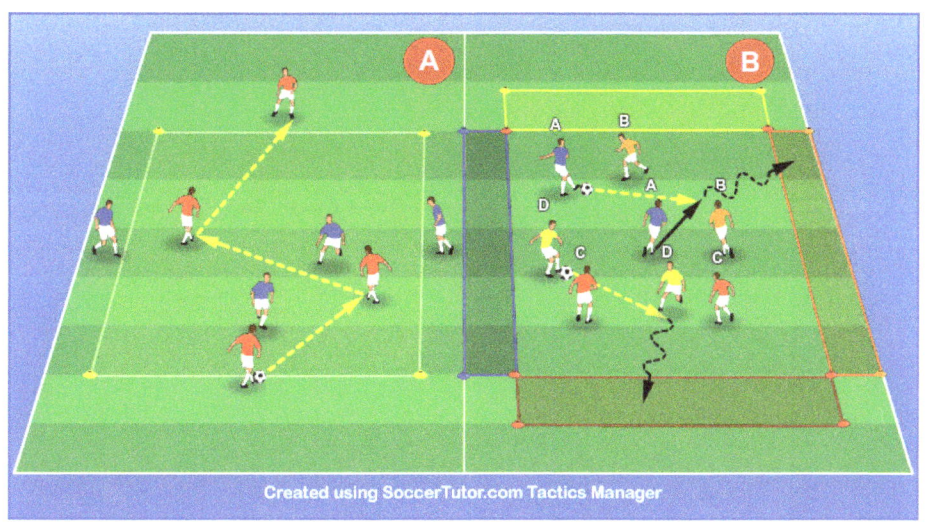

Description

GROUP A: In an area 10 x 10 yards we play a 2v2 game with 2 support players on the outside who play with the team in possession of the ball.

A point is scored every time the ball is passed from one support player to the other using the inside players.

GROUP B: A double 2v2 is played with team A playing against team B from right to left and team C playing against team D from top to bottom. Use 2 balls in this game.

5. Game with a Theme: 6v3 Speed of Play Dynamic Possession Game

15 mins

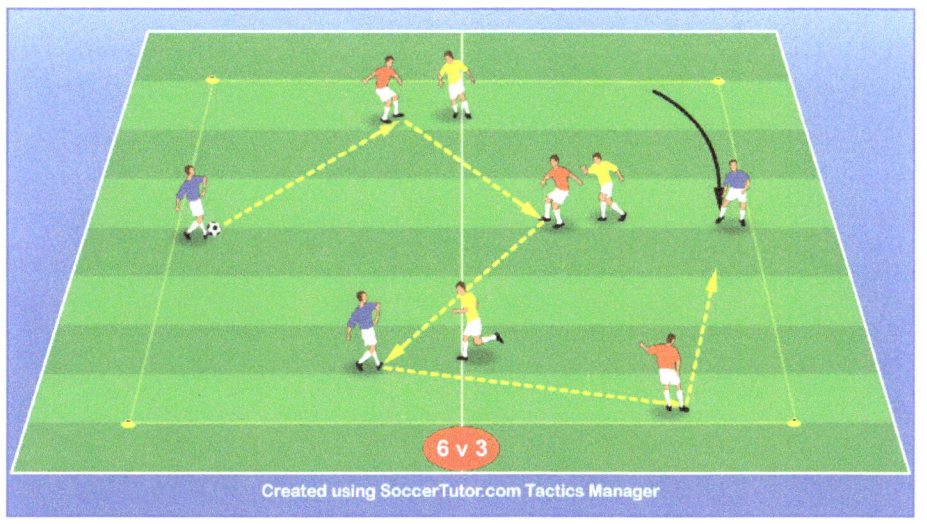

Description

In an area 20 x 20 yards, 2 teams of different colours play against one team creating a 6v3 situation. The objective is to complete 10 continuous passes.

When a player loses possession, his team become the defending team and the other 2 teams aim to complete 10 passes.

Coaching Points

1. The player in possession should always have 2 options so the players need to have intelligent movement to create good angles for the pass.
2. The 3 defenders must press together to close the passing angles making it harder to keep possession.

6. 5v5 Small Sided Games

30 mins

WEEK 5

Shooting

Primary Technical Objective: Shooting and finishing.

Secondary Technical Objective: Feints, changes of direction and passing/receiving.

Coordination Objective: Balance, quickness, space/time adaptation and transformation.

Tactical Objective: Creating space and using width.

Duration of Session: 2 hours 15 mins

1. Warm Up: Technical Block 4   30 mins

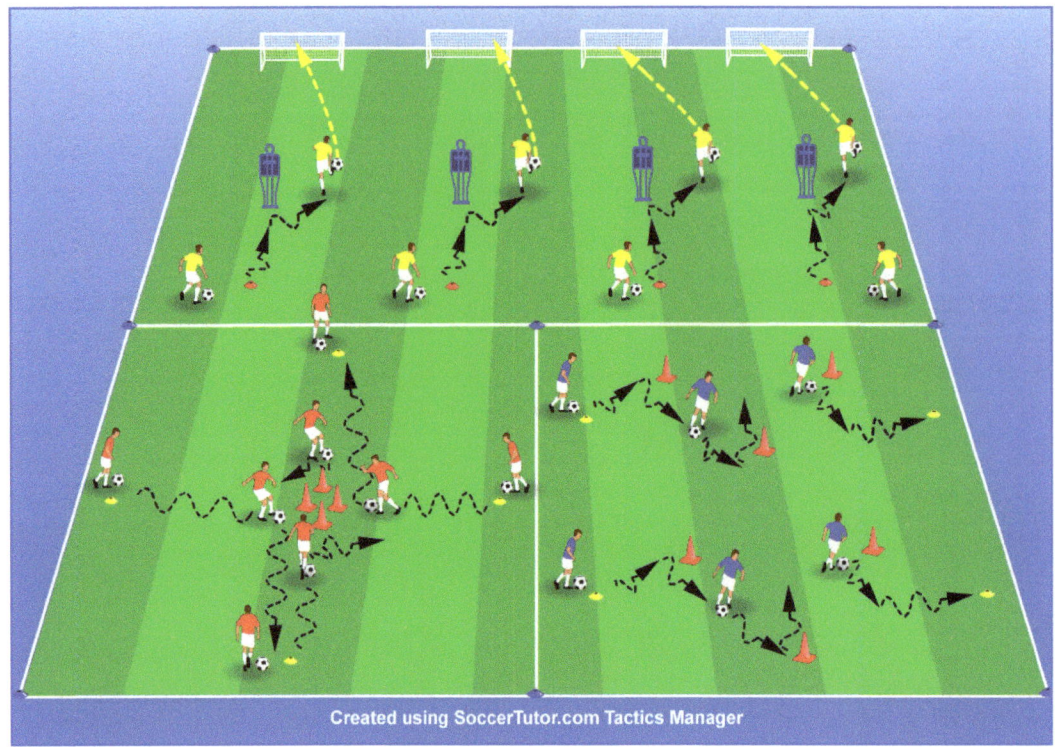

Group A

The red players line up behind the 4 cones as shown. 4 players start at the same time and dribble the ball towards the cone in front of them, perform a feint pre-determined by the coach and move to the cone to the right. Change the type of feint after every completed lap and also change the direction from anticlockwise to clockwise so the players move to the left as well.

Group B

The blue players are divided into 2 groups and practice dribbling with feints to change direction. Initially the players simply use the inside and outside of both feet to dribble and change directions. They then progress to perform a specific feint at each cone which is pre-determined by the coach. Examples of feints include the scissor, the cut back and the chop.

Group C

The yellow players are divided into teams of 3 or 4 and are in a competition to see who can score the most goals. 4 players start simultaneously with a ball, dribble towards the mannequin (or cone), perform a feint to the left or right and shoot in the mini goal. A point is awarded to the player who scores first.

You can decide the type of feint to be used or leave it to the players imagination and freedom.

DAY 04: Shooting

2. Technical: Feints / Quick Movements and Shot — 15 mins

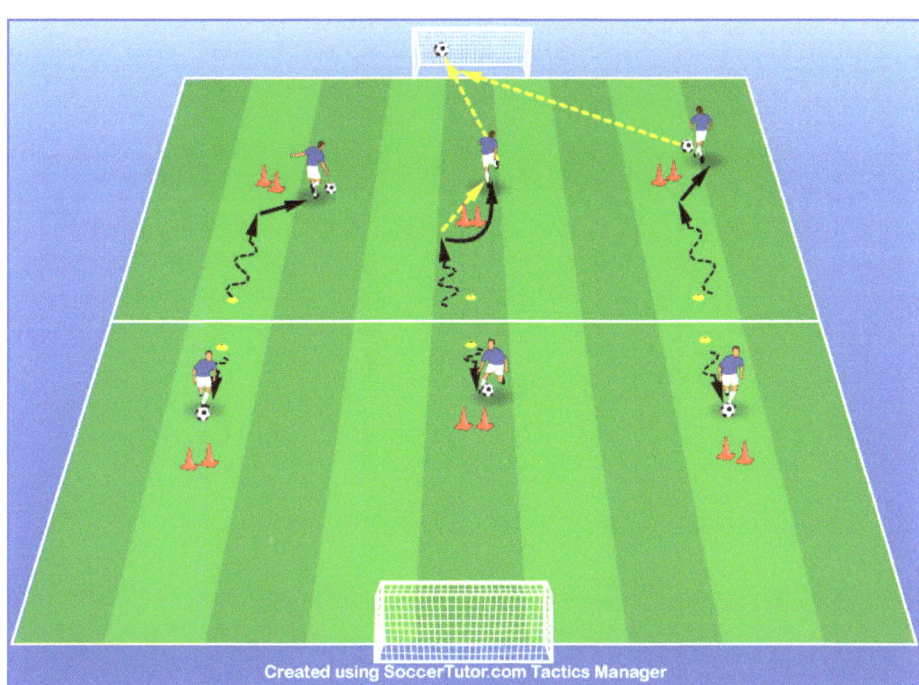

Description

Players practice feints followed by a shot from the positions of the cones.

On the outside cones (left/right), make a feint and go towards the outside of the cones and shoot.

On the central cones, the player passes the ball to the left of the cones, runs round the right of them to meet the ball and shoot.

Coaching Points

1. Feint and then cut inside on the outside cones.
2. Feint from a stationery position and shoot immediately.

3. Coordination: Roll, Dribble and Shoot with a Goalkeeper — 15 mins

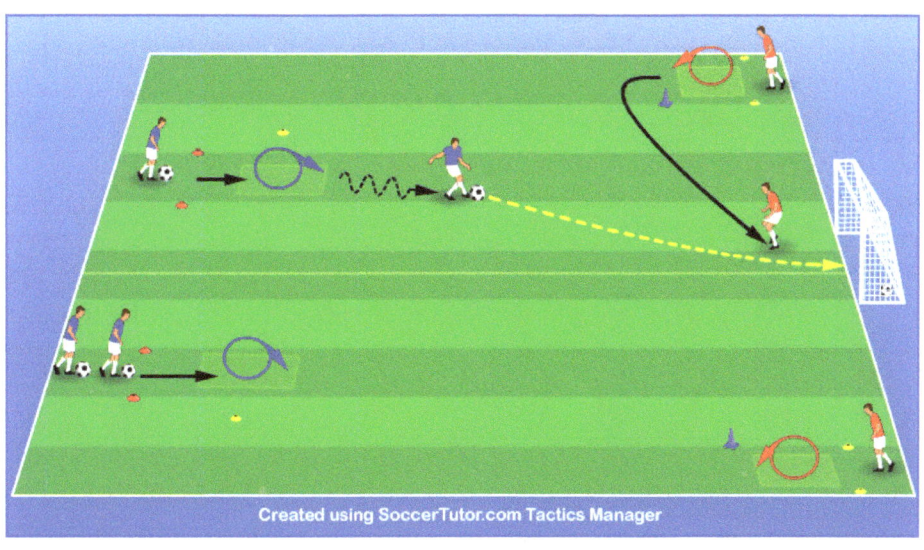

Description

The blue player performs a forward roll, dribbles forward and shoots at goal.

The red player performs a roll, then runs round the cone to become the goalkeeper and stop the blue player from scoring.

Variation

Substitute the forward roll with a side roll.

Coaching Points

1. When performing the forward roll, the players can trap a ball in between their feet.
2. The shot should be taken as early as possible in this practice before the goalkeeper can settle.

WEEK 5

4. Game Situation: Move, Receive and Score in a 1v1 Duel   15 mins

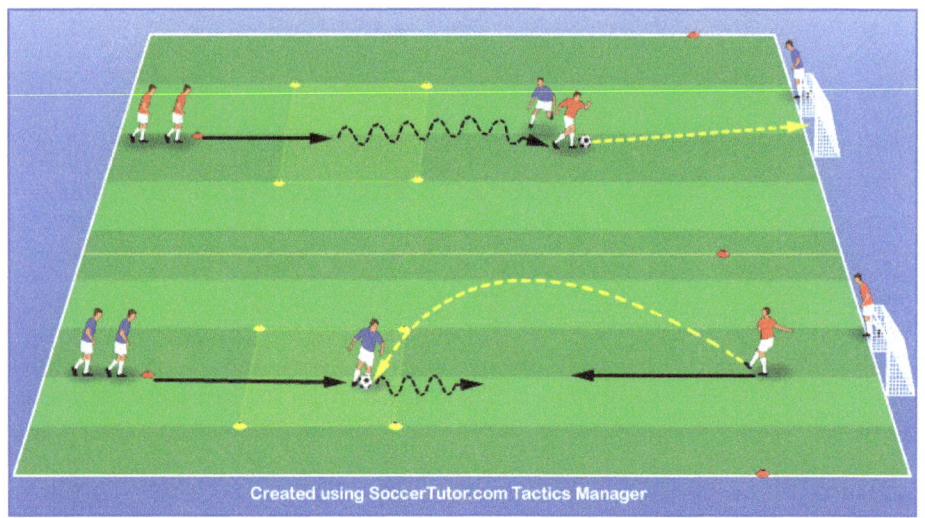

Description

The first players sprint to the square and receive a pass from the opposing player at the other end.

The player receiving the pass has to quickly receive and shoot before the defender can tackle them (1v1 duel).

After 5 turns, switch the roles of the players.

Variation

1. Pass and receive with the weaker foot.

Coaching Points

1. Players should receive facing forwards, with a directional first touch out the front of the square.
2. Strength is needed to prevent the defending players from winning the ball (getting your body in between the opponent and the ball).

---

5. Game with a Theme: Shooting Practice in a 7v7 Possession Game   15 mins

Description

2 teams of 7 play with the aim to keep possession inside the central zone.

The first aim is to keep possession and complete 5 passes. At this point, the last player to receive the ball can shoot without any pressure from the opponents.

The shot must be taken within the central zone.

Variations

1. Change the number of minimum passes.
2. Play possession with a combination of hands and feet.

6. 5v5 Small Sided Games   30 mins

DAY 05: Passing & Receiving in the Air

Passing & Receiving in the Air

Primary Technical Objective: Passing in the air and crossing.

Secondary Technical Objective: Receiving and directional control.

Coordination Objective: Reading the trajectory of the ball, dynamic balance, motor reactions and quickness.

Tactical Objective: 2v1 play, possession and speed of play.

Duration of Session: 2 hours 15 mins

1. Warm Up: Technical Block 5   30 mins

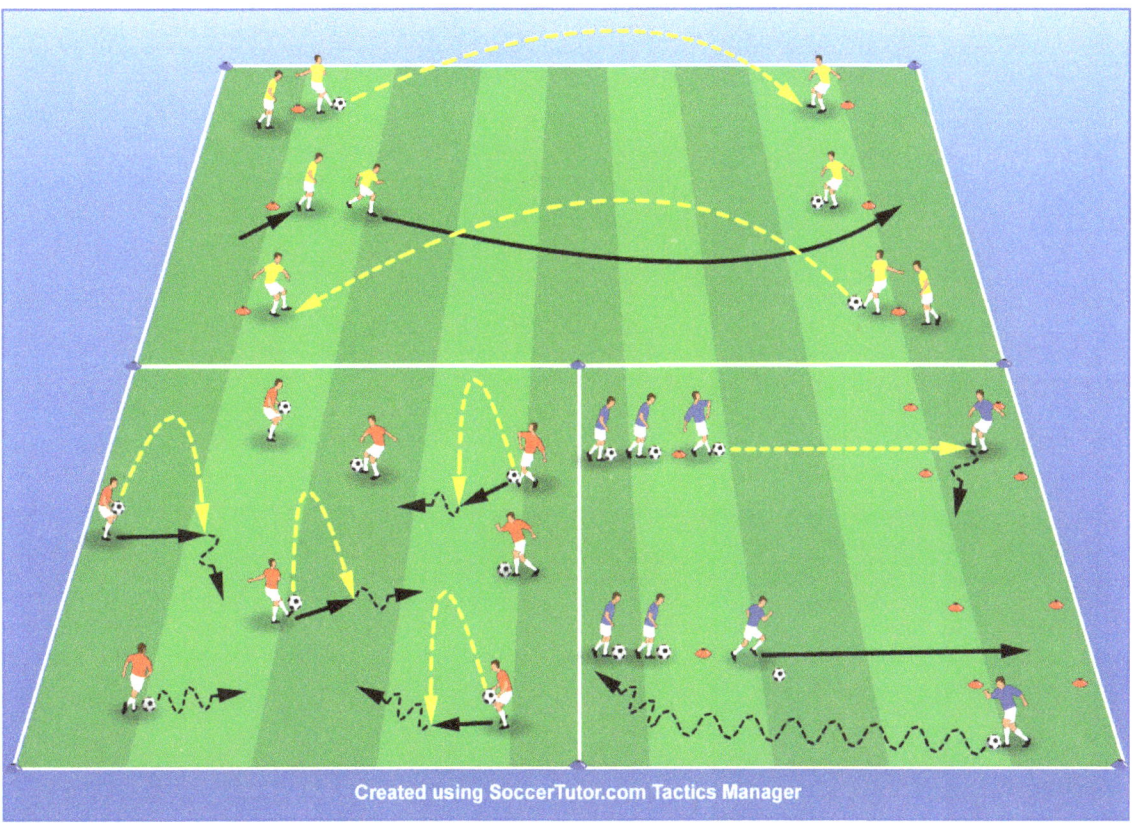

Group A

The red players move freely around the area and control the ball in different ways. The players throw (or kick) the ball up in the air, control the ball and then dribble for a few yards. Vary the type of control used - inside of foot, outside of foot, with the sole, with the laces, thigh, head etc.

Group B

Divide the blue players into 2 groups and set up 5 x 5 yard squares as shown. This is a relay competition with the 2 teams starting simultaneously. The first player passes the ball to the player in the square and then runs into the square. The player in the square takes a directional first touch out the side of the square and dribbles the ball to the next player who repeats the same sequence.

Group C

The yellow players work on passing and receiving high balls at a 25 yard distance. The first player makes an aerial pass to their teammate and then runs 25 yards to their position. The second player controls the ball and then plays the next aerial pass and runs 25 yards to the opposite cone. The same sequence continues.

Vary the type of control used - inside of foot, outside of foot, the sole, the laces, thigh, head etc.

WEEK 5

2. Technical: Accurate Aerial Passing in Pairs

15 mins

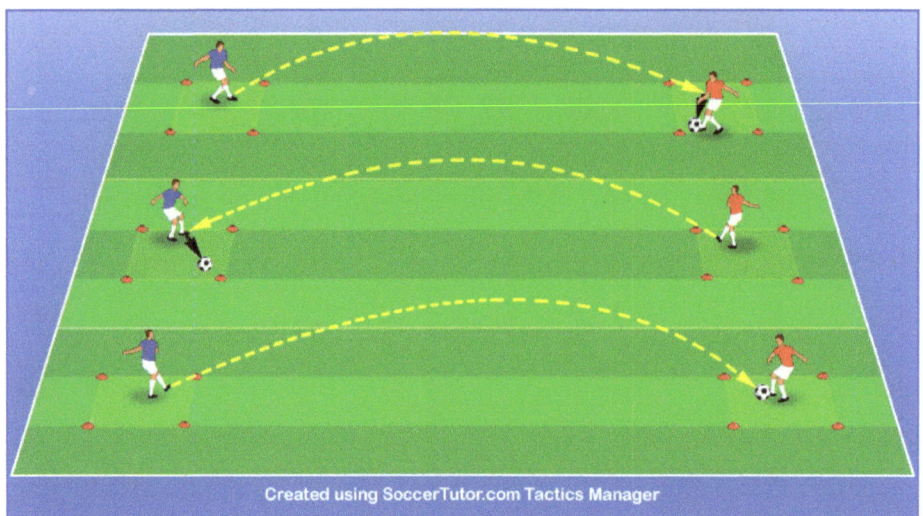

Description

The blue player makes a long pass in the air to the red player and vice-versa.

If a player does not control the ball within the square, the other player gets a point.

If a pass misses the zone, then the player who played the pass loses a point.

Coaching Points
1. The players should try to use all parts of the foot, thigh, chest and head to maximise control of the ball.
2. The aerial passes need to be accurate and played at the right height to receive the ball within the square.
3. Players need to keep their eyes fixed on the flight of the ball, watching it all the way to their foot.

3. Coordination: Quick Reactions & Speed of Play in a 2v1 Duel Game

15 mins

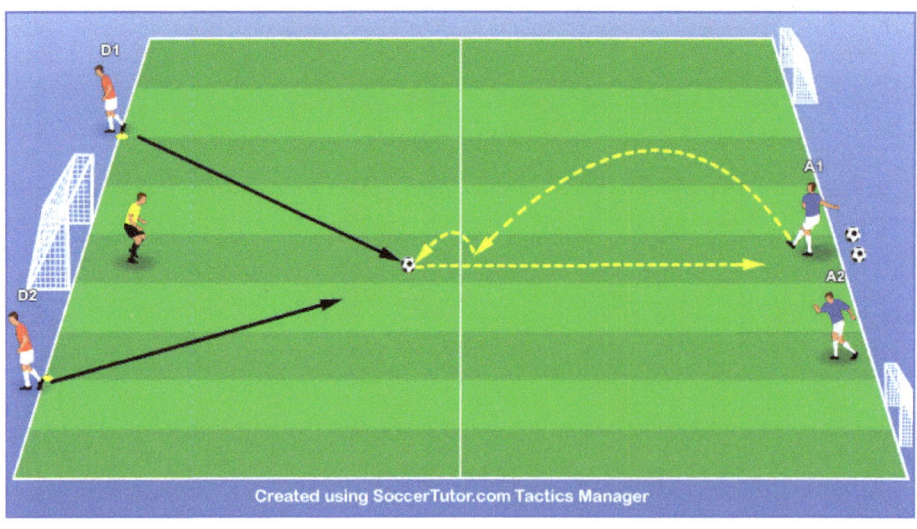

Description

The blue player chips the ball into the middle of the field. The red players stand with their backs to play.

At the sound of the ball being kicked they turn and sprint to the ball. The first player to the ball passes it back to the blue player and a 2v1 situation is created (A1 & A2 v D1 in the diagram).

If the defender wins the ball he can score in either of the 2 mini goals.

Variations
1. Players competing for the ball must perform a coordination exercise before sprinting to the ball.
2. Play with the offside rule.

Coaching Point
To utilise the numerical advantage, the player with the ball should wait for the defender to commit themselves and then pass into space to their teammate.

DAY 05: Passing & Receiving in the Air

4. Game Situation: 2v1 on the Flanks with Accurate Crossing — 15 mins

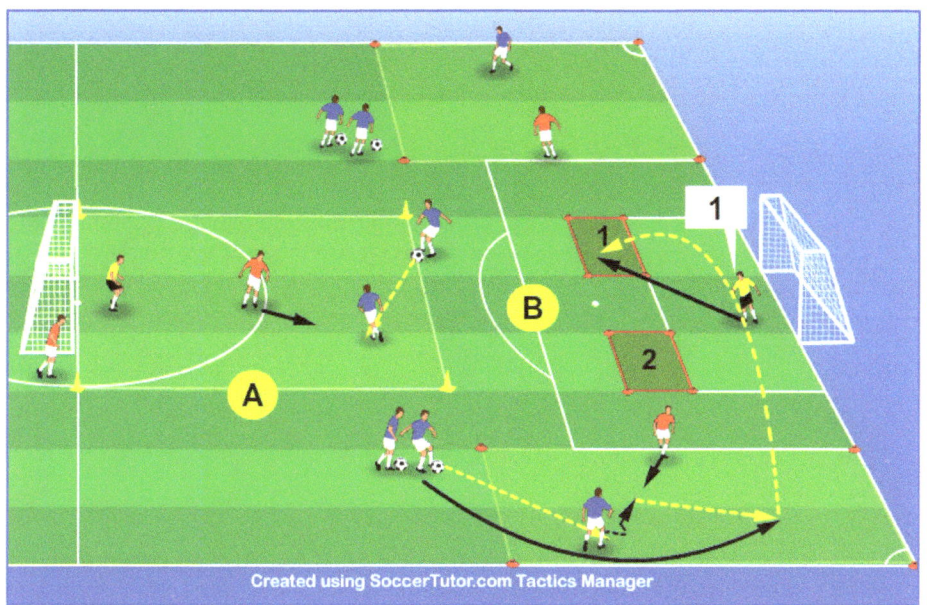

Description

GROUP A: Central defenders and forwards play a 2v1. The attackers must shoot within 4 seconds.

GROUP B: The other players work on situations of 2v1 on the flank with overlapping runs.

The attacking players can score a point if they are able to cross the ball into zone 1 or zone 2 which is called out by the goalkeeper who then moves to catch the ball.

Coaching Points

1. One forwards starts with his back to goal.
2. One forward enters from the outside making a diagonal run to receive.

5. Game with a Theme: 4v4 with Long Accurate Passing — 15 mins

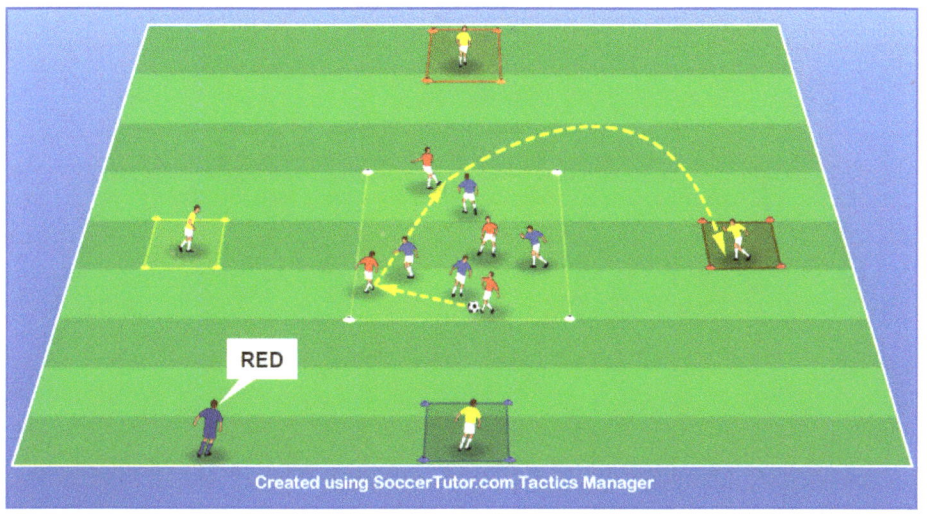

Description

We play a 4v4 possession game in the centre square (20 x 20 yards).

The players wait for the coach to call out a colour and the player in possession of the ball must send a long pass to one of the players in that coloured zone.

A point is scored if the player in the coloured zone successfully receives the pass within the zone.

Coaching Points

1. Correct body shape (open up on the half turn) and positioning is important to view where the next pass goes in the centre square.
2. The lofted pass should be highly accurate and have good height for ease of receiving the ball.
3. The player receiving the lofted pass should utilise all parts of the body to maximise control.

6. 11v11 Matches on a Full Pitch — 30 mins

WEEK 6

DAY 01: Running with the Ball

Running with the Ball

Primary Technical Objective: Running with the ball.
Secondary Technical Objective: Dribbling, turning and shooting.
Coordination Objective: Explosive power, quick reactions and balance.
Tactical Objective: 1v1 Duels and attacking/creating space.

Duration of Session: 2 hours 15 mins

1. Warm Up: Technical Block 1   30 mins

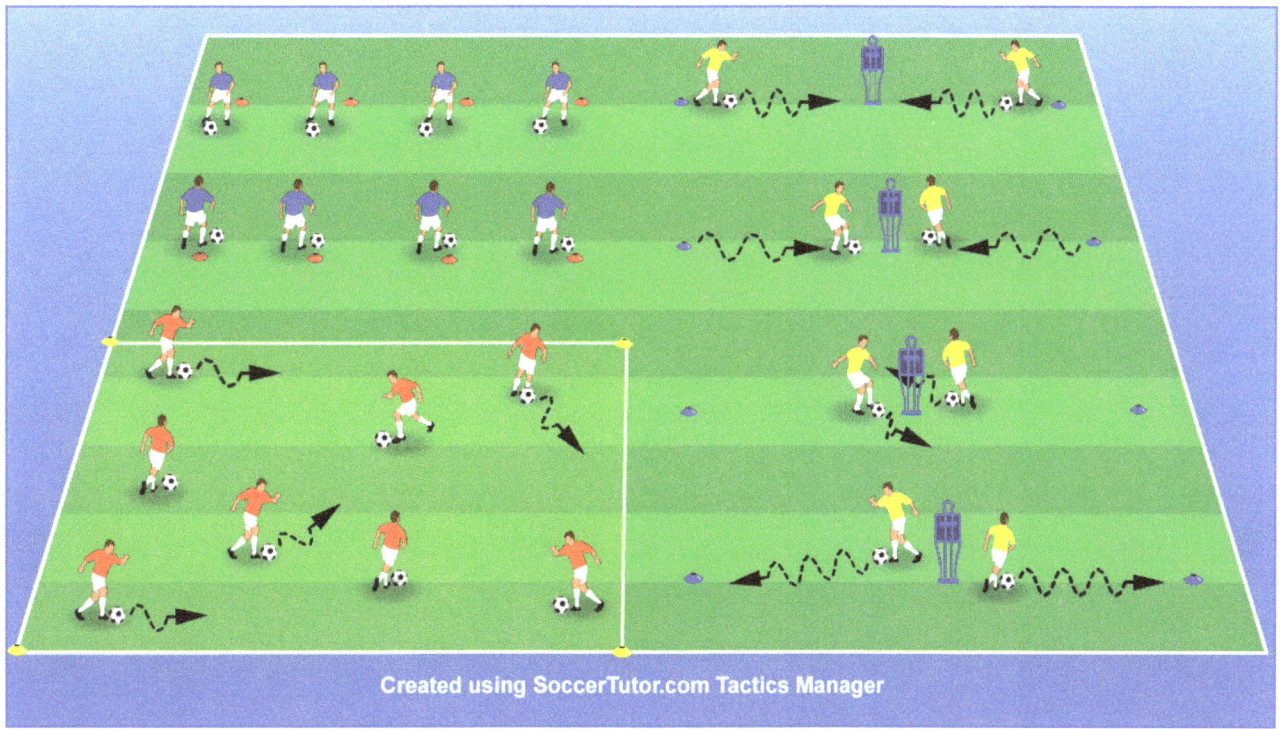

Divide the players into 3 groups with a minimum of 8 players at each station.

Group A

The red players perform different types of dribbling the ball in traffic, making sure to avoid collisions. Keep using variations, making sure that the players use only one foot and then the other when manoeuvring the ball. Vary the part of the foot used - outside, instep, the sole etc. Make sure to also perform different exercises - stretching and joint mobility exercises.

Group B

The blue players are each positioned on a cone. Every player practices different technical ball control exercises on the spot and around the cone. Start slowly and progress to increase the speed of execution. Use exercises such as making an 'L Shape' with the sole, quick outside then inside touches with 1 foot and many more. Each coach can create variants with their own imagination.

Group C

The yellow players line up opposite each other with a mannequin or cone in between them. Each player has a ball and they start simultaneously by dribbling the ball towards the centre and then perform a feint to the right (or left). The coach can determine a specific feint such as a scissor, chop or Maradona move. The players keep the same sequence going and start each time on the coach's whistle.

WEEK 6

2. Technical: **Close Control and Turning with Shot** **15 mins**

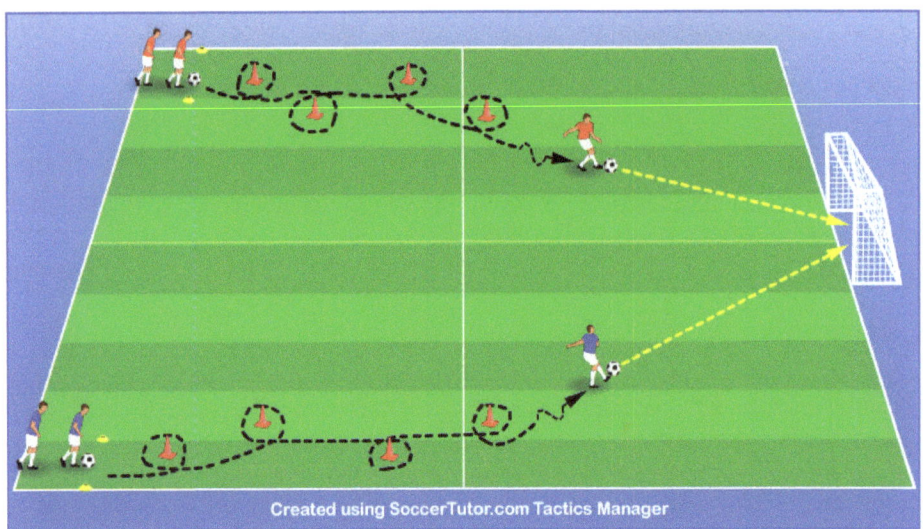

Description

This is a competition between 2 teams. Each player must dribble and turn around the cones as shown in the diagram. They then shoot in the goal.

The players start at the same time and the first player to score a goal gets a point for their team. The next players then need to start at the same time (on the coach's call/whistle).

Variations
1. Dribbling only with the right or left foot.   2. Dribbling only with the outside of the foot.

Coaching Points
1. Players need to use very soft touches and all parts of the foot to turn tightly around the cones.
2. When shooting players should slow down and place their non-striking foot next to the ball.

3. Coordination: **Jump, Dribble and Shoot - 'Who's the Fastest?'** **15 mins**

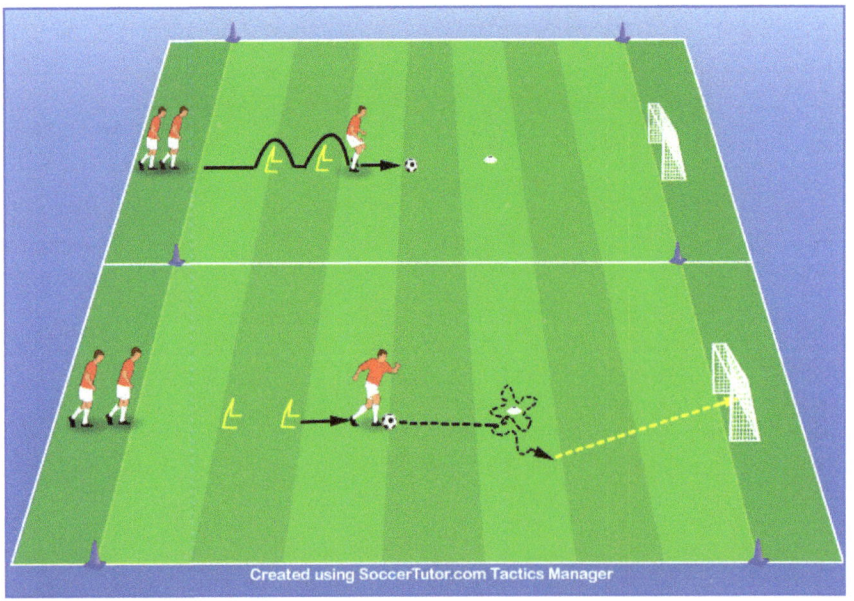

Description

This practice is a relay between 2 teams. Every player must jump over the low hurdles, run to where the ball is (as shown) and dribble the ball around the cone, then shoot on goal.

Running backwards, the player picks up the ball from the goal and places it on the spot, then runs to his teammate for a high five. The next player goes.

The team which scores 10 goals first wins the game.

Variations
1. Increase the number of low hurdles.
2. The player picks up the ball and shoots with a volley for the shot at the end.

Coaching Points
1. Make sure to use hurdles no large than 6 inches for young players (U5-8).
2. Soft touches, keeping the ball close to the feet are needed for going round the cone.
3. Accuracy is the key for the shot on goal, not the power.

©SoccerTutor.com — Football Camp Training Program

DAY 01: Running with the Ball

4. Game Situation: Quick Reactions Dribbling Game

15 mins

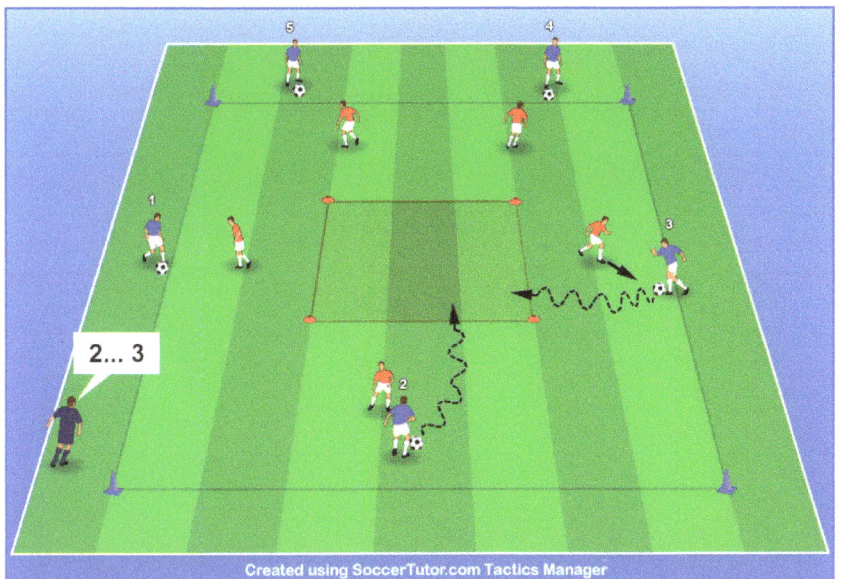

Description

In an area 30 x 30 yards, the blue players are all on the outside with a ball each. The red players are on the inside of the square and must defend the inner box which is 7 x 7 yards.

On the coach's call, 1 blue player at a time tries to dribble the ball into the centre box (to score a point). The teams switch roles halfway through and the team with the most points wins.

Variation

1. Dribbling only with the outside of the feet. 2. Dribble only with the right or left foot.

Coaching Points

1. Quick reactions are needed to dribble into the centre before the defender can position themselves.
2. Use feints/moves to beat to take the ball past the defender.

5. Game with a Theme: 4v4 Rugby Game

15 mins

Description

In an area 30 x 20 yards we play a rugby style 4v4 game with a rugby ball (or football if you do not have one).

Goals are scored by running through the end zone. The ball can only be passed or thrown backwards.

Variations

1. Allow 1 forward pass.
2. Have the players kick the ball out of their hands to pass - volley or half volley.

6. 5v5 Small Sided Games

30 mins

WEEK 6

Feints / Moves to Beat

Primary Technical Objective: Dribbling with the ball and feints/moves to beat.
Secondary Technical Objective: Ball control, dribbling at speed and finishing.
Coordination Objective: Quickness, adaptation, transformation, differentiation, motor combinations and balance.
Tactical Objective: 1v1 Duels, 1v2 play, frontal marking and speed of play.

Duration of Session: 2 hours 15 mins

1. Warm Up: Technical Block 2   30 mins

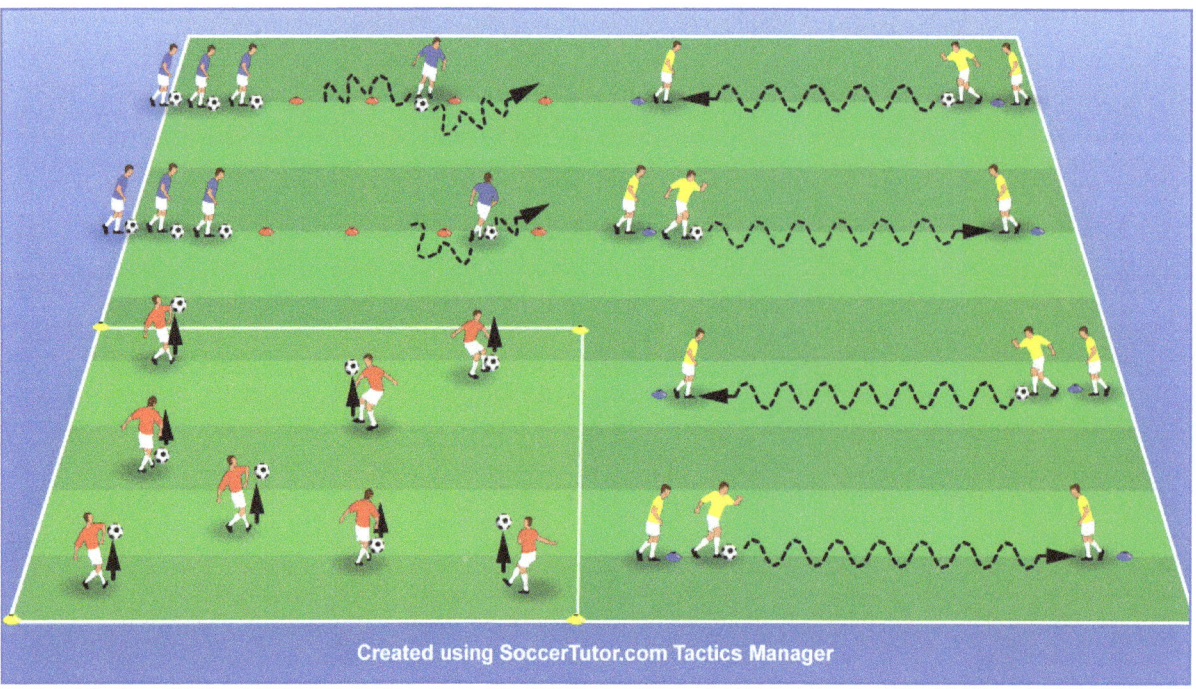

Group A

The red players use a variety of juggling techniques depending on their age/level. If the exercise is too complex for the age/level of their players they can juggle and catch using their hands.

Variations: 1 or 2 touches of the foot and then catch with the hands, juggling with either foot freely, juggle or dribble with alternating rhythm (2 right / 1 left), sequence - foot, thigh, head.

Other Exercises: Juggle at various heights (1 low / 1 high), alternate feet with bounces allowed, juggle followed by acrobatic act e.g. forward roll. You can introduce much more based on ability and propose a points race e.g. first player to complete 20 consecutive alternate touches when juggling.

Group B

The blue players are split into 2 teams and run a relay race dribbling through the cones. When each player arrives at the finish line, they wait there for their teammates to complete. The winning team is the one that finishes quickest. If any player fails to dribble the ball round one of the cones successfully the team receives a time penalty. You can assign rules such as only dribble with left foot, alternate touches etc.

Group C

The yellow players are split into teams of 3 with a ball per team. The first player must dribble the ball to his teammate who is 15 yards away. The player who receives then dribbles the ball to the third player. You can assign points based on whether the players can get the ball to their teammate without losing control of the ball. This exercise can also be done with the players having to juggle the ball.

DAY 02: Feints / Moves to Beat

2. Technical: Ball Control, Feints & Dribbling 'Star'

15 mins

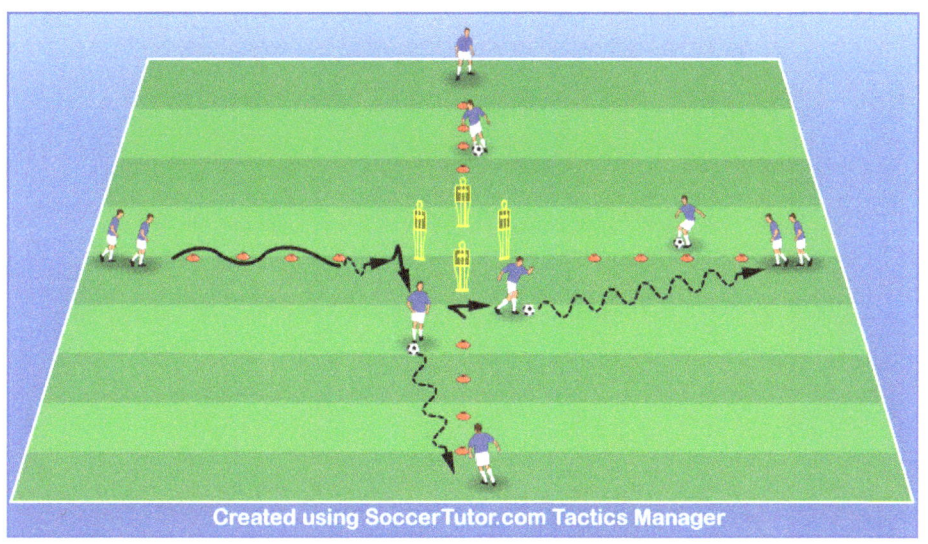

Description

This set up is called "The Star". You can set up one or more stations depending on how many players you have.

4 players start at the same time from all 4 sides of the star; they dribble in and out all the cones. As they approach the mannequin the players execute a move/feint then take the ball to the right and dribble to the next line.

Every 2 minutes the coach will change:

- The dribble sequence - i.e. dribble in and out every 2 cones etc.
- Technique - inside feet only, outside feet only etc.
- Type of move/feint.
- Change the direction from anti-clockwise to clockwise.

3. Coordination: Dribbling at Speed with 'Nutmeg'

15 mins

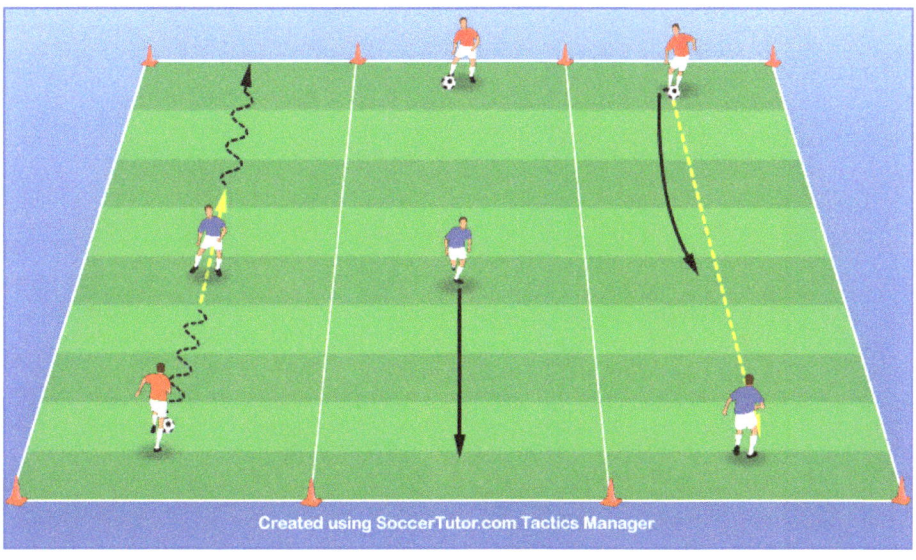

Description

The red player runs with the ball towards the blue player who is standing with his legs open.

The red player plays the ball through the blues' legs, collects the ball behind him and dribbles to the end.

The blue player sprints to the starting position to receive a pass from the red player.

The red player moves into the middle and the same sequence is then repeated with opposite roles.

Variations

1. The defender opens and closes his legs to make it harder for the attacker.
2. Dribble only with the right/left foot, inside/outside of foot, inside of both feet or only with the sole of the foot.

Progression

Make the defender fully active and if they win the ball, they can then score in a mini goal.

WEEK 6

4. Game Situation: Quick Reactions and Finishing in a 1v2 Frontal Marking Duel

15 mins

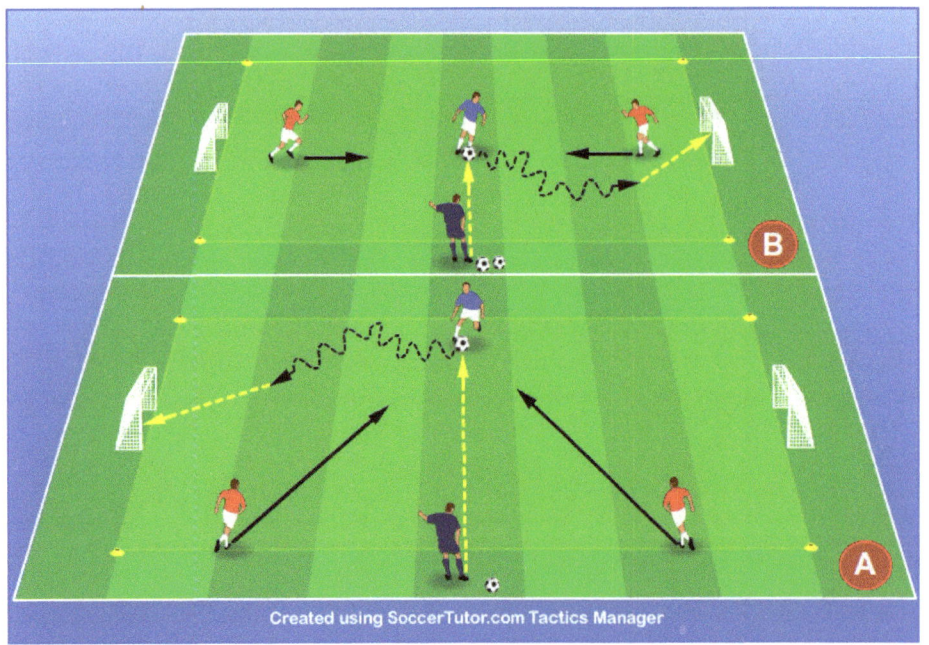

Description

SITUATION A

The coach passes the ball to the attacker who attacks one of the goals.

2 defenders apply pressure as soon as the ball is passed.

SITUATION B

The same situation as A but the defenders start from different positions, as shown in the diagram.

Coaching Points

1. The attacker needs to take a good directional first touch to get in a position to shoot as early as possible.
2. Encourage players to use feints/dribbling to attack the space in behind the defender and score.

5. Game with a Theme: Man Marking 6 Goal Dribbling Game

15 mins

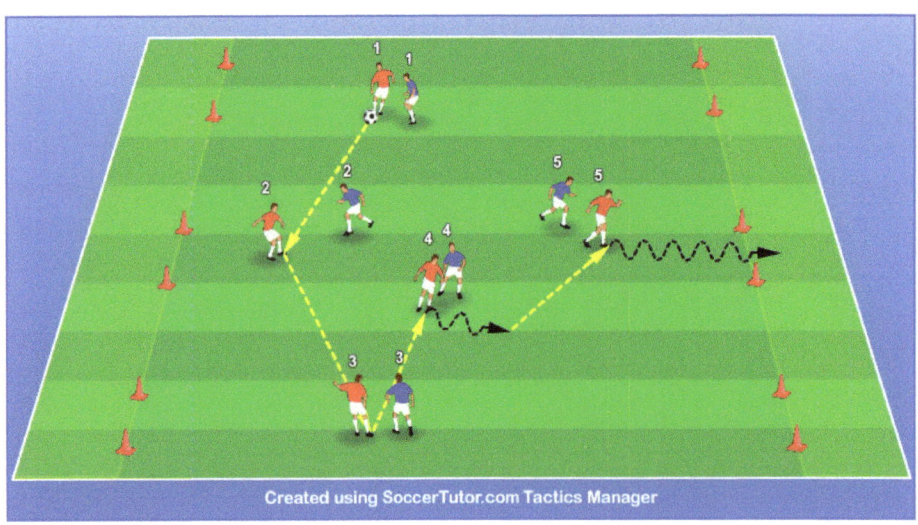

Description

We have a 5v5 game with 3 goals at each end.

Goals are scored by dribbling through the cone gates (goals).

Each player is assigned 1 opponent who they must mark. Players are not allowed to tackle any other player.

Coaching Points

1. Checking away before moving to receive is the key for creating space to receive when man marked.
2. Use feints/moves to beat to take the ball past the defender.

6. 5v5 Small Sided Games

30 mins

DAY 03: Passing and Receiving

Passing and Receiving

Primary Technical Objective: Short and long passing and receiving.

Secondary Technical Objective: Passing and receiving in the air, volley technique, crossing and finishing.

Coordination Objective: Quickness, reactions, agility, explosive power, balance and motor combinations.

Tactical Objective: Speed of play, positional play, movement and possession play.

Duration of Session: 2 hours 15 mins

1. Warm Up: Technical Block 3   30 mins

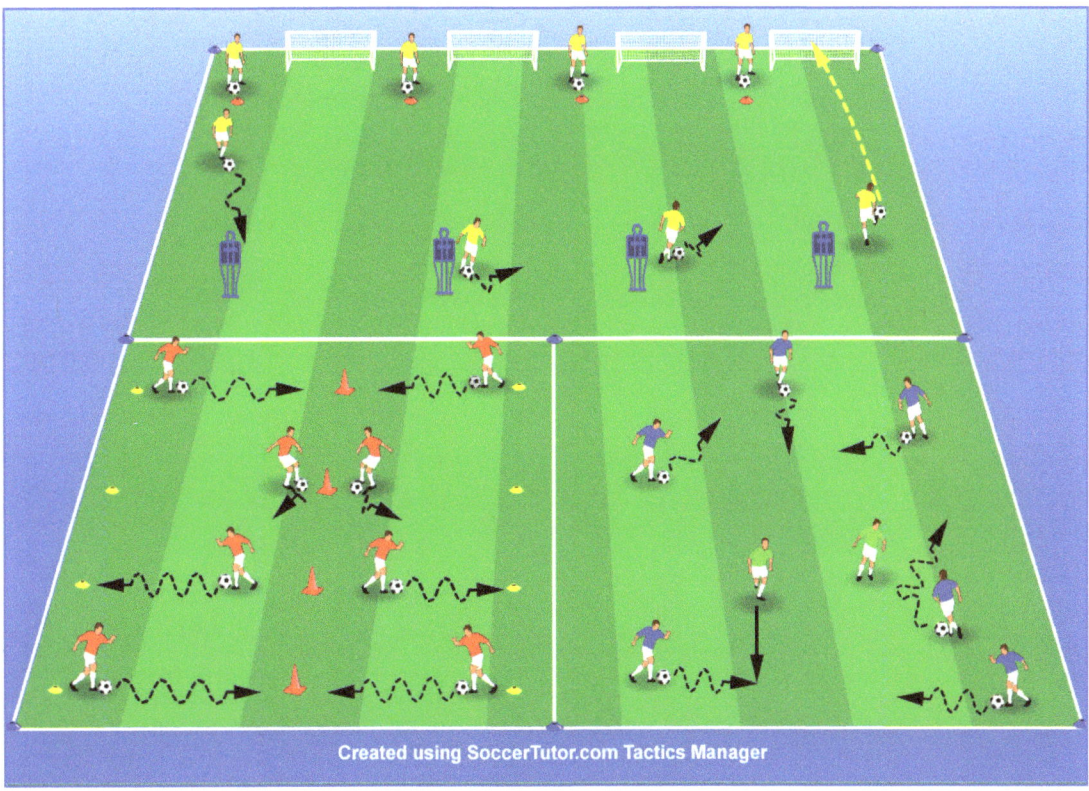

Group A

The red players are in pairs opposite each other 15 yards apart. Both players have a ball and start simultaneously by dribbling the ball towards the centre. At the cone, the players change direction and dribble back to the starting position.

Alternate different types of turns such as turn with the sole, sole 'L' shape, internal cut etc.

Group B

The blue players all have a ball each and move around freely in a 15 x 15 yard area. 2 or more green players are added (depending on the number of players in blue) who try to win the ball from the blue players as quickly as possible. If a blue player loses the ball he is not eliminated, but instead helps the other blue players to maintain possession of the ball. Change the green players every minute.

Group C

The yellow players are divided into 4 groups and compete in a relay competition. Each player dribbles the ball towards the mannequin (or cone) which is 5 yards away, perform a specific turn pre-determined by the coach and then quickly shoot into the goal. The first team to score 10 goals wins the relay.

WEEK 6

2. Technical: Passing and Receiving Square 15 mins

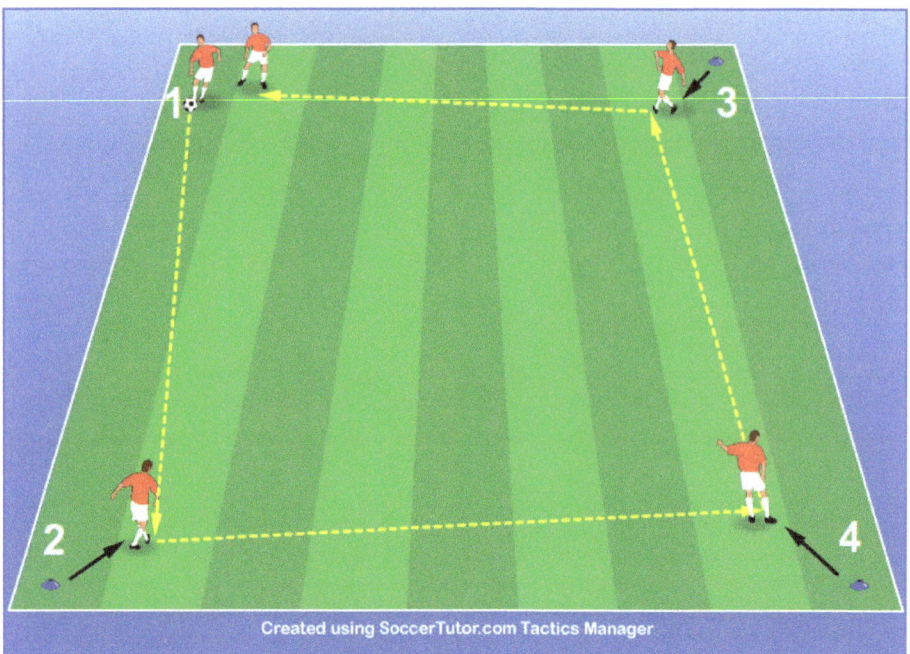

Description
5 players in a 15 x 15 yard square pass the ball in the pattern shown.

Player 1 passes to 2, player 2 to 4, Player 4 to 3 and finally 3 back to the start for the new number 1 to start the sequence again.

Each player moves to the next position after their pass.

Variation
One touch passing.

Coaching Points
1. Players should move to meet the ball and approach it half turned.
2. Change the direction of the drill so the players pass and receive with both feet.

3. Coordination: Hurdle Agility Training & Volley Passes 15 mins

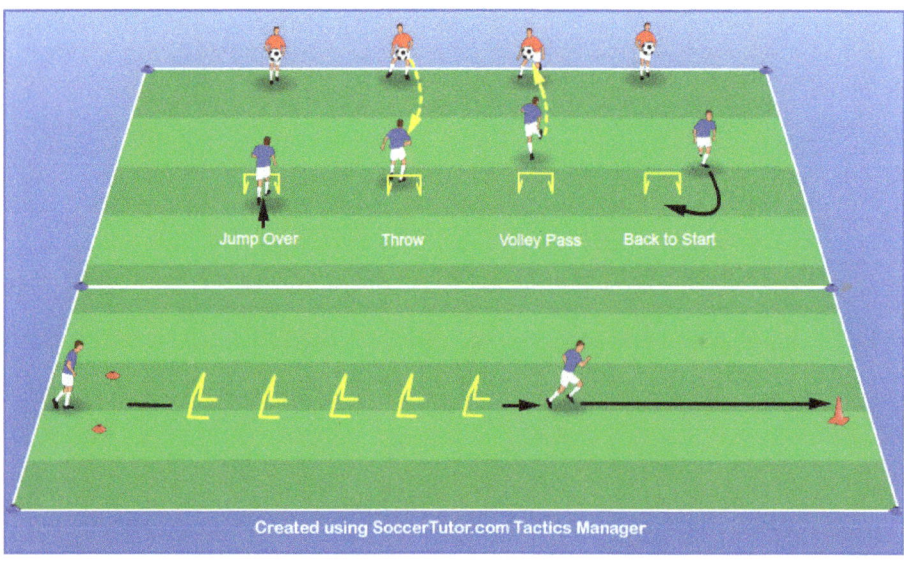

Description
GROUP A: 3 players work on technique in pairs under condition of quickness:

First, the player jumps over the low hurdle, then volley passes back to their teammate who throws the ball, before returning to the start.

Each player works for 30 seconds.

Players execute the following:

Volley with inside of left/right foot, volley with left/right instep, along the ground, half volley and heading.

GROUP B: 2 minutes - Jump over 5 low hurdles, followed by 5 yards of light jogging.

DAY 03:   Passing and Receiving

4. Game Situation: 4v2 Possession - Passing, Receiving & Speed of Play

15 mins

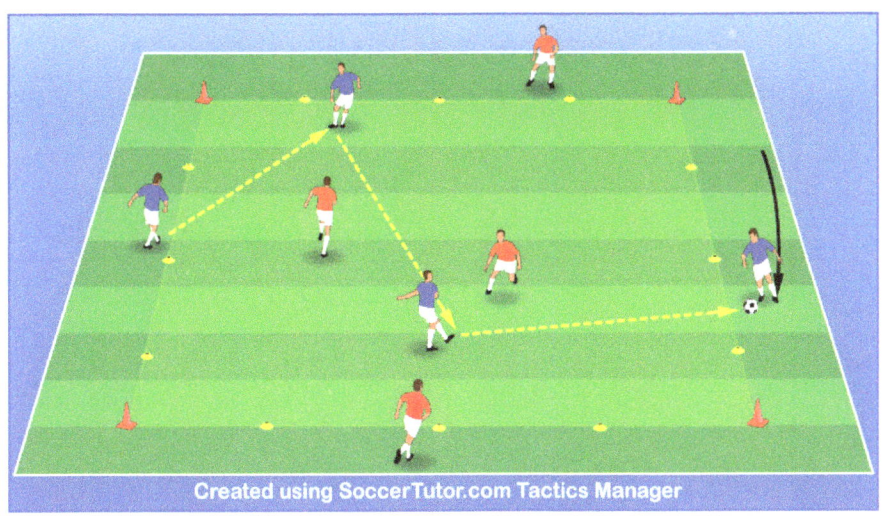

Description

In a square area of 10-12 yards we play 2v2.

Each side has 2 side players who can move up and down their line, but are not allowed to enter the square. This creates a 4v2 situation.

The aim is to maintain possession utilising all 4 players in the team (all are limited to 2 touches).

The aim is to complete 10 passes without the opposition intercepting the ball. The players use the 4v2 advantage while in possession. Every 2 minutes the sides are changed, also rotating the side players.

Coaching Points

1. All players should open up their body to shape themselves in the direction of their first touch and pass to a teammate.
2. Angle of support - provide support with at least 2 viable passing options.
3. Speed up play; reduce the time taken between the first touch and the pass.

5. Game with a Theme: Long Passing, Crossing & Finishing in a 7 Zone SSG

15 mins

Description

Using the area from penalty box to penalty box, we set up 7 zones and play a 9v9 game.

After completing 5 passes the team in possession of the ball can make a long pass into one of the 2 zone A's where one player can run into without any defensive pressure.

The player receiving the ball in zone A must cross the ball into zone B where only 2 attackers and 1 defender are allowed in.

6. 5v5 Small Sided Games

30 mins

WEEK 6

Shooting

Primary Technical Objective: Accurate shooting and volleying.

Secondary Technical Objective: Running with the ball, feints/moves to beat and directional receiving of the ball.

Coordination Objective: Balance, quickness, space/time adaptation and transformation.

Tactical Objective: 1v1 duels, defend the goal and man marking.

Duration of Session: 2 hours 15 mins

---

1. Warm Up: Technical Block 4   30 mins

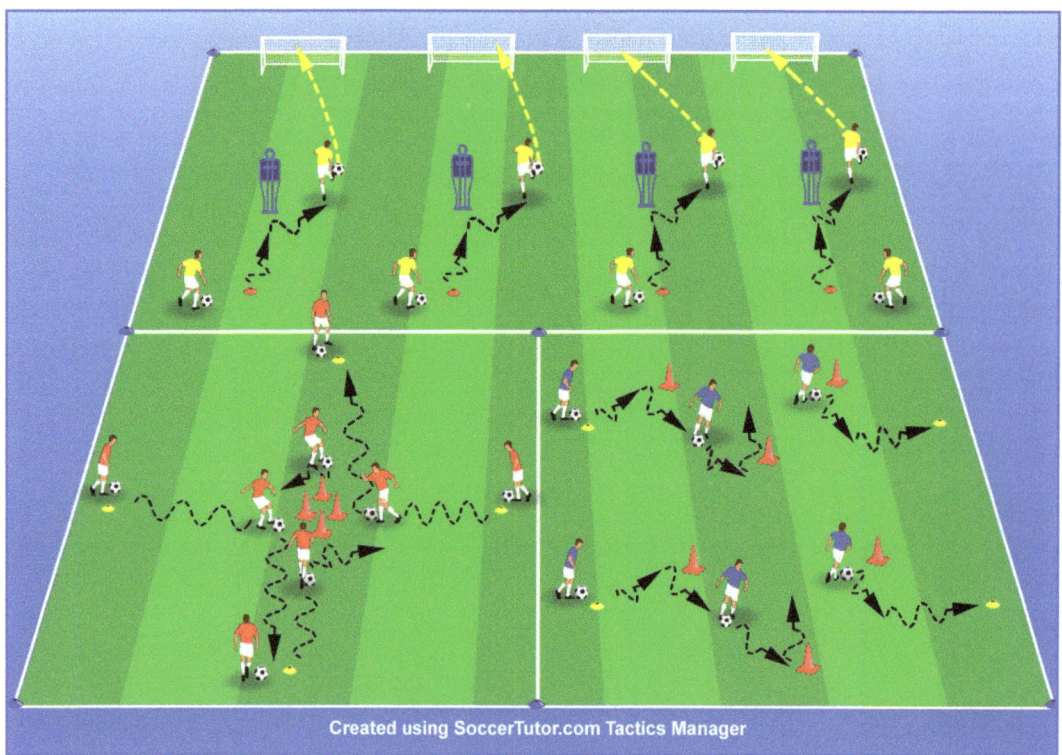

Group A

The red players line up behind the 4 cones as shown. 4 players start at the same time and dribble the ball towards the cone in front of them, perform a feint pre-determined by the coach and move to the cone to the right. Change the type of feint after every completed lap and also change the direction from anticlockwise to clockwise so the players move to the left as well.

Group B

The blue players are divided into 2 groups and practice dribbling with feints to change direction. Initially the players simply use the inside and outside of both feet to dribble and change directions. They then progress to perform a specific feint at each cone which is pre-determined by the coach. Examples of feints include the scissor, the cut back and the chop.

Group C

The yellow players are divided into teams of 3 or 4 and are in a competition to see who can score the most goals. 4 players start simultaneously with a ball, dribble towards the mannequin (or cone), perform a feint to the left or right and shoot in the mini goal. A point is awarded to the player who scores first.

You can decide the type of feint to be used or leave it to the players imagination and freedom.

DAY 04: Shooting

2. Technical: Accurate Volleys & Quick Reactions Exercise   15 mins

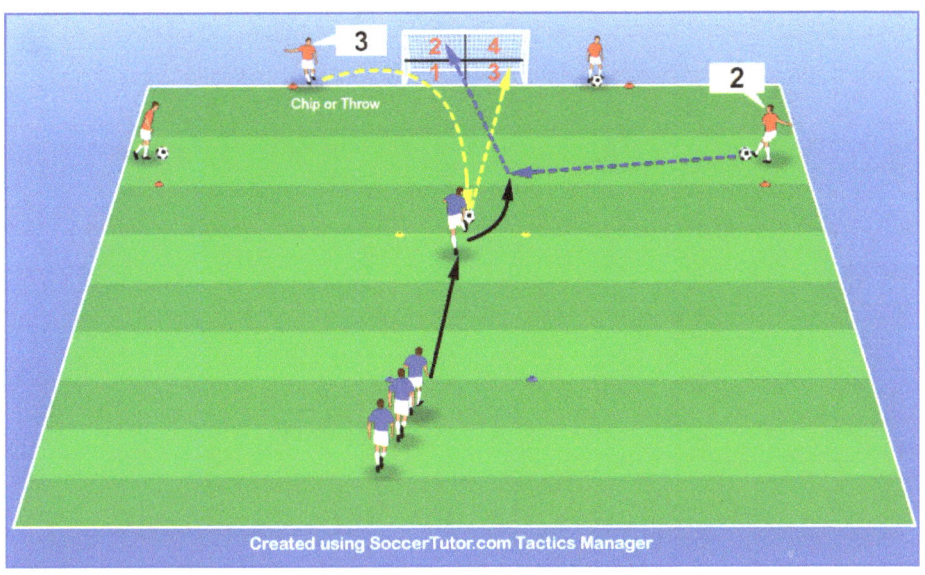

Variations
1. Headers instead of a volley.
2. Half volley.
3. Chip the ball for the first pass (as shown in the diagram).

Description

Players run up to the line as shown and volley the ball from a throw-in by their teammate who is standing at the side of the goal. The thrower calls out a number corresponding to the section of the goal where the player shooting must direct the ball.

A second ball is then passed in from the side and the player must quickly react to shoot first time again. The player who passed again calls out a number corresponding to the section of the goal where the player shooting must direct the ball.

3. Coordination: Sprint, Change Direction and Shooting Race   15 mins

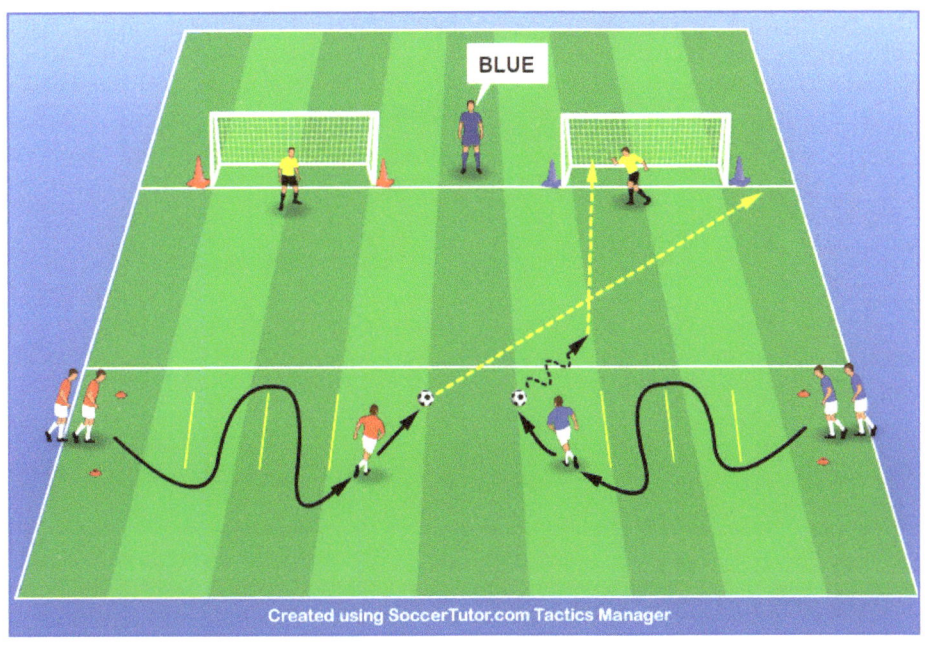

Description

Players are divided into 2 groups and 2 players start the drill at the same time.

The first players in line run round the poles as shown which are laid on the ground and then sprint to the ball.

The coach then calls out the colour of the goal to shoot into and the first player to score gets 1 point for their team.

Variations
1. Use rings instead of poles.
2. Indicate the goal to shoot in with visual signs.

WEEK 6

4. Game Situation: 1v1 Frontal Duel with 3 Goals   15 mins

Description

In an area 10 x 10 yards, we have a 1v1 situation. 1 player starts with the ball and can score in any of the 3 goals.

The defender must challenge the player and if they win the ball they can also score in any of the 3 goals. This stimulates creativity and quick turning/changes of direction.

Variation

The players have to stop the ball on the line of the goal to score.

Coaching Points

1. In 1v1 situations, players need to shield the ball making their body a barrier between the ball and the defender.
2. Reactions are key because if you lose the ball, you have to quickly move to win it back before the opponent can score.
3. Encourage creativity, with both players using all parts of both feet and various feints when dribbling.

5. Game with a Theme: Speed of Play and Shooting SSG   15 mins

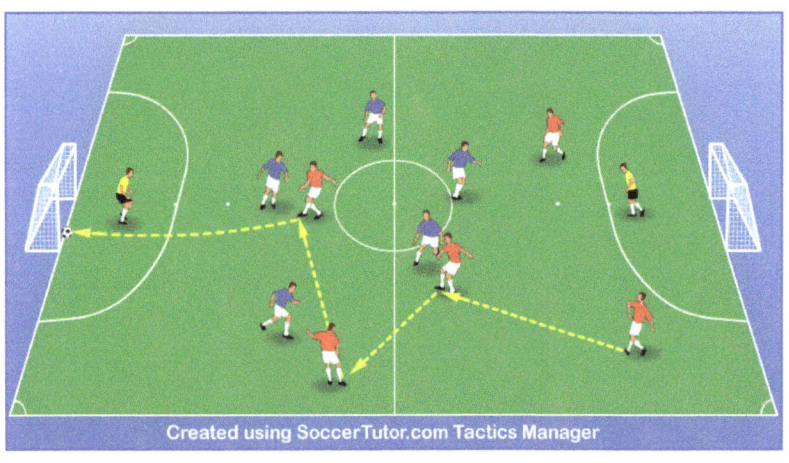

Description

In a 40 x 30 yard area we play a 6v6 game.

The teams must count the amount of passes they have made and must take a shot on goal before reaching 5 passes, otherwise they lose possession.

The practice stimulates quick direct play and quick finishing.

Coaching Point

1. Players should receive the ball half-turned to speed up the transition to the next pass, dribble or shot on goal.
2. Encourage players to think and play quickly, selecting the right pass before receiving the ball.

6. 5v5 Small Sided Games   30 mins

DAY 05: Passing & Receiving in the Air

Passing & Receiving in the Air

Primary Technical Objective: Passing in the air, crossing and heading.

Secondary Technical Objective: Receiving with good control and juggling.

Coordination Objective: Reading the trajectory of the ball, dynamic balance, motor reactions and quickness.

Tactical Objective: Pressing, possession and attacking/defending crosses.

Duration of Session: 2 hours 15 mins

---

1. Warm Up: Technical Block 5 — 30 mins

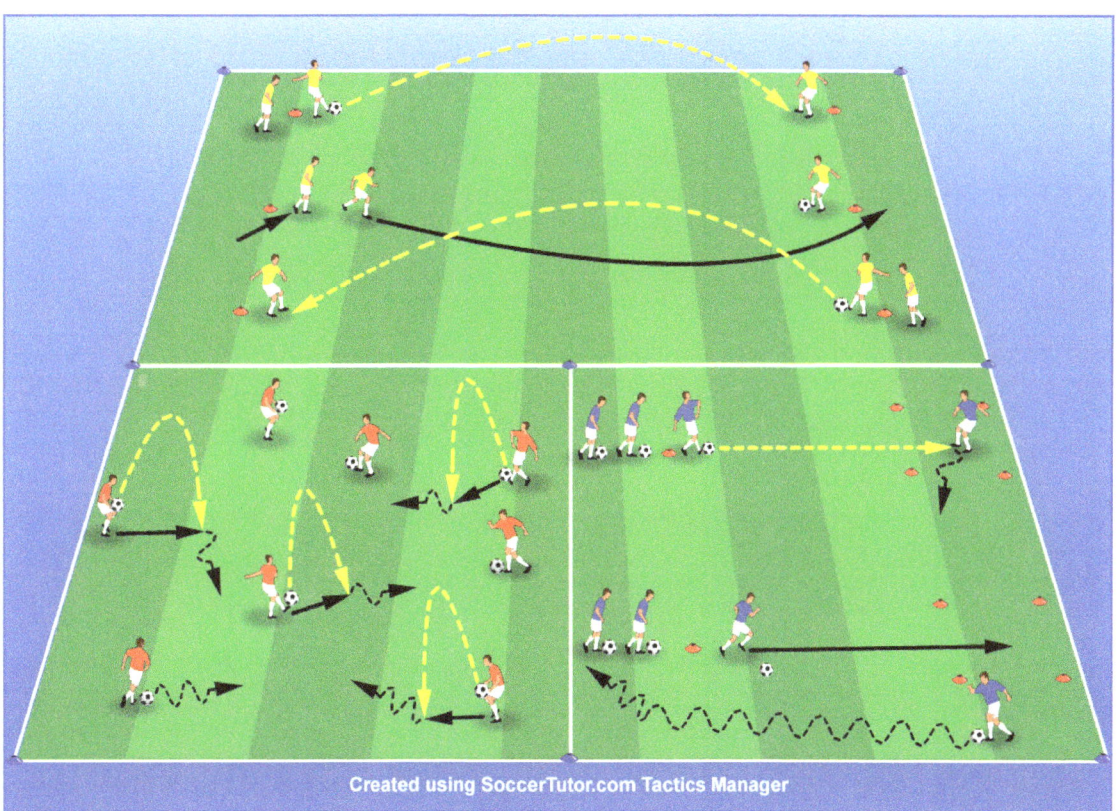

Group A

The red players move freely around the area and control the ball in different ways. The players throw (or kick) the ball up in the air, control the ball and then dribble for a few yards. Vary the type of control used - inside of foot, outside of foot, with the sole, with the laces, thigh, head etc.

Group B

Divide the blue players into 2 groups and set up 5 x 5 yard squares as shown. This is a relay competition with the 2 teams starting simultaneously. The first player passes the ball to the player in the square and then runs into the square. The player in the square takes a directional first touch out the side of the square and dribbles the ball to the next player who repeats the same sequence.

Group C

The yellow players work on passing and receiving high balls at a 25 yard distance. The first player makes an aerial pass to their teammate and then runs 25 yards to their position. The second player controls the ball and then plays the next aerial pass and runs 25 yards to the opposite cone. The same sequence continues.

Vary the type of control used - inside of foot, outside of foot, the sole, the laces, thigh, head etc.

WEEK 6

2. Technical: 2v2 Football Tennis Tournament 15 mins

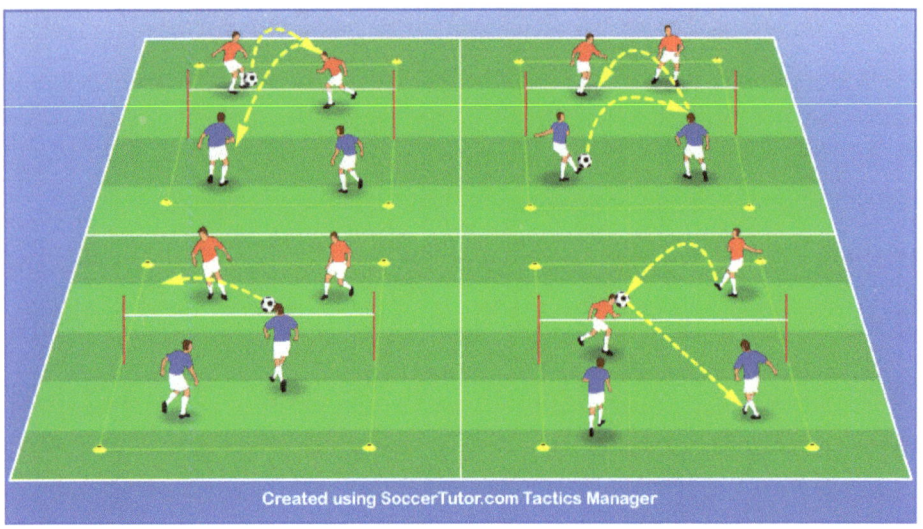

Description

Set up various mini pitches and play football tennis with different rules:

1. A point can only be won with a headed finish.
2. Only allow 3 touches per team and the ball can only bounce once.
3. A player must play the ball to his teammate before playing the ball back over the net.
4. The goals are only valid if the ball is scored in the section called out.

Coaching Points

1. The players should try to use all parts of the foot, thigh, chest and head to maximise control of the ball.
2. The pass to the teammate should have good height for the headed finishes.

3. Coordination: Sprinting & Agility with Crossing & Heading 15 mins

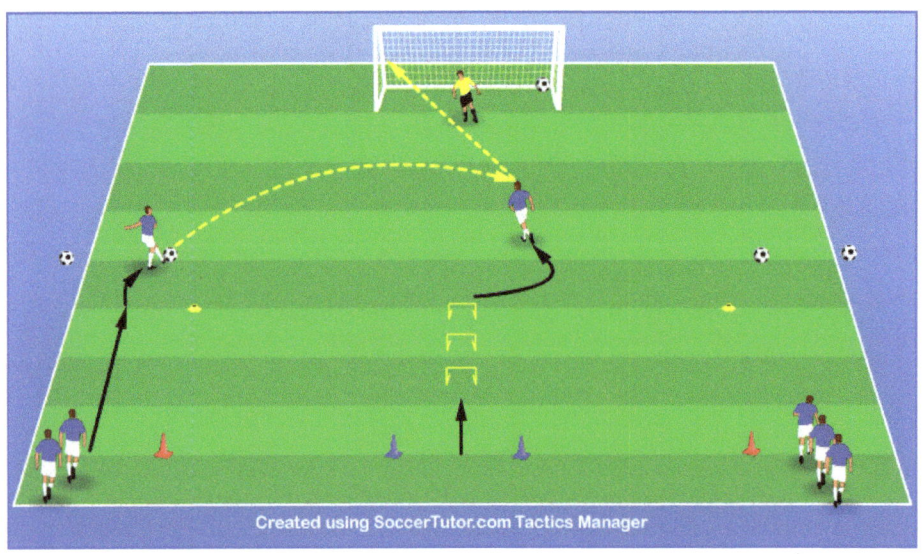

Description

This is a specific exercise for the wingers and full backs, but all players take part.

The wingers and full backs sprint for 20 yards, stop at the cone and re-start the run towards the ball and cross into the middle.

The rest of the players jump over the 3 hurdles performing a heading gesture and then move to head the ball from the cross.

DAY 05: Passing & Receiving in the Air

4. Game Situation: **Applying Quick Pressure in a 3 Zone Game**   **15 mins**

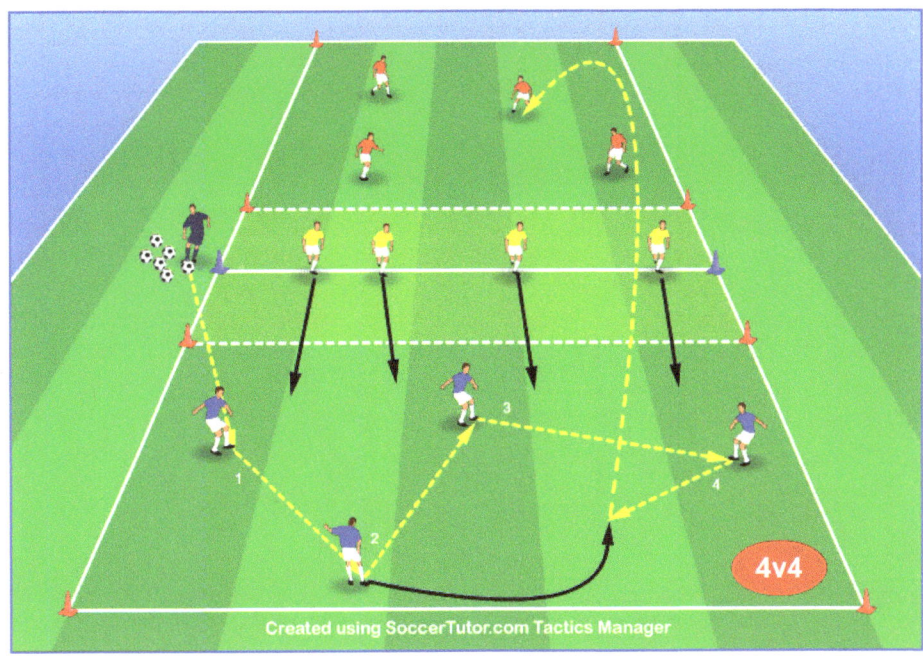

Description

In this practice we have 3 teams of 4 and 3 zones.

The blue team must make 4 passes before making a long pass to the red team.

The yellow team applies pressure to the team in possession. If they win the ball, the team who lost possession become the defending team and must apply pressure to the other team once the long pass has been made.

5. Game with a Theme: **3v3 Attacking / Defending Crosses**   **15 mins**

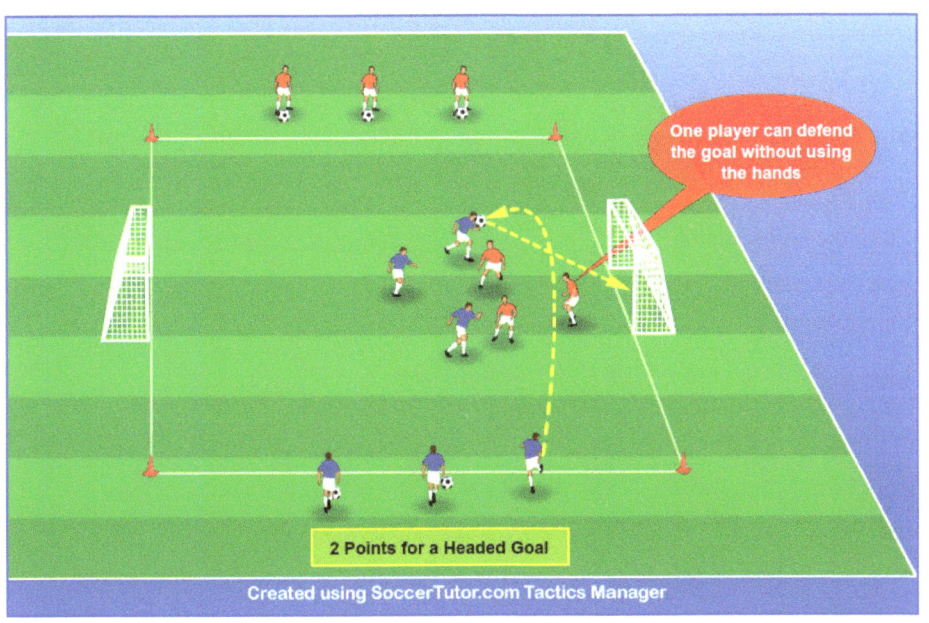

Description

We play with 2 teams of 6 players. There are 3 players positioned on each side to cross the ball for their 3 teammates in the middle to score.

The teams alternate crossing the ball. A goal scored with the head counts as double. 1 player per team can defend the goal but they are not allowed to use their hands.

6. 11v11 Matches on a Full Pitch   **30 mins**

Football Coaching Specialists Since 2001

TACTICS MANAGER
Create your own Practices, Tactics & Plan Sessions!

Available on PC and Mac

Work offline
No need for an Internet connection!

Easy to use
Super quick and easy to use!

One-off fee
Yours to keep for life!

5 Day Free Trial
Take a free trial at soccertutor.com!

Only £59.99!

www.SoccerTutor.com
info@soccertutor.com
+44 (0)208 1234 007

Football Coaching Specialists Since 2001

Soccer Italian Style
Full Colour Books / eBooks & DVD / Videos

FREE SAMPLES

DOWNLOAD FREE COACH VIEWER APP
- Search 'Coach Viewer' at your App Store
- For PC/Mac download at soccertutor.com

www.SoccerTutor.com

info@soccertutor.com

+44 (0)208 1234 007